These Words
upon Our Heart

Every attempt has been made to obtain permission to reprint previously published material. The author gratefully acknowledges the following for permission to reprint previously published material:

CENTRAL CONFERENCE OF AMERICAN RABBIS: Excerpt from "The Guiding Principles of Reform Judaism, Columbus Platform, 1937" is copyright by the Central Conference of American Rabbis and is reproduced by permission; excerpts from "Reform Judaism: A Centenary Perspective" adopted at San Francisco, 1976 are copyright by the Central Conference of American Rabbis and are reproduced by permission; excerpts from "A Statement of Principles from Reform Judaism" adopted at the 1999 Pittsburgh Convention are copyright by the Central Conference of American Rabbis and are reproduced by permission.

PAULIST PRESS: Excerpts from ABRAHAM ISAAC KOOK: *The Lights of Penitence, Lights of Holiness, The Moral Principles, Essays, Letters, and Poems,* translation and introduction by Ben Zion Bokser, from The Classics of Western Spirituality, Copyright © 1978 by Ben Zion Bokser, Paulist Press, Inc., New York/Mahwah, N.J. Used with permission of Paulist Press www.paulistpress.com .

Library of Congress Cataloging-in-Publication Data

Steinbock, Steven E.
    These words upon our heart: a lexicon of Judaism and world religions / Steven E. Steinbock.
        p. cm.
    ISBN 0-8074-0785-2 (pbk. : alk. paper)
        1. Judaism—Terminology. 2. Judaism—Doctrines—Comparative studies.
    3. Religions—Comparative studies. I. Title.

BM50.S73 2003
296.3'9'014—dc22

                                                                            2003061315

Designer: Shaul Akri
Typesetting: El Ot Ltd., Tel Aviv
This book is printed on acid-free paper.
Copyright © 2003 by Steven E. Steinbock.
Manufactured in the United States of America.
10 9 8 7 6 5 4 3 2 1

These Words upon Our Heart

A Lexicon of Judaism and World Religions

Steven E. Steinbock

UAHC Press
New York, New York

Those who look for Scripture's inherent meaning say:
If you wish to know the One by whose word the world
came into being, study *aggadah;* you will thereby come
to know the Holy One, blessed be God, and hold fast to
God's ways.

Sifrei D'varim 49

Acknowledgments

This book was a long time in the gestation stage—like a chrysalis—as the ideas of many books and teachers spun their web into a cocoon inside me. The resources I used are far too numerous to list. But several that were indispensable I'll name here: Charles Panati's entertaining *Sacred Origins of Profound Things* (Penguin, 1996), Mircea Eliade's *Essential Sacred Writings From Around the World* (Harper SanFrancisco, 1992), C.T. Onions' *The Oxford Dictionary of English Etymology* (Oxford University Press, 1983), *What Happens After I Die?* by Rifat Sonsino and Daniel Syme (UAHC Press, 2002), and *Sefer Ha'aggadah* by Bialik and Ravnitzky, translated as *The Book of Legends* by William G. Braude (Schocken Books, 1992). Unlike Bialik and Ravnitzky, I had the benefit of turning to the Internet throughout my research. In checking word origins, I am particularly indebted to www.dictionary.com (Lexico Publishing, LLC), and Melanie and Mike Crowley's Web site Take Our Word For It (www.takeourword.com). I am grateful to members of the UAHC Press editorial board, whose enthusiasm for this project was an inspiration. I am thankful for the close reading and comments of Dr. Carol Ochs of Hebrew Union College–Jewish Institute of Religion in helping to shape the final draft of this manuscript. For the various other readers and copyeditors who made helpful suggestions, including Debra Hirsch Corman, Liane Broido, and Annie Belford, I am appreciative, and my thanks also go to all those who did their part to bring forth this book, including Ken Gesser and Joel Eglash. This volume would not have been possible without the guidance, patience, and gentle prodding of my editor, Rabbi Hara Person, who worked with me throughout the stages of this book's development.

Contents

N O W

the whole

world had

one language

and a common

speech. As men

moved eastward, they

found a plain in Shinar

and settled there. They said

to each other, "Let's make

bricks and bake them thor-

oughly." They used brick instead

of stone, and tar for mortar. Then they

said, "Come, let us build ourselves a

city, with a tower that reaches to the

heavens, so that we may make a name for

ourselves and not be scattered over the face of

the earth." But *Adonai* came down to see the city

and the tower that the men were building. *Adonai*

said, "If as one people speaking the same language

they have begun to do this, then nothing they plan to do

will be impossible for them. Come, let's go down and

confuse their language so they will not understand each

other." So *Adonai* scattered them from there over all the earth,

and they stopped building the city. That is why it was called Babel—

because there *Adonai* confused the language of the whole world.

From there *Adonai* scattered them over the face of the whole earth.

Genesis 11:1–9

Introduction

The Importance of Words and Their Meanings

It is difficult to imagine a world without words. With every passing moment we think, see, and communicate in words. Words help us make sense of the world around us, by giving names and order to the things we see and feel. Words can hurt and words can comfort.

But what is a word, after all? A word is a set of sounds, or symbols on a page, that have been given meaning.

There are many kinds of words.

Some words describe things. The word "banana," for instance, has a very specific meaning. When any two people see or hear that word, they are likely to imagine the same thing: a long, curved yellow fruit.

Other words describe feelings. Words like "love," "hope," "sadness," and "anger" describe emotions that most people share. Even though no two people experience these emotions in exactly the same way, we use these words to communicate how we feel, and the listener will usually understand us.

Another type of word describes concepts. A concept is a set of thoughts or ideas about a specific theme. Concepts are often very hard to define. They are usually intangible, which means that they can't be touched, measured, or perceived with the physical senses. Even the concept of "concept" is hard to describe. Examples of concepts include "patriotism," "economy," "ecology," and "nationality."

Just as in the story of the Tower of Babel, in which speech was changed to confuse people, so have words changed their meanings in ways that confuse people who use them. Religious terms like "cult," "myth," and "sacrifice" have taken on modern meanings that bear no relationship with their original meanings. We often use words from one language to describe ideas taken from another language, for instance using words like "faith," "charity," and "sin" to describe concepts in Judaism for which the

English words have little meaning. We also frequently borrow words from other languages—Hindu words like *karma* and *nirvana,* or Hebrew words like *tzedakah* and *mitzvah*—without understanding what those words really mean in the context of the cultures that first employed them.

> ## Key Terms
>
> **Word**. A set of sounds or printed symbols that are given a meaning.
>
> **Concept**. A word that describes an abstract idea.
>
> **Etymology**. The study of word origins.
>
> **Semantics**. The study of how words are used, and how they are given meaning.
>
> **Translation**. A conversion of a word or group of words from one language to another so that the approximate meaning is preserved.

In this book we will be looking at many words. Most of them are concepts. Some of them are feelings, and a few of them are things. All of them are words that people use to describe religion and religious life. Most of what we'll be examining are Hebrew and English words. But in order to better understand them, we'll also be looking at some words from ancient Greece, India, China, and elsewhere.

The words and ideas that comprise Judaism are many and varied and often difficult to understand. To grasp the meanings behind our words, we'll look at their etymologies, their histories, and their use and misuse. We will learn to appreciate the religious words of other cultures, and in so doing, we will better appreciate our own.

Translation

Ethnologue, a guidebook to world languages and dialects, describes 6,703 different languages. But the editors of *Ethnologue* admit that there are more languages spoken in the world today than anyone can count.

How do we translate? Just look up a word in the dictionary, right?

When a speaker of English says "nice day" to another English speaker, it is fair to assume that the intended meaning of the speaker was understood. Yet the way two people understand "nice day"—the meaning the two people give to the words—will never be exact. One person's idea of a nice day may be different from another's. For one person, "nice day" brings up a vision of sunshine and green fields. For another, it may mean a day filled with many successful accomplishments. A nice day can mean relaxing with a good book all day, or a wild time at a football game.

The subtle differences in meaning are even more pronounced when words are transferred from one language to another. Just as no two people think and feel exactly alike, no two languages use words in exactly the same way. The following chart provides a familiar example:

English	Swahili	Japanese	Hebrew	French
How are you?	*Hujambo?* (Are you fine?) or *Habari?* (What's the news?)	*Ogenki des'ka?* (Your spirit, how is it?)	*Mah sh'lomcha?* (What is your peace?)	*Comment ça va?* (How does it go?)

A translation is not an equation. At best, it is an approximate interpretation of meaning from one language to another. We sometimes use the expression "literal translation" to describe when a translator tries to give an exact word-for-word conversion from one language to another. In truth, no translation can be literal or exact. Translators can only do their best, balancing the sound and the style of the words with mood and meaning, to keep the translation as close as they can to the original.

This is the very process that translators go through when translating the Bible from the original Hebrew. The opening line of the Torah is a familiar one to most people. We usually find it translated from the Hebrew as

In the beginning, God created the heavens and the earth.

The actual Hebrew words are

בְּרֵאשִׁית בָּרָא אֱלֹהִים אֵת הַשָּׁמַיִם וְאֵת הָאָרֶץ.

We can transliterate these words, converting the letters to our own Latin alphabet:

B'reishit bara Elohim eit-hashamayim v'eit-haaretz.

A nearly literal translation would look something like:

At-front-of he-created God *(eit)*-the-skies and-*(eit)*-the-land.

This "literal" translation makes almost no sense in English. The Hebrew word אֵת *(eit)* is used to show which words are the objects of the sentence. There is no counterpart for it in the English language.

As we learn about Jewish concepts and beliefs, we must often rely on translations of ancient Hebrew words. These translations often miss important subtleties and nuances of a word and can lead to misunderstanding of Jewish ideas. In this book we will make an effort to take the limits of translation into account as we expand our understanding.

Semantics

The study of words and their meanings is called "semantics." This word comes from a Greek word, *sema,* which means "sign" or "symbol." In semantics, we study the way words acquire their meanings, how the meanings change, and how words affect people.

The word "semantics" has acquired another meaning. When someone uses words to trick others—trying to get the listener to think something is being said that really isn't—we sometimes call that "semantics."

Etymology

Etymology is the study of the origin of words. Words sometimes have interesting histories. A word may pass from one language to another, changing with each generation.

Two of our most important mathematical words were borrowed from other languages. Our word "geometry" comes from the Greek words **ΓΗ** (gi = earth) and **ΜΕΤΡΩ** (metro = measure), so that geometry (**ΓΕΩΜΕΤΡΊΑ**) is the science of earth measurements.

The word "algebra" comes from the Arabic word *al-jeber,* which means "the reduction of parts." Algebra is the science of making numerical formulas with letters.

The words we use to describe religion and religious experience—both in Hebrew and English—are often adapted from words borrowed from other languages. By breaking words into their original parts, we can sometimes get a broader and deeper picture of what these words mean.

An interesting example of the etymology of a word in the term "Messiah." For modern English-speakers, the word "messiah" generally means "a savior" or "son of God," and specifically, the person of Jesus of Nazareth.

The origin of the word goes back to an ancient Semitic verb meaning "to dab, smear, or paint." The verb מָשַׁח *(mashach)* came to be associated with anointing, the dabbing or smearing of olive oil, which was an ancient custom for marking an object or person as special. Priests, kings, weapons, and religious objects were all dabbed with oil to mark them as ready for their special purpose.

Because kings were so important during the period of the Kingdoms of Israel and Judah, the word מָשִׁיחַ *(mashiach)*—meaning "anointed one"—became an epithet for the king. When the Kingdom of Judah was placed in exile by the Babylonians, Jews began wishing for a return of the kingship, with an anointed descendant of King David on the throne. In time, this hope for an anointed one, or מָשִׁיחַ *(mashiach)*, grew into an idea of an almost superhuman king.

King David playing the harp, Padua, Italy, ca. 1500.

Six hundred years later, now subject to another oppressor, the Jews under Rome still hoped for a מָשִׁיחַ *(mashiach)* to save them. One group of Jews believed that their teacher, Jesus of Nazareth, was the מָשִׁיחַ *(mashiach)*, and after his death, the belief arose that their מָשִׁיחַ *(mashiach)* was not just a king, he was the one son of God and was now an integral part of the godhead.

early meaning → common biblical meaning → rabbinic meaning → Christian meaning

מָשַׁח	מָשַׁח	מָשִׁיחַ	מָשִׁיחַ	מָשִׁיחַ	מָשִׁיחַ
(mashach)	*(mashach)*	*(mashiach)*	*(mashiach)*	*(mashiach)*	*(mashiach)*
to dab, smear, or paint	to anoint with oil	an anointed priest or king	king	savior king	son of God

When Jews and Christians discuss the concept of messiah, they often don't realize that they are coming from two totally different views of what "messiah" means. The Jewish view and the Christian view of messiah are both valid within their own religious perspectives. But they are not the same concept.

Words Grow and Change

As we saw in the above example, the meanings of words like מָשִׁיחַ *(mashiach)* can evolve. The meanings of words sometimes adapt to new situations and needs. Sometimes their meanings completely change, even becoming their own opposites.

Look, for instance, at the words in the following chart:

This word:	Originally meant:	But is now used to mean:
awful	full of awe	terrible, bad
artificial	artistically designed	fake, imitation
gross	large	sickening, grotesque
cosmic	of the world	out of this world

A good example of this in Hebrew is the word גּוֹי *(goy),* which in biblical times meant "nation." In Exodus 19:6, God told the people of Israel that they were a גּוֹי קָדוֹשׁ *(goy kadosh),* "a holy nation." By the time of the Talmud, a time when the Jews were scattered, living in many foreign lands, the word *goy* was used to describe non-Jewish nations and the non-Jewish people who lived in them. In modern times, *goy* has become a negative term to describe non-Jews.

The purpose of this book is to examine the words we use to describe religion—words in English, Hebrew, and sometimes, other languages. Each chapter focuses on a particular theme, such as soul, messiah, holiness, sacrifice, and prayer. After the theme is introduced and the cluster of terms used to describe it are explored, the theme is analyzed as it is variously understood in Judaism and in world religions.

Wherever possible, the Jewish view of the theme is presented, followed by other religions that offer different views of the topic. In some cases, though, this sequence is not always the most logical one to follow. The discussion of the topic of God is so large as to deserve two chapters, with chapter 3 covering the God idea in other religions, and chapter 4 entirely on God in Judaism. Certain ideas in Judaism have evolved from or are reactions against ideas that existed in other religions. Therefore, in order to understand the background and development of these ideas, as in the case of messiah (chapter 6), afterlife (chapter 7), and sacrifice (chapter 11), it is important to present the ancient religious ideas that influenced Judaism before introducing the Jewish position. For the topics of holiness (chapter 8) and mythology (chapter 9), anthropological and philosophical connections are introduced before presenting the approach to these ideas in Judaism.

We hope that you will use this book as a guide, reference, or textbook to better understand the words that we use to describe religion, to better know and appreciate our own religion, and to strengthen your ability to use and explain these words upon our heart.

Chapter One

אֱמוּנָה

Emunah

Defining Religion

> These words, which I command you today, shall be
> upon your heart. You shall teach them faithfully to your
> children, and shall talk of them when you sit in your
> house, when you are going about your way, when you
> lie down, and when you rise up.
>
> Deuteronomy 6:6–7

As we begin this study of the words and concepts that give shape to Jewish religion, our first step is to examine what we mean when we say "religion."

For most Westerners—people brought up and influenced in European and American culture—"religion" is defined as "a system of believing in God." We often use the words "faith" and "religion" interchangeably, as when we refer to the "Muslim faith" or the "Buddhist faith." This linking of faith with religion is largely a Christian idea, coming out of Christianity's emphasis on perfect faith in God.

In practice, however, world religions vary so much that it is difficult to call them all faiths. For many, belief in a god is a very minor part of the religion.

While the religions of the world have many elements in common, religions are like fingerprints; no two religions are alike. Each has a different set of beliefs and practices.

In most cases, we can find a central principle that defines the particular religion:

- Confucianism emphasizes proper behavior as a way of preserving universal order.
- Taoism (pronounced "dow-ism") teaches that harmony in nature is the means of preserving universal order.
- Islam teaches that there is one God, and submission to God's will is the key to salvation.

- Christianity emphasizes that faith and faith alone is what God wants of us.
- Classical (Theravada) Buddhism teaches that desire is the cause of suffering and that by eliminating desire, suffering ceases.

Word Histories

In this section we take a closer look at the etymologies (word origins) of several key Hebrew and English terms. We also examine how their meanings have evolved over time.

Faith. The word "faith" comes from a Latin root, *fidere,* which means, "trust," and the Old English *bidon,* meaning "to wait trustingly." We find the same root in words like "confidence," "fidelity," and "affidavit," as well as in "federal," "federate," "abide," and "bid." Faith is an act of having trust, patience, or confidence in a certain person, belief, or idea.

Particularly in Christianity, "faith" has come to mean acceptance of a religious statement without the benefit of proof. In Christian philosophy, faith and reason (logical, scientific, provable beliefs) have often been regarded as opposites. Faith in God, it has been thought, cannot be proven, but must be accepted as a "leap of faith." Some philosophers—Jewish, Christian, and Muslim—have proposed using logical proofs to defend God's existence. Others have found a middle ground, suggesting that faith and reason are different, but not in opposition to each other, and that science and religion are two different windows to finding the same truths.

In modern usage, as mentioned at the beginning of the chapter, the word "faith" is often used as a synonym or substitute for the word "religion." Relationships between people of different religions are referred to as "interfaith." A person who marries someone of a different religion is said to be marrying "outside of the faith."

Belief. From the Old English root *lieb* (meaning "love"), "belief" originally meant "to desire or care for something, to hold it dear." Over the ages, the meaning of

> ## Key Terms
>
> **Faith.** Trust or confidence in something. Sometimes used as a synonym for "religion."
>
> **Belief.** An idea that is embraced. To believe is to hold dear that idea, to desire or care for something.
>
> **Religion.** A set of beliefs and practices that derive from a common history.
>
> **Cult.** A system of religious beliefs and rituals; a religious community associated with a specific set of rituals; often a subset of a religion.
>
> **Myth.** A higher truth or teaching told through stories.
>
> **דָּת (dat).** A judgment, rule, or custom. In modern Hebrew, the word *dat* is translated as "religion."
>
> **אֱמוּנָה (emunah).** Belief; affirmation. An idea that one upholds (holds upward, maintains).

"belief" has changed from an emotional response to an intellectual one. Today, "to believe" nearly always means "to accept something as true." Consider the phrases "seeing is believing," "believe it or not," and "I don't believe in UFOs."

Religion.   There is some debate about the origin of the word "religion." One source (Cicero in 60 B.C.E.) suggested that it meant "to read again," as we repeat stories and prayer verses. Another source (Augustine in around 400 C.E.) explained that it meant "to bind tightly," as in holding a community together through rigidly practiced rules and rituals.

What distinguishes a religion from philosophies and individual beliefs is that religion is institutional. An institution is a belief, practice, or organization that is important to a large group of people. Institutions belong to a society or culture and are often associated with buildings, such as schools, hospitals, and places of worship. While a person may hold individual beliefs or be well versed in religious ideas, it's fair to say that one cannot participate in religion without partaking of its institutions.

Cult.   The word "cult" comes from the Latin word *cultus,* meaning "worship," and has the same root as the words "culture," "cultivate," and "colony," as well as "circle" and "cycle." "Cult" can refer to any collection of rituals and the circle of people who observe them. A group of people who regularly meet at synagogue for daily services can be called a cult. The system of sacrifices that took place at the Temple in ancient Israel was also a cult.

An interesting modern use of the word "cult" refers to popular fads or crazes, particularly with books, movies, and television programs. When *Star Trek* first appeared on television in the late 1960s, the critics and network executives didn't particularly like it, but it developed such a strong "cult following" that it has spawned numerous other television shows, movies, games, clubs, and conventions.

It's unfortunate that the word "cult" is often used to describe extremist modern religious movements with dictatorial leaders who use psychological manipulation. Religious groups like Hare Krishna, Church of Scientology, and the Unification Church ("Moonies") are sometimes referred to as cults. The term is also used to label violent doomsday groups such as the Branch Davidians (who battled with Treasury agents in Waco, Texas, in 1993), Aum Shinrikyo (which released poisonous sarin gas into the Tokyo subway system in 1995), and Heaven's Gate (the UFO-based religious group that committed mass suicide in 1997). The use of the term "cult" in this way is often an oversimplification. Any group that uses rituals—including Judaism and the Roman Catholic Church—can be labeled a cult.

Myth.   Today people tend to use the word "myth" in two ways, both of which take us away from the real meaning. The first use is "a primitive story about imaginary gods and heroes." The second use is "an idea or belief that is commonly accepted even though it is false." If we could wash these poor definitions from our consciousness, we might begin to get a better idea of what a myth really is. A myth, in fact, is nearly the opposite of what these two definitions suggest: it's a story that is *truer* than fact.

The Greek word μῦθος *(muthos)* means "word" or "speech." Contrary to the way "myth" is often used today, the type of word or speech meant by *muthos* is that which is specifically true, real, and big. In ancient Greece it was used to refer to speeches, lectures, and sayings about important matters. "Myth" came to mean any story that had a special purpose, a story told to teach a message. We will use "myth" to describe a higher truth or message told through story.

דָּת *(dat)*.   *Dat* comes from the same root as the Hebrew word *din,* meaning "judgment," "rule," or "custom." During talmudic times, דָּת came to mean "Jewish custom" or "Jewish law." In modern Hebrew, the word *dat* is translated as "religion."

אֱמוּנָה *(emunah)*.   The Hebrew word *emunah,* "belief," comes from a root meaning "to support." Other related words include *amon* (architect), *omnah* (pillar), *emet* (truth), and *amen* (said after a prayer and meaning "I agree or affirm that"). In talmudic Hebrew, it meant "honesty," "trust," or "surety." In modern usage, *emunah* is usually translated as "belief" or "faith."

Jewish Doctrines

Over the ages, Jewish scholars and teachers have taught that there are three related themes central to Judaism: God, Torah, and Israel. Different groups, in different ages and different regions, have understood these three elements in various ways, but they have always been a consistent part of Judaism. Any time a group tried to remove one of these elements, the group ceased to be Jewish. This pattern of God–Torah–Israel will reappear throughout our study of Judaism.

Of the many beliefs embraced by Jews, none is more central than the belief in the Oneness of God that we find expressed in the *Sh'ma* prayer:

שְׁמַע יִשְׂרָאֵל יְהוָה אֱלֹהֵינוּ יְהוָה אֶחָד!

Sh'ma Yisrael, Adonai Eloheinu, Adonai Echad!
Listen Israel, *Adonai* is our God, *Adonai* is One!

Deuteronomy 6:4

In this short Hebrew phrase, the *Sh'ma* reminds the Jew throughout the day to listen—to pay attention—to God. In the first-person plural, it reminds us that God is our God. That God is One suggests not only that God is a unity, a single and unique Being, but also that God should be first—primary—in our minds, our hearts, and our actions.

In order to teach the people Israel, God gave them the Torah, a guidebook that encompasses everything from holiday observance and ritual offerings to ethical conduct. Central among these rulings are what is known as the Ten Commandments. According to tradition, there are actually 613 commandments (or mitzvot) in the Torah. The prophet Micah distilled the meaning of the Torah into the following formula:

> God has told you, O human, what is good,
> And what *Adonai* requires of you:
> Only to do justice, to love goodness, and to walk humbly with your God.
>
> Micah 6:8

Nearly a thousand years later, another great Jewish teacher, Hillel, gave the following formula when a non-Jew asked him to summarize the meaning of Torah:

> That which is hateful to you, do not do to your neighbor.
> That is the whole Torah. The rest is commentary.
> Now go and study.
>
> Babylonian Talmud, *Shabbat* 31a

Hillel's message has been repeated often, in one way or another, as the Golden Rule: Love your neighbor as yourself. Hillel is suggesting that the central theme of Torah is the ethical behavior between people. Since these ethics are often gray rather than black and white, Hillel emphasizes the importance of Torah study as a means to being a good person. Although the prophet Micah and the great teacher Hillel were each able to distill the essence of Torah into a concise teaching, Jewish philosophers and teachers have compiled their own lists of the most important elements of Judaism. One of these philosophers is Maimonides.

Thirteen Principles of Faith by Maimonides

Moses ben Maimon, known as Maimonides or The Rambam, was born in Spain in 1135. He was a surgeon, philosopher, politician, and Torah scholar. According to Maimonides, the thirteen essential beliefs of Judaism can be defined by the following formula:

I believe with complete faith:

1. That God continually creates and guides all creatures,
2. That God is unique and there is no one like God in any way, that God alone was, is, and will ever be,
3. That God is not physical and is not affected by physical phenomena, that nothing can be compared to God,
4. That God is infinite,
5. That God is the only One to whom one should pray, and to no other,
6. That all the words of the prophets are true,
7. That the prophecy of Moses is true and that he was the greatest of the prophets, before or after him,
8. That our current Torah is the same as the one given to Moses,
9. That the Torah will not be changed or added to,
10. That God knows all the deeds and thoughts of human beings,
11. That God rewards those who observe mitzvot, and punishes those who violate mitzvot,
12. That the Messiah will come, however long it takes, I look forward to it every day,
13. That there will be a resurrection of the dead when God wills it.

As you read over Maimonides' Thirteen Principles of Faith, take note of which beliefs seem most important to you. Take note also of whether the beliefs are still valid, nearly a thousand years later. Some of the ideas may seem at first to be out-of-date. Rather than dismissing those ideas, you may follow Maimonides' example of turning ideas and images over and over until fresh meanings could be drawn from them. In addition to Maimonides' Thirteen Principles, there have been other sets of doctrines and creeds expressed by Jews over the ages, some containing elements common to Maimonides', and others with very little overlap.

Reform Jewish Beliefs

Over the years that Reform Judaism has had its impact on Jewish life, Reform rabbis and leaders have been called on several times to write statements about what a Jew should believe and how a Jew should behave.

Reform Judaism developed as a result of political changes that were happening in Europe. In France and Holland in the late 1700s, Jews were granted citizenship in those countries—something that had never before happened in Europe. As a result of this new freedom, Jews were exposed to new ideas, customs, and social norms. They began adopting some of these elements into their religious life, and in 1796, a synagogue in Amsterdam began eliminating several prayers from the worship service and added a sermon (read in Dutch). These may seem like minor changes, but they were original and daring at the time.

During the 1760s and 1770s, a philosophical movement began to develop with German-born Moses Mendelssohn at its center. Its members called the movement הַשְׂכָּלָה (Haskalah), "enlightenment," from the Hebrew word שֵׂכֶל *(seichel),* "reason" or "intellect." The goal of Haskalah thinkers *(maskilim)* was to bridge the chasm between Jewish life and the world of mainstream European culture. Haskalah encouraged the study and writing of literature, philosophy, and political science, usually in Hebrew, and applying modern Western ways of thinking to understanding Judaism and Jewish Scriptures.

In 1801, a Jewish school in Seesen, Germany, began including German translations of some of the prayers and invited guest speakers to its Shabbat services. No Jewish service had ever been performed in anything but Hebrew, and when word got out, many Jews began flocking to the Seesen school's Shabbat services. In 1817, in Hamburg, Germany, a Reform society was established to promote religious discussion and to explore modernizing Jewish worship. New prayer books and synagogues soon followed.

Abraham Geiger, an important rabbi and religious leader in Breslau, Germany, established some important liturgical changes that included making the sermon the centerpiece of the service and adding organ music and orderly recitation of prayers to establish a tone of decorum. He also removed particularistic and nationalistic phrases from the prayer book (such as the notion of "Chosen People") and gave greater emphasis to the universal mission of Judaism to spread ethical monotheism.

In 1845 in Frankfurt, and in 1846 in Breslau, rabbinic conferences were held, attended by Geiger and other important figures, which affirmed the ideas of the new Reform Judaism. At these conferences, rabbis recommended abolishing dietary laws and the wearing of the *kippah, tallit,* and *t'fillin.* References to sacrifice, a "return to Zion," personal Messiah, and resurrection of the dead were removed from the prayer book. There was even debate about abolishing circumcision and the use of Hebrew in prayer, but these traditions remained.

In 1842, a synagogue in Baltimore, Maryland, became the first new synagogue to be organized as Reform in America. By 1871, the Reform Movement was firmly established in America and declared itself the Union of American Hebrew Congregations (UAHC) in 1873. The rabbis who affiliated with this movement formed the Central Conference of American Rabbis (CCAR) in 1889.

In 1885, a meeting of Reform rabbis and community leaders in Pittsburgh, Pennsylvania, met to discuss guidelines for Jewish Reform. The result was a statement called the Pittsburgh Platform, a statement containing eight "planks":

1. God is central to Judaism, but the God-idea belongs to all nations and peoples.
2. The Bible is a sacred record of the Jewish mission but must be interpreted and understood in light of modern scientific discoveries.
3. Jewish moral laws and ceremonies that "elevate and sanctify our lives," are accepted but "all such as are not adapted to the views and habits of modern civilization" are rejected.
4. All dietary laws, laws of priestly purity, and laws of dress are rejected.
5. While the idea of a "messianic age" is accepted, all ideas of a return to Jerusalem and a restoration of Temple sacrifices are rejected.
6. Judaism is growing and changing with the world and respects its partnership with Islam and Christianity in spreading the message of ethical monotheism.
7. While the idea that the human soul is immortal is accepted, the ideas of bodily resurrection and of reward and punishment in heaven and hell are rejected.
8. Social justice is "the great task of modern times," to solve society's problems "on the basis of justice and righteousness."

For the framers of this platform, these statements seemed solid and permanent. But fifty years after the signing of the Pittsburgh Platform, Jewish life in North America was in a totally different situation. Reform had become the establishment, rather than a revolutionary movement. The Jewish population in America had increased more than tenfold. The condition of Jews in Europe was vexed by poverty and violent anti-Semitism. The Great War (World War I) was past, but a new war was brewing in Europe. In light of these changes, a conference of Reform rabbis declared the Columbus Platform in 1937. Following are some of the highlights of that statement:

In view of the changes that have taken place in the modern world and the consequent need of stating anew the teachings of Reform Judaism, the Central Conference of American Rabbis makes the following declaration of principles. It presents them not as a fixed creed but as a guide for the progressive elements of Jewry....

Judaism is the historical religious experience of the Jewish people. Though growing out of Jewish life, its message is universal, aiming at the union and perfection of mankind under the sovereignty of God....

In Judaism religion and morality blend into an indissoluble unity. Seeking God means to strive after holiness, righteousness and goodness. The love of God is incomplete without the love of one's fellowmen. . . .

[Judaism] aims at the elimination of man-made misery and suffering, of poverty and degradation, of tyranny and slavery, of social inequality and prejudice, of ill-will and strife. . . .

These timeless aims and ideals of our faith we present anew to a confused and troubled world. We call upon our fellow Jews to rededicate themselves to them, and, in harmony with all men, hopefully and courageously to continue Israel's eternal quest after God and His kingdom.

In 1976, the CCAR issued another statement of Reform beliefs, titled "A Centenary Perspective." In the years since the Columbus Platform, many aspects of Jewish life had again altered. While anti-Semitism hadn't disappeared, it was not nearly as widespread as it had been in the 1930s. At that time, in an effort to affirm their affiliation with America, Reform leaders had been largely indifferent to Zionism and often strongly opposed it. However following the Holocaust and the establishment of the State of Israel, Reform leaders recognized the importance of Israel to the Jewish people:

We are bound to that land and to the newly reborn State of Israel by innumerable religious and ethnic ties. We have been enriched by its culture and ennobled by its indomitable spirit. We see it providing unique opportunities for Jewish self-expression. We have both a stake and a responsibility in building the State of Israel, assuring its security, and defining its Jewish character. We encourage *aliyah* for those who wish to find maximum personal fulfillment in the cause of Zion.

Social changes of the 1960s and 1970s resulted in ethnic pride among many minorities, including Jews. American Jewry felt it was no longer necessary to hide Jewish identity through assimilation. Members of the Reform Movement began reclaiming some of the traditional accoutrements that their parents had discarded: Hebrew, kashrut, and *kippot* were finding their way into Reform synagogues. We can see this change in the following statement taken from the Centenary Perspective:

Judaism emphasizes action rather than creed as the primary expression of a religious life, the means by which we strive to achieve universal justice and peace. Reform Judaism shares this emphasis on duty and obligation. Our founders stressed that the Jew's ethical responsibilities, personal and social, are enjoined by God. The past century has taught us that the claims made upon us may begin with our ethical obligations but they extend to many other aspects of Jewish living, including: creating a Jewish home centered on family devotion; lifelong study; private prayer and public worship; daily religious observance; keeping the Sabbath and the holy days; celebrating the major events of life; involvement with the synagogue and community; and other activities which promote the survival of the Jewish people and enhance its existence. Within each area of Jewish observance Reform Jews are called upon to confront the claims of Jewish tradition, however differently perceived, and to exercise their individual autonomy, choosing and creating on the basis of commitment and knowledge.

The above statement teaches that observance of mitzvot (commandments, ethical and ritual laws) should be important for Reform Jews. Still, Reform Jews should not follow with blind acceptance; rather we should be "choosing and creating on the basis of commitment and knowledge."

The most recent statement of principles for Reform Judaism, like the first one, was adopted in Pittsburgh, Pennsylvania. In May 1999, members of the CCAR issued a statement that reaffirmed the importance of the "three gems" of Judaism: God, Torah, and Israel:

This "Statement of Principles" affirms the central tenets of Judaism—God, Torah and Israel—even as it acknowledges the diversity of Reform Jewish beliefs and practices. It also invites all Reform Jews to engage in a dialogue with the sources of our tradition, responding out of our knowledge, our experience and our faith. Thus we hope to transform our lives through קְדֻשָׁה (kedushah), holiness.

God
We affirm the reality and oneness of God, even as we may differ in our understanding of the Divine presence.

We affirm that the Jewish people is bound to God by an eternal בְּרִית (b'rit), covenant, as reflected in our varied understandings of Creation, Revelation and Redemption. . . .

Torah
We affirm that Torah is the foundation of Jewish life.

We cherish the truths revealed in Torah, God's ongoing revelation to our people and the record of our people's ongoing relationship with God. . . . We are committed to the ongoing study of the whole array of מִצְווֹת (mitzvot) and to the fulfillment of those that address us as individuals and as a community. Some of these מִצְווֹת *(mitzvot),* sacred obligations, have long been observed by Reform Jews; others, both ancient and modern, demand renewed attention as the result of the unique context of our own times.

Israel

We are Israel, a people aspiring to holiness, singled out through our ancient covenant and our unique history among the nations to be witnesses to God's presence. We are linked by that covenant and that history to all Jews in every age and place.

Judaism has meant many things to many people. Within the Jewish people, groups and individuals have defined religion and Jewishness in many different ways. While belief in One God is the most universally accepted central idea of Judaism, it can be said that Judaism has many centers.

- For some, Judaism is a link with our culture and heritage.
- For some, Judaism is a God-given set of guidelines for living a good and proper life.
- For some, Judaism is a mission to better the world through social and political activism.
- For some, Judaism is a mission to preserve ancient and sacred traditions.
- For some, Judaism is a living and active community and civilization.

All of these things are valid, true ways in which Jews understand and express their Jewishness. Every Jew is challenged to find his or her own center in Judaism and to be prepared for that center to grow and change.

Religious Doctrines of World Religions

Christianity

The Christian religion is centered around the devotion to Jesus of Nazareth, believed by Christians to be the Christ (anointed one), the son of God, and the saver of human souls. For several centuries there was debate among Christians about the nature of Christ. In 325 C.E., three hundred years after the death of Jesus, the Roman Emperor Constantine organized a council of bishops and other Christian leaders to discuss and determine essential Christian beliefs. Meeting in Nicea, they came up with the Nicene Creed, which states:

I believe in one God the Father, and in one Lord Jesus Christ, the only begotten son of God, who came down from heaven, incarnate as a man for us and for our salvation; he was crucified, he suffered and was buried, and after three days he rose; and he shall come again. And I believe in the Holy Spirit, and in the Church, and in baptism for the pardon of sins; I look for the resurrection of the dead, and the life of the world to come. Amen.

From the Nicene Creed

One of the ideas that was determined is that the nature of the Trinity (God the Father, the Son, and the Holy Spirit) is not three separate beings, but three aspects or faces of one God. The Nicene Creed also emphasized that Jesus was sacrificed in order for sin to be taken away from human nature and that baptism is a means of being reborn to a life without sin.

Islam

As in Judaism, Islam emphasizes the oneness of God. In fact, of all religions, Islam seems to have the strongest message of monotheism. Founded by Muhammad in 622 C.E., Islam incorporated Jewish stories and beliefs into Arabic culture in a religion that spread throughout the Middle East and into Africa and Asia. The core belief is that God (Allah) is one, and that the faithful Muslim must submit to God's will and follow the right path. They believe that:

> There is no god but Allah, and Muhammad is His Prophet.

The Shahada

Islam also teaches that there has been a long succession of prophets, people who have served as God's messengers, who have included Abraham, Moses, Jesus, and the last of the prophets, Muhammad.

Hinduism

The "religion" of India (*hindu* means "Indian" in Sanskrit and Persian) truly tests our definitions of what a religion is. At close examination, Hinduism appears to be many religions. Individual sects such as Vaishna-

Indra, Bronze figure, 13th century C.E.

vism, Shivaism, Shaktism, Bhaktivedanta, and Tantrism each have their own sets of rituals, beliefs, goals, and objects of worship. In the Bhagavad Gita, the god Krishna explains to the soldier-prince Arjuna:

> Some yogis (persons practicing yoga) pray to the gods as their worship.
> Some offer worship by burnt offerings.
> Others offer their senses in the fire of self-denial.
> Others offer the senses what they desire, in the fire of the senses.
> Others offer actions of the senses and of the breath in a fire kindled by wisdom of the practice of self-restraint.
>
> Bhagavad Gita 4:25–28

While beliefs, rituals, and definitions vary from sect to sect, the basic beliefs of Hinduism include the following:

1. The life we are living is a life of illusion. All beings—gods, humans, and animals—are trapped in an endless cycle of rebirths *(samsara)* in this world.
2. All of our actions (karma) attach themselves to our self (atman) and come back to us either in this life or a later incarnation.
3. It is these attachments that bind us to the cycle of rebirths *(samsara).*
4. The individual person (atman) is a reflection of the universal world soul (Brahman). When the individual (atman), through practice and meditation (yoga), reunites with the world soul (Brahman), that individual breaks the wheel of karma and achieves salvation (nirvana).

The earliest Hindu writings are the Vedas (meaning "Wisdom"), poems of praise to various Hindu gods, such as Agni, Indra, and Soma. The focus of the Vedas is sacrifice to the gods. The most important collection of these poems is the Rig Veda, which contains 1,028 individual hymns. The following verses, dedicated to the fire-god Agni, will give an idea of the Vedas' contents:

> Lord of powers, master of sacrifice,
> Put on robes, and take our sacrifice.
> Sit, young Agni, our favorite priest.
> Through our hymns and our heavenly words.
> May Varuna, Mitra, amd Aryaman, proud of their powers,
> Sit upon our sacred grass, like Primal Man.
> You, ancient herald, enjoy our company and listen to our songs.

When we offer sacrifice to this god or that god, we are offering it to you.

May he be our beloved lord and priest,

May we have a worthy fire and be loved by him.

When the gods have a good fire, they bring us what we wish for.

So let us pray to you with a good fire.

May praises flow back and forth between us mortals and you, Immortal One.

Agni, son of strength, with all fires, find pleasure in our sacrifice, and our words.

Rig Veda 1:26:1, 2, 4–10

Buddhism

The word "Buddhism" comes from a Sanskrit word meaning "to wake up." Buddhism can be traced to the teachings of Siddhartha Gautama, who in 534 B.C.E. left the privileged life as a prince in India to find the reasons for death and human suffering. While sitting beneath a bodhi tree, he "woke up" or became "enlightened." After this enlightenment, Siddhartha Gautama came to be called Shakyamuni (Sage of the Shakya tribe) and Buddha (Enlightened One). His enlightenment meant discovering that the proper lifestyle is a middle path between luxury and asceticism and that all suffering comes out of our desires.

> All life is suffering.
> Suffering is caused by desire.
> Suffering may be stopped by removing desire.
> Desire may be removed by following the Eightfold Path.
>
> The Four Noble Truths

The Buddha taught that the means of ending suffering and achieving enlightenment was following the Eightfold Path of (1) proper understanding, (2) proper thought, (3) proper speech, (4) proper action, (5) proper livelihood, (6) proper effort, (7) proper mindfulness, and (8) proper concentration.

Although Buddhism was founded in India, today most Buddhists can be found in Asian countries outside of India.

Siddhartha, ca. 4th century C.E.

Confucianism

The Chinese sage K'ung-Fu-tzu (known in English as Master K'ung or Confucius) lived from 551 to 479 B.C.E. and taught that the purpose in life is to maintain harmony in the world by following the Tao (way) of proper discipline, respect, and goodness. In contrast to the Tao of Taoism (see below), the Confucian Tao is a philosophy of cultural order. Many of the teachings found in the Analects of Confucius are guides for politicians on the methods of proper leadership:

Confucius, 17th century
Chinese scroll painting.

> 2:3 Confucius said: "If you govern the people legalistically and control them by punishment, they will avoid crime, but have no personal sense of shame. If you govern them by means of virtue and control them with propriety, they will gain their own sense of shame, and thus correct themselves."

> 2:20 Chi K'ang Tzu asked: "How can I make the people reverent and loyal, so they will work positively for me?" Confucius said, "Approach them with dignity, and they will be reverent. Be filial and compassionate and they will be loyal. Promote the able and teach the incompetent, and they will work positively for you."
>
> Analects

The practical lessons found in his Analects remind us of the Hebrew Book of Proverbs, the Mishnah tractate *Pirkei Avot*, or even the teachings of Benjamin Franklin. Notice how numbers are used to emphasize the importance of being a good person:

> 5:15 Confucius said that Tzu Chan had four characteristics of the Superior Man: In his private conduct he was courteous; in serving superiors he was respectful; in providing for the people he was kind; in dealing with the people he was just.

> 16:10 Confucius said: "There are nine patterns which are awarenesses of the Superior Man. In seeing, he is aware of clarity; in listening, he is aware of sharpness;

in faces, he is aware of warmth; with behavior he is aware of courtesy; in speech, sincerity; in service, reverence. In doubt, he is inclined to question; when angry, he is aware of the inherent difficulties. When he sees an opportunity for gain, he thinks of what would be Righteous."

Analects

For Confucius, Tao is a way of justice, fairness, and preserving a stable society. One way of understanding Tao is as "balance" or "harmony." Society's harmony can be maintained by polite and respectful relations between people and by following the rules of the society. At first glance, this seems more like a political or civil movement than a religion. But along with the importance of following proper protocol (correct conduct based on hierarchy and established procedures) and decorum (conduct based on proper manners and graceful appearance), Confucianism emphasized piety toward elders, ancestors, and ancient kings and teachers. Its ethics, rituals, and civil order were spiritual experiences, cosmically ordained.

Taoism

Like Confucianism, this other great Chinese religion teaches that the goal in life is to pursue the harmony of the Tao. However, where Confucius emphasized harmony in human interaction, the Taoist teacher Lao-tzu taught of the harmony in nature:

> The great Tao flows everywhere, to the left and to the right.
> Ten thousand things depend on it; it holds nothing back.
> It fulfills its purpose silently and makes no claim.
> Tao Te Ching 34

Lao-tzu taught that two principles of the universe should always be in balance. These principles go by the Mandarin Chinese terms *yin* and *yang*.

Yang is the active element of nature, represented by the sun and light. Yin is the passive element, characterized by the moon and shadows. Yin is feminine energy, while yang is masculine. These two principles, represented in harmony as the light and dark halves of a circle, symbolize the balance, the way of nature: the Tao.

For the Taoist, the purpose in life is to do all things in accordance with the laws of nature. Observing and respecting natural beauty, and keeping a balance of all things in life, are the keys to "going with the flow" of Tao.

As the two primary religions native to classical China, Taoism and Confucianism complement each other in much the same way yin and yang complement one another.

The rituals, social protocols, and forms of worship of these two religions exist together in harmony, alongside Buddhist traditions, which became popular during the Han dynasty (206 B.C.E.–220 C.E.). The traditions and rituals of these three religions intermingled in the lives of families, communities, and kingdom.

The following table summarizes the religions explored in this chapter:

	Community of Believers	Deity/Deities	Core Beliefs	Core Teaching or Sacred Text	Human Mission
Judaism	Israel	God *(Y-H-V-H)*	There is one God who is our Creator, Redeemer from slavery, and Giver of Torah	Torah	To live an ethical and spiritual life in accordance with the Torah by observing mitzvot; to perfect the world
Christianity	Church	God as Father, Son, and Holy Spirit	Jesus is the way, the path to redemption from sin	The Bible; the person of Jesus Christ	To prepare the world for the return of Christ
Islam	Umma	God (Allah)	There is no god but Allah, and Muhammad is His Prophet	Quran, Hadith literature	To act according to the will of God
Hinduism	Unlike other religions that seek to unite the entire religious community, Hinduism divides its adherents into *varnas* (castes) and *jatis* (village societies)	Brahma, Vishnu, Shiva, Agni, Indra, Hanuman, Ganesha, and others	Life is an endless cycle of rebirths Action (karma) has consequences in this life or the next Nonviolence (ahimsa) The individual (atman) is the universe (Brahman)	Vedas, Upanishads, Bhagavad Gita	Nirvana, enlightenment: merging of the individual soul with the world soul
Buddhism	*Sangha*	Buddha Bodhisattvas	To eliminate desire is to free oneself of suffering	Dharma Tripitaka (Three Baskets), three collections of Sutras—"threads" of sacred writing attributed to the Buddha	Enlightenment: release of desires, merging with the Buddha-mind

Confucianism	The community for Confucians is the Chinese nation	Jade Emporer (Yu Huang—the ultimate god of Taoism and Confucianism) Various nature gods, city gods, and mythical ancestors	The way of the universe is the way of the kings of old	Analects	Cultural harmony through kindness, respect, protocol, and decorum
Taoism	By and large, Taoism is practiced by individuals and families at home and at local shrines; there is no distinct community of believers	Jade Emporer (Yu Huang—the ultimate god) Yuan-shih T'ien-tsun (first principal) Tien-kuan, Ti-kuan, and Shui-kuan (rulers of heaven, earth, and water) Various immortal heroes and teachers	The way of the universe is balance of opposing natural forces	Tao Te Ching	To find harmony with the way of nature

Chapter Two

נְשָׁמָה

N'shamah

The Breath of God,
the Soul of the World

And the breath of God hovered over the face of the
depths.

Genesis 1:2

God formed a man out of dust from the ground
and breathed into his nostrils the breath of life; and
man became a living being.

Genesis 2:7

What do we mean when we use the word "spirit"? Is soul something that is a part of us? Or is it something beyond and apart from our physical beings? Is spirit the thing that makes us human? Or is spirit something that is completely apart from humanity?

In this chapter, we will look at the words associated with soul and spirit.

Often these words are used interchangeably, to describe an aspect of a person where emotional and religious consciousness can be found. Soul and spirit are usually seen as the part of us that, while contained in our bodies, goes beyond our physical being and is somehow eternal.

An individual's soul or spirit is his or her life essence or inner being.

Soul and spirit are often defined as being transcendent, which means "going beyond" or "rising above." When we say something is transcendent, we are suggesting that it is outside of, greater than, and distant from normal everyday matters. A piece of music may have a transcendent affect on us if it moves us beyond our daily experience. The view of a tall mountain peak can, if we're in the right mood, have "transcendent beauty" for us.

We often find the word "spiritual" used as an adjective to describe religious matters. People sometimes use the words "spiritual" and "religious" interchangeably. What distinguishes these words is that a religion, as we saw in the last chapter, is bound to specific customs, practices, and institutions. Religious events and institutions may often be spiritual. But something that is spiritual may or may not be associated with a religion.

Word Histories

The surprising thing about the key words in this chapter is that they all have origins meaning "to breathe." Even the mysterious word "soul," whose origins are clouded by time, came into use as a substitute for the Latin word *anima*, which meant "breath."

Soul.   The origin of the word "soul" is a mystery. The sound of the word reminds us of the Latin words *sol* (sun, solar) and *solus* (one, singular, solitary), but there doesn't seem to be any proof that the words are connected. Whatever its origins, the soul is the central or integral part of something. In Western thought, epitomized by Plato, a human soul is the immaterial part, the opposite of body. Judaism doesn't make such a distinction. The soul is understood to be the source of

---

Key Terms

Soul. The immaterial aspect of human beings; the central or integral part of something.

Spirit. The life force or inner energy of a person; invisible beings such as ghosts, gods, or angels.

Enthusiasm. A feeling of excitement or lively interest in a subject or cause. The state of being filled with God.

Inspiration. Stimulation of the mind or emotions in a way that leads to increased activity. Breathing in.

נְשָׁמָה (*n'shamah*). Hebrew for breath, divine or human.

נֶפֶשׁ (*nefesh*). Hebrew for soul, living being, person, or self. From a root meaning "breath," "blood," or "life."

רוּחַ (*ruach*).   Wind or spirit.

---

our thoughts and emotions. The soul is also often considered the immortal and immaterial part of a person.

When we talk about the soul of something, we are addressing something that is very hard to put into words. We can't see, touch, or measure a soul. But presumably, we can feel it. When a piece of music strikes at our very core, we can say that the music is soulful. African American culture uses the word "soul" to label things that are special to the people, as in "soul music," "soul food," and "soul brother."

The expression "soul mate" refers to a relationship between two people that transcends the physical. A person might think of a soul mate as a predestined friend, partner, or lover, someone with whom a person shares deep understanding. In some circles, soul mates are believed to be people who shared a relationship in a previous life.

"Soul" can also be used as a synonym for "person," as in "he's a good soul," "she's the soul of discretion," and "Old King Cole was a merry old soul."

Spirit.   The word "spirit" comes from a Latin form, *spiritus,* "breath." It is related to words like "aspire," "expire," "inspire," and "perspire," as well as "sprite" (elf or fairy) and "sprightly" (full of life, animated). In early Christian writing, the Latin *spiritus* came to mean "soul."

"Spirit" can refer to an aspect of any living creature, or as something supernatural. The realm of the dead is sometimes called the "spirit world," and ghosts or disembodied souls are called spirits.

"Spirit" can also describe emotions, energies, or characteristics ("that's the spirit," "in the spirit of kindness," "keep up the spirit," and Charles Lindbergh's famous airplane, "the Spirit of St. Louis"). Furthermore to "spirit something away" is to take it in secret, or hide it, expressing the mysterious element of spirit. Just as African American music of the 1960s and 1970s was known as soul music, the music of nineteenth-century slaves was known as negro spirituals.

A religious experience that is highly moving is often referred to as spiritual. And so, when we are discussing the human experience of God and holiness, we often call it spirituality.

Enthusiasm.   While the word "enthusiasm" is usually applied to the energy, excitement, or interest a person shows toward a particular sport, hobby, or profession, the origins of this word are very religious. It is made up of the root *theos* ("god," as in "theology" and "theism") with the prefix *en* ("in" or "entered"). To be enthused or enthusiastic means to have God inside oneself, to be possessed by God.

Inspiration.   As with "enthusiasm," the word "inspiration" usually describes an energy that a person has for a particular job or task, especially with regard to the influence writers and artists sometimes find in doing their work. Also like "enthusiasm," the word originally meant "being filled with God." "Inspiration," which comes from the same root as "spirit," literally means "to breathe in." According to Jewish mythology, humanity was brought to life when God breathed into Adam's nostrils the breath of life.

We also used the word "inspired" when describing how holy books such as those in the Bible were written. When we say that a book is "divinely inspired," we are suggesting that the writer was guided by God's spirit, and so the book is, in part, written by God.

נְשָׁמָה *(n'shamah).* The Hebrew word *n'shamah* comes from a root that means "blow," "breath," or "pant." In the Bible, it is used to describe God's breath as well as human breath. Breath is the element that God gave us that made us come alive. Breath is the part of us that leaves the body when we die. God's breath and human breath are somehow mystically linked, as we see in Proverbs 20:27, where we are told:

נֵר יְהוָֹה נִשְׁמַת אָדָם.

Ner Adonai nishmat adam.
The lamp of *Adonai* is the *n'shamah* of humanity.

This passage implies—figuratively or perhaps literally—that the light of God can be found in the breath of every human being, that within each person is the flame of God's lamp.

נֶפֶשׁ *(nefesh).* The word *nefesh* comes from a Hebrew root that, like *n'shamah,* means "breath," as well as "blood," "life," and "soul." *Nefesh* is used frequently in the Bible, most often to mean "person," "living being," or "soul." When considered as "soul," it is often described as the part of a person that is the source of appetites, desires, emotions, and strong mental acts.

רוּחַ *(ruach).* *Ruach* is another Hebrew word whose root means "breath" or "blow." It is used in the Bible to describe human breath through mouth or nose, as well as "wind"—north wind, rushing wind, sea wind, and so on. *Ruach* also means "courage," "temper," "disposition," or "spirit." *Ruach* can mean "God's presence." *Ruchani,* an adjective from the same root, is the Hebrew word for "spiritual."

The Soul in Judaism

For Jews of all ages, soul is our breath and our inner being. The soul is a link to God found within our bodies. Through our function of breathing, we are bound to the Creator who breathed life into us.

In the first chapter of Genesis, we are told that on the sixth day of Creation, God made the entire human race, male and female, in God's image. In the second chapter of Genesis, we get a closer look at what it means to be made in the divine image. "God formed a man out of dust from the ground," we are told (Genesis 2:7). This is true both metaphorically and biologically. Human beings, like all life on earth, are made up of carbon, water, and various minerals. As a metaphor, this reminds us that we come from earth, from dirt, from the ground, and will one day return there. This is what is meant by the expression "feet of clay." None of us is perfect. We are all composed of dirt.

Yet we are also more than dirt. Not only do we have God's image, but we have God's spirit, God's *n'shamah,* breathed into us. The second part of Genesis 2:7 teaches that God "breathed into his nostrils the breath of life; and man became a living being." We may be made of dirt, but we have God's breath running through our bodies. That bit of God inside us, as some Jews understand it, is the soul.

Body and Soul

Plato and most Western thinkers who followed him accept a duality of body and soul. They say that our spiritual beings are distinct from our physical bodies, which serve as temporary shells. Our bodies may get old, sick, and eventually die and decay, but our souls are eternal.

Judaism does not argue against these beliefs, though it does stress that body and soul are both part of us and together form one whole. It is our task to integrate body and soul, to bring them together rather than to separate them in order to deny the physical. As in Native American religions, in Chinese Taoist philosophy, and in Tai Chi (a Chinese exercise intended to coordinate mind, body, and spirit), Judaism works to find spirit in the natural world.

The way Judaism does this is through mitzvot. Many, if not most, of the mitzvot found in Torah are meant to raise normal mundane experience to a spiritual level. Everything from the way we eat to the way we conduct business—even the way we make love—is done in ways that raise our spirituality. Judaism is one of the few religions that teach that sex is a holy act. Even the most basic biological function—going to the bathroom—is transformed into a soulful and sacred act by saying the prayer *Asher Yatzar,* in which we thank God for having the wisdom to have created us with the ability to relieve ourselves. The prayer reminds us that our bodies are a sacred balance of openings and closings, vessels and passageways, that allow us to continue living, providing us with the chance to thank God.

Prayer as a Breathing Meditation

Hinduism emphasizes that by chanting holy syllables, particularly the mantra "om," an individual can break down the bounds of selfhood and merge with Brahman, the world soul. The Hindu can effectively find himself by losing his self. As Jews, we have similar beliefs. Our prayers, like the Vedas and mantras, are said as offerings to God. When we give them, we are praising God, asking God for favor, and in the very act of saying the prayers, elevating our own souls.

The important distinction is that in Hinduism, as well as in other Eastern religions, as we'll see later in this chapter, the task is for the individual to lose his or her selfhood and to merge with the collective world soul, the Buddha-mind, or the Tao. The highest point in these religions is to achieve nothingness, a void. In *moksha* or nirvana the individual ceases to exist. In Judaism, by contrast, "spiritual enlightenment" is experiencing the link between our souls and God in an act of asserting the self. In Eastern religions, one seeks union with God, while in Judaism and other Western religions, the emphasis tends to be making communion with God—sharing and partnering with God—while maintaining individual identity.

Look at some of the ways in which Hebrew prayers serve as tools or mantras to bring our souls closer to God. The first, and most obvious, is the *Sh'ma*. Like the sacred word "om" in Hinduism, the word *sh'ma* can serve as a mantra, teaching us lessons while guiding us in a meditation.

The first sound of the word *sh'ma* is "sh"—the sound of white noise, all tones blended together, instructing us to be quiet, while at the same time reminding us of chaos, of a world not in order, like a radio caught between stations unable to focus.

The second sound is "m"—calling us to focus the chaos, to bring things together. "M" is a nurturing sound. It asks us to gather all the sparks of Creation together as a shepherd gathers his flock. "M" is the quiet sound of humming within our souls.

The final sound—flowing outward from the focusing "m"—is the expanding sound of "ah." It is the sound of breath, reminding us of God and God's Oneness. The sound "ah" has no ending; once begun it is infinite.

Each time we say the word *sh'ma,* we are being told to pay special attention—to listen. We are making a testimony to God, retracing Creation from chaos to unity, and awakening our souls to the spirit of God and the universe.

Another part of Jewish prayer that teaches us lessons about the soul is the אֱלֹהַי נְשָׁמָה *Elohai N'shamah*—a prayer said each morning thanking God for giving us our souls. This prayer has an almost magical sound to it;

Page from Jewish prayer book, Vienna, 1716–1717.

without even paying attention to the meaning, one can hear the meaning in the vowels and consonants that are used. As you read the Hebrew of the first seven lines, below, notice how frequently the sounds "h" and "ah" are used. One can't read this prayer aloud without being aware of one's breathing.

Elohai n'shamah	אֱלֹהַי נְשָׁמָה	O God, the soul
Shenatata bi	שֶׁנָתַתָּ בִּי	That You have given me
T'horah hi.	טְהוֹרָה הִיא.	It is pure.
Atah b'ratah	אַתָּה בְּרָאתָהּ	You created it
Atah y'tzartah	אַתָּה יְצַרְתָּהּ	You formed it
Atah n'fachtah bi	אַתָּה נְפַחְתָּהּ בִּי	You breathed it into me
V'atah m'shamrah b'kirbi.	וְאַתָּה מְשַׁמְּרָהּ בְּקִרְבִּי.	And within me You sustain it.
Kol z'man shehan'shamah	כָּל זְמַן שֶׁהַנְּשָׁמָה	So long as I have breath
b'kirbi	בְּקִרְבִּי	in me
Modeh ani l'fanecha.	מוֹדֶה אֲנִי לְפָנֶיךָ.	I give thanks to You.

The Four-Letter Name of God

God's most mysterious name is the four-letter name יהוה *(Y-H-V-H)*, often referred to as the Tetragrammaton (from the Greek meaning "four-letter word"). The High Priest spoke this special name during Yom Kippur within the confines of the Holy of Holies back in the days when the Temple stood in Jerusalem. No one alive knows exactly how this name was pronounced. It is so sacred that when we see this word in the prayer book or the Torah, rather than trying to pronounce it, we say *Adonai.* The four-letter name may come from the Hebrew root ה-י-ה *(h-y-h)*, meaning "to be." Thus, God's name may mean "Is" or "That Which Is."

The letters of the four-letter name also give us a metaphor for our own breathing:

י–*Y–yod*—our bodies in their small state, with all air blown out of the lungs;

ה–*H–hei*—inhale, the ה resembling our windpipe, and its sound that of flowing breath;

ו–*V–vav*—body in large state, lungs full of air, back straight;

ה–*H–hei*—exhale, and the cycle is ready to repeat.

Rabbi Abraham Isaac Kook

Abraham Isaac Kook was born in Latvia in 1865 and served as the Chief Rabbi of Jerusalem from 1919 until his death in 1935. Rav Kook was a scholar, a diplomat, a mystic, and a poet. Below are the texts of two poems by Rav Kook that express his view of the nature of the human soul and the "world soul":

My soul aspires
For the mysteries,
For the hidden secrets of the universe.
It cannot be content
With much knowledge
That probes
The trivialities of life.

Rav Abraham Isaac Kook, in *Abraham Isaac Kook:*
The Lights of Penitence, Lights of Holiness, trans. Ben Zion Bokser (Paulist Press, 1978), p. 371

The words of this poem give a feel of the soul rising up, trying to reach toward God. In this next poem, we also get a sense of the human soul rising. But we also get an image of the spirit of God, expressed in the world soul, a universal spirit like the Buddha-mind or the Hindu idea of Brahman.

Radiant is the world soul,
Full of splendor and beauty,
Full of life,
Of souls hidden,
Of treasures of the holy spirit,
Of fountains of strength,
Of greatness and beauty.
Proudly I ascend
Toward the heights of the world soul
That gives life to the universe.
How majestic the vision,
Come, enjoy,
Come, find peace,
Embrace delight,
Taste and see that God is good.
Why spend your substance on what does not nourish
And your labor on what cannot satisfy?
Listen to me, and you will enjoy what is good,
And find delight in what is truly precious.

Ibid., p. 376

In "Radiant Is the World Soul," Kook shows us how we can reach out and find the spirit of God in the world. While we aspire to get closer to God, we find beauty in the world around us.

The Soul in World Religions

Hindu

The Hindu belief is that while two souls exist—the individual soul and the world soul—they are really one soul. Hindu philosophy teaches that Brahman, a being present at Creation, is the world soul that encompasses the entire universe. Often portrayed in human form, Brahman is Everything, Infinity, All-Being. The soul or identity of individual people is referred to as atman, or self. The paradox that is often repeated in the Upanishads—a body of Hindu philosophical writings composed around the seventh and eighth centuries B.C.E.—is that atman equals Brahman; the individual is the universe.

> In the beginning this world was only Brahman, and it knew only its self [atman]. It thought, "I am Brahman," and thereby became the Whole.... This is true even now. If a man knows "I am Brahman" he becomes the whole world. Not even the gods can stop it, for he becomes their self. So when a man worships a god, and thinks, "He is one, I am another," he does not understand.
>
> Brihadaranyaka Upanishad 1:4:10

Breathing is a form of spiritual exercise or yoga in Indian religion. When we breathe, we are celebrating the link that our atman has with Brahman. Saying certain sounds, especially the Vedic chant "om," has special meaning both in showing devotion to the gods and in helping to connect atman with Brahman. The sound "om" is formed from the different parts of breath and is considered the High Chant. The following passage from the Chandogya Upanishad teaches the meaning of "om" by using linguistic wordplay:

> This breath in here and that sun up there are exactly the same. This is warm, and so is that. People call this *svara* [sound] and that *svara* [shine]. ... Therefore one should venerate the High Chant as both this here and that there.
>
> Chandogya Upanishad 1:3:2

From Hindu religion, we learn several things about the soul: (1) soul (atman) is connected with our breath and with our voices; (2) an individual's soul (atman) is not only parallel to the world soul (Brahman), it *is* Brahman; and (3) a truly enlightened person recognizes that there is no separation between individual soul and world soul, and in making this recognition, he is set free.

Plato and the Soul

Plato is the most famous and one of the most influential philosophers of all time. He lived from approximately 427 to 347 B.C.E., and most of his writings present his ideas about knowledge, nature, and humanity in the form of imaginary dialogues between his own teacher, Socrates, and various other philosophers.

Plato by Giovanni Pisano, 13th century.

More than any other scholar, prophet, or theologian, Plato put into concrete terms many of the ideas about the human soul that exist today. The soul that modern thinkers talk about, even when they claim that it doesn't exist, is the soul defined by Plato. His ideas about the eternal soul also had an important influence on Christian beliefs.

Much of what Plato said about the soul addresses afterlife, or what happens to the soul after we die. This is a subject we will examine in detail in chapter 7. In *Phaedo,* his dialogue about the death of his teacher, Socrates, Plato explains the nature of the human soul. The setting of *Phaedo* is a prison cell, where Socrates was being held for "impiety." As Socrates awaits punishment by poison, Simmias, Cebes, and other students visit him to ask him about what is to happen when he dies.

> "Do we think there is such a thing as death? Is it anything more than the separation of the soul from the body?" said Socrates. "Death is, that the body separates itself from the soul, and remains by itself apart from the soul, and the soul, separated from the body, exists by itself apart from the body. Is death anything but that?"
>
> *Phaedo 63b–65a*

The soul, for Plato, is eternal. Every person's soul existed before they were born and will continue to exist after that person dies. Each soul has knowledge and wisdom that go far beyond that of which we are aware. Trapped in our physical bodies, our souls are unable to recall all of the teachings and experiences of infinity. "Our souls existed long ago, before they were in human shape, apart from bodies, and then had wisdom."

So what is the soul? According to Plato, it is

> the unseen part of us, which goes to another place noble and pure and unseen like itself, a true unseen Hades, to the presence of the good and wise God, where, if God will, my own soul must go very soon.
>
> *Phaedo 79c–81b*

The soul is part of the unseen world, "the divine and the immortal and the wise" (Plato).

Native American Spirituality

For the most part, the indigenous people of North America do not have a strong concept of personal soul. The individual is thought to be made up of many souls, souls of nature and of ancestors that dwell around and within us.

Rather than focusing on the self, Native American religion emphasizes group souls and the spirit that flows through nature and ancestors. The soul of the community/tribe/ nation is bound to the soul forces of nature, as we see in the following prayer from the Oglala Sioux holy man Black Elk:

Tobacco, an Oglala Chief by George Catlin, 19th century.

> "Grandfather, the Great Spirit, behold me! To all the wild things that eat flesh, this I have offered that my people may live and the children grow up with plenty."
>
> Neihardt, *Black Elk Speaks* (Morrow, 1932), p. 65

When explaining the soul of the universe to John Neihardt, Black Elk holds up a pipe as a symbol. The four ribbons hanging from its stem represent the four winds, four spirits, the four compass points, and the four elements of rain, cleansing, wisdom, and power.

"But these four spirits are only one Spirit after all, and this feather here is for that One, which is like a father, and also it is like the thoughts of men that should rise high as eagles do."

Ibid., p. 2

Native Americans are, as a people, less concerned with the individual soul or spirit than with the soul of the community and the spirits of the ancestors that exist all around.

Pentecostal Christianity

The image of the Holy Spirit entering the bodies of humans is a persistent one in Christianity. To be "possessed" by God is among the greatest heights a Christian can obtain. Many Christian stories describe how a person is transformed after God has entered them. One Christian movement—Pentecostalism—has focused on this part of the religious experience.

The Pentecostal movement gets its name from the Greek word for the festival of Shavuot. The traditional Jewish observance of Shavuot includes all-night study sessions in order to be awake and studying Torah on the anniversary of the receiving of the Torah at Sinai (which, according to tradition, took place early in the morning). One of the most unusual stories in the Christian Bible involves the Shavuot observance of a group of early Christians, the apostles, and how their study resulted in the flowing of God's spirit:

> When the day of Pentecost [Shavuot] had come, they were all together in one place. And suddenly a sound came from the heaven like the rush of a mighty wind, and it filled all the house where they were sitting. And there appeared to them tongues of fire, one resting on each of them. And they were all filled with the Holy Spirit and began to speak in tongues, as the Spirit gave them utterances.

Acts 2:1–4

The precise meaning of this story, particularly the idea of "speaking in tongues," is unclear to modern readers. But it is clear that the Holy Spirit had a powerful effect on the apostles. This spirit, presenting itself in the form of wind and fire, transformed the apostles to their very souls. This is the literal meaning of "inspiration" and "enthusiasm." It was the very entering of God's spirit into their bodies that transformed them.

There are modern Christian denominations that call themselves Pentecostalists who emphasize Holy Spirit in their worship. For these groups, formal liturgy (prayer services) is less important than spontaneous soulful expression. People pray "as their souls move them," calling out, dancing, spinning without any form or pattern other than the belief that they are being directed by the Holy Spirit.

As we look at the ways in which other religions understand the idea of soul, we can not only better understand how the Jewish views are unique, but we can also build a better framework for understanding *what it is* that we as Jews believe.

Chapter Three

Elohim

God—Part One:
What Is a Deity?

Who among the gods is like You, *Adonai*?
Who is like You—majestic in holiness, awesome in glory,
working wonders?

Exodus 15:11

"God" is the ultimate concept. Of all the things that cannot be seen, touched, or measured, God is the highest of the high. But what do we really mean when we use that word? How do we describe that which is cannot be observed or measured? In calling God a "being," are we saying that God is a personality? An emotion? An energy? An idea?

Human beliefs about God and gods range from personal, anthropomorphic images and ideas to very abstract concepts. In this chapter we will examine how different cultures have developed ideas of the Divine to fit their condition and how these cultural ideas inform our understanding of Jewish theology.

Many religions include belief in, and worship of, more than one god. We call this "polytheism," a term that includes ancient and modern religions such as Babylonian, Greek, Roman, Hindu, and Native American religions. Other religions espouse belief in only one God, which we call "monotheism." Judaism, Christianity, and Islam are all examples of monotheistic religions.

Throughout this chapter we will be referring to the gods of polytheistic religions using the word "god" with a lowercase "g." For the sake of discussion, we are assuming that the monotheistic religions (Islam, Christianity, and Judaism) all worship the same God. We differentiate this God of monotheistic religions by spelling it "God" with an uppercase "G." When talking about God as an abstraction, and when our discussion applies equally to one God as it does to many gods, we will also use "God" with a capital "G."

When we describe God, we often use human terms. We call this kind of description "anthropomorphism" (changing to human). In the Bible you may find expressions like "the hand of God," "the voice of God," and "the throne of God." Since God has no form or body, God cannot have a hand, a voice, or a throne in any literal sense; however, we can understand these images as representing the control, the message, and the presence of God.

An important problem when we are talking about God has to do with gender. In polytheistic religions, there are male gods, female gods, and gods that can be neither or both. Christianity traditionally asserts that God is masculine, whether describing God the Father or God the Son. Conversely, Judaism, Islam, and certain strands of Hinduism, teach that God, having no physical form, is neither male nor female.

Nevertheless, Jews have traditionally used masculine language to describe God. Part of the reason for this is that every noun and verb conjugation of the original Hebrew text is either male or female. As a result, words like "King," "Father," "He," "Him," and "His" recur throughout English translations and reinforce the tendency to view God as masculine. Although English has male, female, and neutral nouns and verb conjugations, religious thinkers and translators find it difficult to use the neutral pronoun "It" when describing God. This book provides no easy solutions to the problem. When we describe God, gender-neutral language is used except when quoting texts.

Word Histories

God. The similary between the words "God" and "good" has led people to mistakenly assume that they come from

---

Key Terms

God. A being of supernatural powers or attributes, believed in and worshiped by a people. Adapted from the Indo-European root *ghut* ("called" or "invoked").

Lord. A man of high rank in society. Taken from the root *wor* (watchful), a person who was watchful, on guard, or in charge. As a title of respect, it is often used as a substitute for "God" or "god."

Deity. A god or supreme being, from the Latin word *deus*, meaning "god."

Theology. The study of the nature of God; a system of opinions or beliefs about God.

Monotheism. The worship, doctrine, and belief in one God.

Polytheism. The worship, doctrine, and belief in more than one god.

Pantheism. Often used as a synonym for "polytheism," pantheism (pan = all + theism) can mean belief in *all* gods, as well as belief that God is *in* all things. "Pantheon" means the listing of all gods of a particular religion.

Monism. A belief, found in various philosophies and religions, that all things are part of a unified One.

the same source. The source of the word "God" is an ancient Indo-European root, *ghut,* meaning "call upon," "invoke," or "implore." God is thus the being or entity upon whom we call.

Lord. Although in American standard English, this word is almost exclusively used as a synonym for God, its meaning is originally and primarily human. From a root word meaning "guardian," the word "Lord" originally meant a head of household, a husband, or a landowner. In medieval Europe, "Lord" meant the master of an estate or manor. It was commonly used as a title, similar to Duke, Baron, Earl, or Count, referring to high political, military, or commercial figures. In England, a Lord is a member of the upper class of British society, as in the title House of Lords. Yet, like its ancient Hebrew counterparts בַּעַל *(baal)* and אָדוֹן *(adon)*—both of which mean "lord," "master," or "husband"—the word "Lord" has also been used to describe God and gods from earliest times. Names of Hindu gods as well as teachers are often prefaced with the word "sri" (similar in meaning, but probably unrelated to the English "sir"), which is usually translated as "Lord" (as in "Lord Krishna").

Deity. From the Latin root *deus* (god), "deity" is a generic term for a god or God. It is related to the words "divine," "divinity," and "diva." "Deity," in turn, is the root of many religious terms including "theology," "theism," "atheism," "monotheism," and so on.

The Gods of World Religions

Whenever and wherever people have come together, religion happens. And where there is religion, there are usually (but not always) gods to be worshiped. Most world religions, ancient and modern, are polytheistic, believing in more than one god.

It's natural for Jews, Christians, and Muslims to view polytheism—the belief in more than one god—as being primitive and inferior to monotheism. There is no question that, from our point of view, belief in a single God is a higher step in the evolution of ideas and worship of idols is a wrongful practice. But it is also important for us to respect and appreciate the beliefs of polytheistic religions for what they are and what they can teach us about our own beliefs.

As we will see, the gods of polytheistic faiths often show the same characteristics of our own God. Many polytheistic gods would be understood and labeled as angels, prophets, or saints if we used the same definitions that we apply to our own religion.

Are there other ways to harmonize the idea of one God with the idea of many? To a certain extent, yes. Just as a school has many classes and a house has many rooms, so does God have many aspects, attributes, or faces. Later in this chapter we will look at the Hindu story of Vidagdha, a student, who learns from his teacher that the thousands of gods that are worshiped can all be boiled down to a single God. Similarly, Christianity teaches the idea of a Trinity—Father, Son, and Spirit—as three aspects of one God.

The Gods of Ancient and Tribal Communities

From earliest times, human beings have worshiped the very things they most needed and most feared. Water is the most basic of human needs, but can also be a devastating cause of death and destruction in the form of floods, tidal waves, and accidental drowning. Therefore, there is an abundance of sea gods, examples of which include Poseidon (Greece), Njord (Norse), Neptune (Rome), Varuna (India), Idliragijenget (Inuit), and Tiamat (Babylonia).

Beasts are both a source of food and a dangerous threat. Snakes, bulls, and birds of prey are often used as images of gods. Animal gods include Anyiewo (snake god of Togo, Africa), Anansi (spider god of West Africa), Apis (the sacred bull of Egypt), Bast (Egyptian cat goddess), Horus (Egyptian falcon god), and Ganesh (the elephant god of India).

Horus, shown as a falcon, Temple of Seti I, Abydos, Egypt, 13th century B.C.E.

As infants, we see our parents as sources of food, comfort, and security. It's no accident that many cultures have gods that are depicted as parents. The function of such gods is often expanded to being a patron god of a specific tribe or city. Related also is the ancestor worship that is found in many African, Asian, and Native American religions. Gods associated with sky or heavens such as Apollo, Odin, Zeus, and Marduk are typically portrayed as father gods. Earth deities such as Isis (Egypt), Eithinoha (Iroquois), Demeter (Greece), and Eseasar (Africa) are often depicted as mother gods.

In addition to gods of earth, sky, and water, most polytheistic religions identify a god or goddess who rules the underground, usually associated with death. These include Hades (Greece), Ereshkigal (Babylon), Pluto (Rome), Osiris (Egypt), Hella (Norse), and Miclantechupi (Aztec).

Gods and goddesses were frequently associated with specific places and tribes, as well as psychological and social phenomena. The Greek goddess Athena was the patron of the arts and of the city-state of Athens. The Philistine god Dagon was closely associated with Gaza. Southern Italy was thought to be the realm of the Roman god Saturn. Chinese religion included patron gods for nearly every occupation, including butchers, masons, fishermen, and wig salesmen. The Indian elephant god, Ganesha, is the patron of wisdom and prosperity. Japanese gods include Usu-dori (goddess of singing), Shoten (god of commerce), Okuni-Nushi (god of medicine), and Monju-Bosatsu (god of education).

The Gods of the World

	Sumerian	Babylonian	Egyptian	Greek	Roman	Hindu	Norse
Creator	Enki	Apsu Tiamat	Ptah	Cronus Gaea		Brahma	Odin
Sky/heaven	An	Anu Marduk	Nuit	Uranus Zeus	Apollo	Indra	Odin
Earth	Ki	Ea	Isis	Demeter	Terra	Vishnu	Jord
Sun	Utu	Shamash	Ra	Apollo	Sol	Surya	Frey
Fire	Gibil	Gerra	Ptah	Hephaestus	Vulcan	Agni	Heimdall
Water	Nammu	Tiamat Apsu	Anuket	Poseidon	Neptune	Varuna	Njord
Underworld	Endukugga	Ereshkigal	Osiris Anubus	Hades Persephone	Pluto	Yama	Hel
Air	Enlil	Ellil	Shu	Aeblas Aether	Mercury	Vaya	
Moon	Nanna	Kingu	Bast	Artemis	Diana	Chandra	Freyja
War	Ashur Akkad	Ninurta	Sakhmet	Ares	Mars	Shiva	Thor Tyr
Love	Inanna	Ishtar	Hathor	Aphrodite	Venus	Lakshmi Kama	Freyja
Intoxication	Ashnan	Ninkasi	Tenenit	Dionysus	Bacchus	Soma	Aegir

Mesopotamian Gods

Jewish theology grew out of ancient Israelite ideas about God. These ideas, in turn, were more often than not shaped by reaction against the religions of the nations of ancient Mesopotamia.

"Mesopotamia" is a geographical term meaning "between the rivers." It refers to the land between the Tigris and Euphrates Rivers in what roughly is now Iraq. The Sumerians were a non-Semitic people who had a strong presence in the area from 3300 to 1900 B.C.E. They were a confederacy of several city-states, each with its own patron god. Myths arose about these gods that explained natural and social phenomena and provided a common worldview. When the Amorites conquered the region in 1900, much of Sumerian religion remained, including numerous myths and gods. Around 1600 B.C.E., the city-state of Babylon became the prominent power in the region. A Babylonian empire grew, and the Babylonian national identity included gods and myths adapted from Sumeria.

The primary Sumerian gods include An (sky—male), Ki (earth—female), Nammu (water—female), and Enlil (air—male). The sky god An—whose worship was centered in the city of Uruk—was originally the supreme god of the pantheon. But when the city of Nippur succeeded Uruk as capital of Sumeria, Enlil replaced An as the chief god of the pantheon.

Other gods included Nanna—the moon god and son of Enlil. Nanna was the father of Utu, the sun god, and Inanna, the queen of heaven. Inanna, as goddess of wisdom, love, and war, was very important in the belief and worship of the Sumerian people, together with the worship of Inanna's lover, the bull-shepherd god Dumuzi (god of vegetation and farming).

The Babylonians borrowed gods and myths from Sumeria, changing names as necessary, and supplanting certain old gods with their own new ones. The chief god of Babylonia was Marduk, an agricultural god similar to the Sumerian Dumuzi. The Babylonian versions of the cosmological epic *Enuma Elish* ("When on High") describe how, in the beginning, Apsu (fresh water) and Tiamat (the depths of the sea, depicted as a dragon) led a quiet life as husband and wife. They had several children—including the gods Kingu (moon), Anu (sky), and Ea (earth)—whose noisy playfulness annoyed their father. When Apsu threatened his children, he was killed by his son Ea. Angered by her husband's death, the dragon queen Tiamat attacked the lower gods. It was her grandson, Marduk, who heroically slayed Tiamat by slicing her body down the middle, making the heavens from one half and the earth from the other. The fluid from her pierced eyes became the Tigris and Euphrates.

Greek and Roman Pantheons

Just as the Babylonians borrowed and adapted the mythology of Sumeria to develop their own myths, so did the Romans copy many of the gods and stories of ancient Greece. The Greek Zeus became the Roman Jupiter. Ares and Poseidon were renamed Mars and Neptune. Dionysus became Bacchus, and Aphrodite was reborn as Venus. The lives of the Greek and Roman gods are told by sculptures and temples that remain today as archeological relics, as well as in the writings of Homer, Hesiod, Ovid, and others who related the acts of people and gods in epic poetry.

Greek and Roman gods were surprisingly human. The stories of the gods reflected many social and physical elements of human experience, including the pettiness, deceit, and whimsy that sometimes plague human society. Although often depicted as being bigger than humans, the Greeks and Romans created their gods in their own image. The myths of the Greek gods form a story tied to the creation of the world and the origin of humanity. It is a history of fighting, petty intrigue, and underhanded plots. The gods are not immune to jealousy, greed, and revenge. The myths tell of several generations of gods.

In the beginning, according to the myths, the world was filled with chaos. Out of the chaos, Gaea, the earth mother, emerged. Gaea had a son, Uranus, who became the sky father and married his mother. They had many children, most of whom were gigantic monsters such as the Cyclopes. Twelve children of Gaea and Uranus were called the Titans, which included Rhea (mother of the gods), Prometheus (humanity's friend and giver of fire), Atlas (who carried the world on his shoulders), Oceanus (god of the oceans), and Cronus (leader of the Titans). Fearing that they would take control of the universe, Uranus had all the Titans locked up inside Gaea's body. Cronus escaped to save his mother and free the other Titans. He killed his father and became the new supreme god.

Cronus married his sister Rhea, and they had six children. Fearing that his children would do to him what he had done to his own father, Cronus swallowed each of his children. Rhea managed to hide her youngest son, Zeus, who returned when he was grown, forced his father to vomit up the other children, and then slew Cronus with a thunderbolt. The next generation of gods were the Olympians, named for Mount Olympus, their home. The Olympians included the following (Roman names in parentheses):

Zeus (Jupiter)—son of Cronus and Rhea, and leader of the Olympians
Hera (Juno)—daughter of Cronus and Rhea, wife to Zeus, goddess of marriage
Poseidon (Neptune)—son of Cronus and Rhea and god of the sea

47

Demeter (Ceres)—daughter of Cronus and Rhea, goddess of agriculture

Apollo (Apollo)—son of Zeus, god of the sun, music, and the arts

Artemis (Diana)—twin sister to Apollo, goddess of the moon, hunting, and children

Athena (Minerva)—daughter of Zeus, goddess of wisdom

Aphrodite (Venus)—goddess of love and beauty

Hermes (Mercury)—son of Zeus, messenger of the gods, protector of travelers and merchants

Ares (Mars)—son of Zeus and Hera, god of war

Hephaestus (Vulcan)—son of Zeus and Hera, god of fire and metalwork

Dionysus (Bacchus)—son of Zeus, god of wine and celebration

On one level, Greek and Roman mythologies are pure entertainment. These are enjoyable and exciting stories about love, jealousy, and adventure. On another level, the ancients used these stories of their gods to explain natural and psychological events. The story of Demeter and her daughter Persephone, for instance, explains the seasons of the earth, how humanity learned to farm, and why crops do not grow in winter. Persephone, the daughter of Demeter and Zeus, was forced into marriage with her uncle, Hades, ruler of the underworld, the realm of the dead. Demeter was so distraught over the loss of her daughter that she went into a deep depression, causing all vegetation to cease growing. As the earth grew barren, an arrangement was made that enabled Persephone to return to her mother once a year, bringing forth spring. Demeter was so grateful that she taught human civilization how to cultivate the land. But each autumn, as Persephone would return to Hades, the land would dry up and crops would stop producing.

Some gods were personifications of abstract ideas, like Eros for love, Chronos for time, and Psyche for the soul. Fate is depicted

Athena, Greek sculpture.

as three sisters, Clotho, Lachesis, and Atropos, who spend eternity weaving human destiny. Clotho would spin the thread, determining how people are born. Lachesis was responsible for measuring, determining the length of our days. Atropos was in charge of cutting, deciding the moment of death.

Gods in the Names of Days, Months, and Astral Bodies

While the seven-day week is certainly a Jewish invention, most of the world has adopted that system, adding to it their own religious bent. Most cultures and languages name the days of the week based on their theology, astronomy, or chemistry.

	Norse/Anglo-Saxon origin	Italian (from Latin)	Japanese
Sunday	Sun's day	Domenica (Sun)	Sun day
Monday	Moon's day	Lunedí (Lunar)	Moon day
Tuesday	Tiu's (Norse war goddess) day	Martedí (Mars)	Fire day
Wednesday	Odin's day	Mercoledí (Mercury)	Water day
Thursday	Thor's day	Giovedì (Jove, Jupiter)	Tree day
Friday	Freyja (or Frigg's) day	Venerdì (Venus)	Gold day
Saturday	Saturn's day (from Latin)	Sabado (Sabbath)	Earth day

The Gods of India

India—as well as most of the rest of East Asia—is a land of many gods and many religions. Religious Asians may observe household rituals of one religion, regularly attend a temple of another religion, follow marriage rituals of a third religion, and practice funeral customs of a fourth. The word "Hindu," in fact, doesn't refer to a single religion, but simply means "Indian" and includes a variety of religious practices and beliefs.

There are too many forms of Hinduism to discuss in these pages, so we'll focus on three forms that are part of the central traditions of Indian religion but are each quite different from one another. The forms, or disciplines, are Veda, Vedanta, and Bhaktivedanta.

Veda. Vedic religion involves worship—based on collections of hymns (called Vedas, from the Sanskrit word for "wisdom")—to various Vedic gods.

Vedanta. Vedanta (literally meaning "after Veda") is an intellectual and philosophical form of observance involving the study and discussion of the nature of gods and reality. The most common Vedantic texts are the many collections of teachings called the Upanishads.

Bhaktivedanta. "Bhakti" means "devotion." This form of Hinduism involves having the individual strive for a personal loving relationship with a particular god, typically an avatar of Vishnu or Shiva.

The Hindu word for god is *deva*. The *devas* are generally perceived as looking like humans, though sometimes larger, with differently colored skin, and/or with additional limbs or eyes or other body parts, and are generally immortal. Sometimes they are in the form of animals, as the elephant god Ganesha or the monkey god Hanuman. The earliest Hindu gods, like

Ganesh (or Ganesha), New Delhi, India.

the early gods of Mesopotamia and Greece, were a sky father and an earth mother. The influence of these gods was not very significant in written records. Far more important, at least as far as the written records show, are the gods of the Vedas.

The Vedic Gods

The Vedas were collections of hymns devoted to various Indian gods. Rig Veda, written sometime around 1500 B.C.E., may be the oldest religious work ever composed. The gods most commonly found in the Vedas are Indra, Agni, and Varuna.

Indra, a sky god, is the chief among the Vedic deities. Like Apollo, Zeus, and the Norse god Thor, Indra is god of thunder and a symbol of strength and leadership. Indra is a warrior king, often portrayed riding on a chariot or upon the back of an elephant.

Agni is the god of fire. Because Agni serves as the link between earth and the gods, he is the most widely worshiped god in classic Vedic Hinduism. Like the Greek Hermes or the Roman Mercury, Agni serves as messenger of the gods and the mediator between gods and humans. Often pictured as a red-skinned old man with seven arms, Agni is at the center of Hindu sacrificial rituals.

Varuna is god of the sky, as well as being associated with oceans, rivers, and rain. Varuna is the four-armed, all knowing sustainer of life. He is often pictured carrying a noose or lasso (sometimes a snake in the form of a lasso), reminding the Hindu that Varuna is the chief judge and upholder of moral law.

Surya, the Vedic sun god, is the giver of light, source of heat and healing. He is often portrayed riding a chariot drawn by a seven-headed horse.

Soma is unique in that it is not a divine being, but a divine thing. Soma is a hallucinogenic drink made from the juices of certain plants. As part of a sacrificial ritual, people would drink the energizing juice, and a portion was shared with the gods. It is said that soma is the favorite drink of Indra.

Surya, Temple of the Sun, Konarak, Orissa, India, 13th century C.E.

In later years, three Vedic gods emerged as the most important in understanding the world. Known as the Hindu Trinity, they are Brahma, Vishnu, and Shiva—the creator, the sustainer, and the destroyer.

Brahma is the creator god, responsible for the birth of the world, depicted as a man with four heads and four arms. Interestingly, Brahma is not widely worshiped.

Vishnu is the god who sustains the world. He is the blue-skinned teacher and savior of the universe, often seen carrying a conch shell, a disk, a mace, and a lotus flower, and wearing a garland of flowers around his neck. Among the most widely worshiped gods in India, Vishnu is believed to have come to earth in human form numerous times. His most famous incarnation (avatar) is **Lord Krishna.**

Shiva is the dancing god, responsible for guiding the world from destruction to rebirth. Despite his destructiveness, Shiva is not seen as a bad god. Rather than being an evil deed, Shiva's dance of destruction is understood as part of the natural cycle of deaths and rebirths. Shiva is a great judge, and it is within him that the universe sleeps between creation cycles.

God in the Vedanta Hinduism

The early Vedas centered on the interaction of gods and humans through rituals of sacrifice and drinking soma. By the end of the Vedic period, Hindu scriptures began to focus more on individual spiritual philosophy.

The Upanishads were a type of holy book that bridged the Vedas with the Vedanta ("after Vedas" or "end of the Vedas"). The name "Upanishad" means "sitting near," referring to students sitting at the feet of their teachers. Among the many themes explored in the Upanishads is the knowledge of Brahma—the Infinite One that pervades and transcends all existence. Another theme is that the individual person (atman) is a reflection of the One (Brahma).

One of the earliest Upanishads is the Brihadaranyaka (Great Forest Text) Upanishad, composed around 700 B.C.E. The following story, adapted from the Brihadaranyaka Upanishad (3:9), tells of a student, Vidagdha, asking his teacher, Yagnavalkya, about the number of gods:

> Vidagdha Sakalya asked him: "Tell me, Yagnavalkya, how many gods are there?"
>
> He replied: "As many as are mentioned in the invocation of the hymn of praise addressed to the All-gods: three and three hundred, three and three thousand."
>
> "Yes," he said, and asked again: "But Yagnavalkya, how many gods are there really?"
>
> "These three and three hundred, three and three thousand represent the various powers of the gods. In reality there are only thirty-three gods. The eight Vasus, the eleven Rudras, and the twelve Adityas. They make thirty-one, and Indra and Pragapati make the thirty-three."
>
> "Yes," he said, and asked again, "How many gods are there really, Yagnavalkya?"
>
> "Six," he said. "They are Agni [fire], Prithivi [earth], Vayu [air], Antariksha [sky], Aditya [sun], Dyu [heaven], they are the six, for they are all this, the six."
>
> "Yes," he said, and asked again: "How many gods are there really, Yagnavalkya?"
>
> "Three," he said. "These three worlds, for in them all these gods exist."
>
> "Yes," he said, and asked again: "How many gods are there really, Yagnavalkya?"
>
> "Two," he said. "Food and breath."
>
> "Yes," he said, and asked again: "How many gods are there really, Yagnavalkya?"
>
> "One and a half," he said. "The purifying wind that is blowing here."
>
> "Yes," he said, and asked again: "How many gods are there really, Yagnavalkya?"
>
> "One," he said. "Breath [prana], and he is Brahman."

Although the above text is clearly not a reflection of monotheism, it does express something that can be called "monism"—that all things can be reduced to a singularity. There is a close similarity between this Hindu idea of monism and the monotheism that we will see in Judaism and Islam.

Bhaktivedanta

The Vedas met a practical and civic need. The Upanishads served the intellectual and spiritual needs of the educated classes. A third form of Hinduism fulfilled a deeply personal and individual need of the Indian people, reflecting a need in all human beings. The word "bhakti" comes from a Sanskrit root meaning "to share" or "revere." "Bhakti" is often translated as "devotion," and its focus is on engendering a personal relationship with a god through love and devotion.

The earliest forms of Bhaktivedanta—or Bhakti yoga—primarily involved worship of the god Shiva as well as his lover Parvati and their son, the elephant-headed Ganesha. But the Bhakti movements that have dominated Hinduism over the past two thousand years have been devoted to Vishnu, usually in the form of his two incarnations—or avatars—as Rama and Krishna.

Through stories, poetry, prayer, and painting, the devotees would experience closeness to their gods by repeating the god's name in song and generating feelings of love for the god as one would for one's lover or one's child. Stories and paintings of Krishna often depict him as a cute baby sneaking a taste of butter or as a sexy young man courting the shepherdess Radha.

A familiar example of Bhakti is found in former-Beatle George Harrison's 1970 song "My Sweet Lord":

My sweet Lord
I really want to see you
Really want to be with you
Really want to see you Lord
But it takes so long, my Lord

I really want to know you
Really want to go with you
Really want to show you Lord
That it won't take long, my Lord

Hm, my Lord (hare krishna)
My, my, my Lord (hare krishna)
Oh, my sweet Lord (krishna, krishna)
Oh-uuh-uh (hare hare)

Krishna as a child with his mother, Bombay, India, 18th century C.E.

53

Now, I really want to see you (hare rama)
Really want to be with you (hare rama)
Really want to see you Lord (aaah)
But it takes so long, my Lord (hallelujah)
My sweet Lord (hare krishna)

Bhakti—or devotional religion—is not very common in Judaism but is a very prominent form of religious expression in Christianity and some sects of Buddhism. Christian depictions of Christ's nativity, as well as attention to the Madonna (Jesus' mother), the wearing of the cross, and the popular bumper sticker "God is Love" are all expressions of devotionalism. To this day, when Roman Catholic nuns and priests take their vows, they are said to be married to Jesus and wear a ring on their finger symbolizing that marriage.

Ancient Persia—the Dualism of Zoroaster

Indian religion had little direct influence on Judaism, but India's distant cousins, the Persians, came to have a strong impact on Judaism, Christianity, and Islam. Like Hinduism, Persian religion arose among ancestors of Aryan invaders (who entered India ca. 1500–1200 B.C.E., and invaded Persia ca. 1000–800 B.C.E.).

The primary religion of ancient Persia is called Zoroastrianism, named for Zarathustra (or Zoroaster, as his name was translated in Greek), who founded the religion sometime around 600 B.C.E. Probably a priest and a descendant of the Aryan invaders, Zoroaster reported having a vision in which the god Ahuramazda (Wise Lord) spoke to him. The essential teachings of Zoroastrianism are that Ahuramazda is the one true god, the god of truth, who created the world and all good things in it, including humanity. Ahuramazda is the only god worthy of worship. Ahuramazda also told Zoroaster that the bloody sacrifices that were popular in ancient Persia were a false and evil ritual. True sacrifice for the Zoroastrian took the form of the lighting and tending of a pure fire, a ritual that is retained today by the few remaining Zoroastrians (now called Parsees) living mostly in India.

In opposition to Ahuramazda is the spirit being Ahriman—"The Lie"—the wise Lord's evil counterpart, analogous to Satan in Christian tradition. Since the beginning of time, good and evil, in the form of Ahuramazda and Ahriman, have been waging a war.

Truly, there are two primal Spirits, twins renowned to be in conflict. In thought and word, in act they are two: the better and the bad. And those who act well have chosen rightly between these two, not so the evildoers. And when these two Spirits first came together they created life and not-life, and how at the end Worst Existence shall be for the wicked, but the House of Best Purpose shall for the just man.

Yasna 30:3–4

The war between Ahuramazda and Ahriman would end in a final battle in which truth would rule out over falsehood, and evil would be defeated forever. Ahuramazda would pass judgment over all humanity. The good would enter a kingdom of everlasting joy and light, while those who lived under the false god would suffer in darkness.

What precisely is the theology of Zoroaster? Is it a polytheism that praises a supreme ethical god? Is it a monotheism affirming the truth of one God over the falsehood of many? Is it a dualism in which twin gods, one good and the other evil, are responsible for everything in our universe? Accepting any one of these answers as the true understanding of Zoroastrianism would be too simplistic to be accurate. In truth, it is a bit of all three.

During the period in which the Persian king, Cyrus the Great, liberated the Jews from the Babylonian exile in 538 B.C.E., it is likely that some of these ideas rubbed off on the people of Judea. The notion of a final battle, reward in a kingdom of God, and a resurrection of the dead would become important in prophetic Judaism. The dualism of God battling an evil counterpart and the idea of a Final Judgment would become prominent in Christian beliefs.

God in Christianity

In addition to the religious traditions examined so far, all of which arose independently of Judaism and outside of Jewish influence, there are two religions that grew directly from Judaism. The first began as a Jewish sect and evolved to become a global religion; the other began as an Arab cult inspired by the stories and beliefs of neighboring Jews.

Christianity is based on the person of Jesus of Nazareth, a Jew who was executed by Roman authorities in 30 C.E. and is believed by Christians to be the embodiment of God. (*Christ* is the Latin word for "anointed"; see chapter 6.) During its first several centuries, there was much debate in Christian circles about the nature of Jesus and the difference between Jesus and God. In the Christian Bible, Jesus is reported to have said, "I and the Father are one" (John 10:30). This seemed to suggest that Jesus and God were one and the same, an idea that was (and still is) perplexing in monotheistic circles.

Christian teachings suggested that (1) there is only one God, that (2) Jesus was the son of God, and that (3) Jesus was God. The solution to this paradox came when Church leaders met in Constantinople in 381 C.E. They taught that just as a flame contains different colors of light, so does God contain different faces. The Christian Bible commanded that Jesus' disciples be baptized "in the name of the Father and of the Son and of the Holy Spirit" (Matthew 28:19). At the Council of Constantinople, theologian Athanasius affirmed that God is One, but that the One is made up of three equal partners, three divine beings:

1. Spirit, the creative, transcendent presence of God;
2. Father, the law-giving ruler; and
3. Jesus Christ, the Son of God, offered as a sacrifice, given to the world as the Messiah promised in Judaism to bring the Kingdom of God to earth.

For the Christian, God is primarily worshiped in the form of Jesus Christ. Rather than emphasizing the seeming paradox of monotheism and trinity, Christians view God-in-Christ as a sacrifice made by God for the benefit of believers. God took human form, and then sacrificed that human form, in order to save humanity. This was the ultimate act of love. Jesus represents all of God's love embodied in human form.

Thus, for Christians, belief is more than a logical acceptance of God's existence; it is an emotional attachment to God. As with Bhaktivedanta in Hindu religion, Christian devotion is a rich experience of personal love of the believer toward Jesus and the self-sacrificing love (agape in Greek) of God toward humankind.

Nowhere is the message of God's love more apparent than in the First Epistle of John (I John) in the Christian Bible. "This is love," wrote John. "Not that we loved God, but that he loved us and sent his Son as an atoning sacrifice for our sins" (I John 4:10). John goes so far as stating several times that God is love: "Whoever does not love does not know God, because God is love" (I John 4:8) and "We know and rely on the love God has for us. God is love. Whoever lives in love lives in God, and God in him" (I John 4:16).

God in Islam

In contrast to Christian theology in which God takes human form, and Christian devotion in which God is love, the Islamic conception of God is one that is ultimately formless, and devotion involves submission rather than love.

Developing among Arabic-speaking people some 600 years after the emergence of Christianity, Islam is based on the revelations of the prophet Muhammad (born 570 C.E.). Like Zoroaster in Persia a thousand years earlier, Muhammad kept a record of his encounters with God (called Allah in Arabic). These records come down to us as the Quran (also spelled Koran).

The God of Islam is presumably the same as the God of the Jews. The name "Allah" is related to the Hebrew word *Elohim*. The stories and characters that appear in the Quran include many that

The Quran, being revealed to Muhammad, page from a manuscript.

appear in the Hebrew Bible—Adam and Eve, Noah, Abraham, Moses, King David—as well as the Christian figure of Jesus (presented as a prophet rather than as a messiah).

The message of the Quran is one of steadfast submission to the will of God. The word "Islam," in fact, means "submission," and a Muslim is "one who submits" to God. Unlike Christianity, whose artwork and idea of the Trinity seem to play loose with the ideas of monotheism and the prohibition against making likenesses of God, Islam takes a firm and unwavering position regarding the oneness of God and extends the biblical prohibition against likenesses to creating any representational art. Thus, Islamic art consists of geometric patterns and decorative renderings of sacred texts. The first of the Five Pillars of Islam is the commandment to announce, several times each day, the *Shahada* Creed (similar to the Jewish *Sh'ma* prayer): *La ilaha il Allah, Muhammad ur Rasool Allah,* "There is no god but Allah, and Muhammad is His Prophet."

The attention that Islam places on God is so strong that Muslim law forbids speculation *(al takyeef)* about God, and making analogy *(al tamtheel)* between God's attributes and those of humans. However, the Quran stresses three intermingled aspects of power, justice, and mercy. Although in Islam there can be no icons, symbols, or sacraments that represent God, the Quran has the highest authority in the life of a Muslim in that it is believed to be the direct word of God. Submission to God— the goal of every Muslim—is an act of utter humility and devotion. It is to recognize God's absolute authority, that God alone possesses all power, and that no person or entity possesses any power that is independent of God. The Muslim's duty, then, is to devote worship to God alone and to devote one's life to following God's will as expressed in the Quran.

Chapter Four

Elohim

God—Part Two:
Jewish Views of God

Listen Israel, *Adonai* is our God, *Adonai* is One!

Deuteronomy 6:4

The Jews, more than any other nation or culture, brought the idea of one God to the world. But paradoxically, no religious word causes more discomfort for the modern Jew than the word "God." At parties and in lunchrooms you'll find people of various religious backgrounds—believers, agnostics, skeptics, and atheists—chattering about everything from politics to fashion. But generally, Jews become silent when the discussion turns to God.

Having explored, in the previous chapter, the various ways other religions view the idea of God and gods, we will now focus on the Jewish notion of God. Jewish theology spans more than three thousand years, yet we will find that certain ideas about God have remained consistent for most of Jewish history.

What does Judaism teach us about the nature of God? Among the common threads in Jewish theology are the following:

1. There is one God.
2. God is involved in the world.
3. God desires ethical behavior.
4. Human beings and God can be in dialogue.
5. God has a special relationship with the people Israel.

Word Histories

אֱלֹהִים *(Elohim)*. *Elohim* is the generic word for "God" in Hebrew, used to describe the gods of other nations, as well as the God of Israel. Interestingly, it is a plural form, yet when signifying the one God, it is treated grammatically as a singular noun. The origin of this word is uncertain. Scholars have suggested that אֱלֹהִים *(Elohim)* comes from the root אֱלֹהַּ *(eloha)*, "fearsome" or "revered," while its synonym אֵל *(El)* comes from the root אוּל *(ol)*, meaning "strong." The question of whether or not these two roots are related is an issue of ongoing scholarly debate.

While אֱלֹהִים *(Elohim)* normally refers to deities, a related word, אֵילִים *(eilim)*, means "mighty ones" and applies to humans (see II Kings 24:15; Ezekiel 17:13; 31:11; 32:21). The phrases בְּנֵי אֵלִים *(b'nei eilim)* and בְּנֵי אֱלֹהִים *(b'nei elohim)*—both of which can be translated as "sons of God" or "sons of gods"—are often used in the Bible to describe angels (Psalms 29:1; 89:7; Job 1:6; 38:7).

יהוה *(Y-H-V-H)*. This combination of letters *(Y-H-V-H)* is called the Tetragram-

---

Key Terms

God. A being of supernatural powers or attributes, believed in and worshiped by a people. Adapted from the root *ghut* ("called" or "invoked").

Lord. A man of high rank in society. Taken from the root *wor* (watchful), a person who was watchful, on guard, or in charge. As a title of respect it is often used as a substitute for "God" or "god."

אֱלֹהִים *(Elohim)*. Generic term for God or deity. Although it has a plural ending, when applied to the one God, it is understood as singular. Possible origin is ancient word for "strong," "mighty," or "revered." Related to the shorter form אֵל *(El)*.

יהוה *(Y-H-V-H)*. The unpronounceable name of God. Often referred to by the Greek word "Tetragrammaton" (four-letter name). The proper personal name of the God of Israel. When reading the name aloud, it is traditional to substitute the word *Adonai* (Sir) or *HaShem* (the Name).

הַשֵּׁם *(HaShem)*. Literally, "the Name." An alternative to *Adonai* used to represent the Tetragrammaton (see above).

הַמָּקוֹם *(HaMakom)*. Literally, "the Place." Another name for God.

הקב״ה *(HKB"H)*. Abbreviation for *HaKadosh Baruch Hu*, "The Holy One, Praised Be He." Another appellation of God.

---

maton (four-letter name), *HaShem* (the Name), and the Ineffable Name of God.

The mysterious, unpronounceable name of God first appears in the Torah in Genesis 2:4. Up to that point, God is referred to as אֱלֹהִים *(Elohim)*. In subsequent passages, both names are used, sometimes in combination with other names and with each other. While the name appears many times, it isn't until Genesis 15:7 that God uses this name, when God tells Abraham, "I am *Y-H-V-H* who brought you from Ur of the Chaldees to give you this land." God uses the Name again during Jacob's dream of the ladder: "I am *Y-H-V-H,* the God of Abraham your father and the God of Isaac"

(Genesis 28:13). When God appears to Moses in the Burning Bush, asking Moses to return to Egypt to free the Israelites, Moses complains to God that the people will not believe him. "'When they ask me "What is His name?" what shall I tell them?' God said to Moses, 'I Am That I Am' [אֶהְיֶה אֲשֶׁר אֶהְיֶה, *Ehyeh Asher Ehyeh,* which can also be translated 'I Will Be What I Will Be']. And He said, 'Tell the Israelite people, "I Am has sent me to you."'" (Exodus 3:13–14).

According to tradition, this name was only spoken aloud once a year. During Yom Kippur, the High Priest would call out the Name from within the Holy of Holies—the inner chamber of the Temple—where no one else could hear it. Since the destruction of the Temple in 70 C.E., the Name has never been officially evoked, and its correct pronunciation has been forgotten.

When reading holy texts containing the Name, Jews would substitute the word אֲדֹנָי (*Adonai,* "my Lord" or "Sir"). To help remind people to substitute this word, the Masorites (600–1100 C.E.) began adding the vowel symbols from אֲדֹנָי (*Adonai)* to the name יהוה.

> ### The Documentary Hypothesis
>
> During the 1800s, several scholars began paying particular attention to how the words *Elohim* and *Y-H-V-H* were used in the Five Books of Moses.
>
> In 1878, German scholar Julius Wellhausen proposed that the Five Books of the Torah were made up of two separate documents, one that used the word *Elohim* for God, and the other that used the name *Y-H-V-H* for God. These two documents (he called them J and E) were carefully woven into a single text.
>
> Later scholars, following on this document theory, identified two other sources of the Five Books that they named P (Priestly) and D (Deuteronomist).

Scholars generally assume that the Name was pronounced "Yahweh." But because of a misunderstanding of the substituted vowels from *Adonai,* medieval Christian scholars tried spelling the Name in forms such as "Yohoua," "Iohouah," and "Jehovah." This is the source of the inaccurate translation of the Name to "Jehovah."

One possibility is that the Name, derived from the Hebrew root היה (*h-y-h,* "to be"), means "the One that calls existence into being." Some mystical thinkers have suggested that the Name—composed of open-mouthed spirant sounds—is uttered every time a person breathes.

Defining the Indefinable

How can we describe that which we haven't seen with our eyes or touched with our hands? The very nature of God is unknowable. Yet it is our task to gain a better understanding of the Being that has had such a close relationship with our ancestors and, by extension, with us.

When theologians (people who discuss and study the nature of God) talk about God, they sometimes use negative labels—descriptions that tell what God *isn't*. Some of the common descriptions of God in monotheistic religions include the following:

- Infinite—God is without limit or end. God cannot be limited or measured.
- Immutable—God cannot be changed.
- Incorporeal—God has no body or physical form.
- Unknowable—The human mind cannot fully comprehend God.
- Ineffable—God is something that is incapable of being expressed by words, unspeakable.

Theologians also use a number of positive labels that attempt to describe certain aspects of God:

- Unity—God is One, unique, complete.
- Perfect/Supreme—God is the highest of the high, the greatest of the great.
- Prime Mover/First Cause—This philosophical expression describes God as being the force that put all other forces into motion; in the endless chain of cause and effect, God is the Force that has no cause.
- Omniscient—God sees, knows, and understands everything.
- Omnipotent—God is all-powerful, capable of doing anything.
- All Good—God is moral.
- Transcendent—God is beyond all things, above time, space, and physical description.
- Creator—God is responsible for all creation; God created the universe from nothing (the Latin term for this is *creatio ex nihilo*).
- Purposeful—God has a plan, intention, or purpose; creation is not random.
- Savior—God takes an active role in human events, communal and individual.

God in Judaism

The Bible is filled with stories and verse that describe God. The most direct experience of God is a "revelation," a direct encounter between God and a person in which God is "revealed" to the prophet through visions and instructions. In the passages that follow, from revelations of Moses and Isaiah, most of the attributes of God are given note.

In the third chapter of Exodus, Moses is tending his father-in-law's flock in the Midian hills when God speaks to him through a bush that is burning without being consumed:

> "I am...the God of your father, the God of Abraham, the God of Isaac, and the God of Jacob....I have marked well the plight of My people in Egypt and have heeded their outcry because of their taskmasters. Yes, I am mindful of their sufferings. I have come to rescue them from the Egyptians and to bring them out of that land to a good and spacious land, a land flowing with milk and honey."
>
> Exodus 3:6–8

Moses balked at the responsibility. Even when assured that God would be with him, Moses asked how the Israelites would know God. By what name would they know God?

> God said to Moses, "*Ehyeh Asher Ehyeh* [I Am That I Am]." God continued, "Thus shall you say to the Israelites: '*Ehyeh* has sent me to you.'" God said further to Moses, "You should say to the Israelites: '*Adonai* [Y-H-V-H], the God of your ancestors, the God of Abraham, the God of Isaac, the God of Jacob, has sent me to you. This shall be My name forever. This is My appellation for all eternity.'"
>
> Exodus 3:14–15

In God's meeting with Moses we learn that God has a relationship with the Israelites, that God is concerned about their plight in Egypt, that God intends to rescue them, and that God's name is "*Ehyeh Asher Ehyeh.*" The name seems to be the most perplexing part of the revelation, until we recognize the similarity between *Ehyeh* and *Y-H-V-H.* The four-letter name, *Y-H-V-H,* is the proper name of the God of Israel throughout the Bible. Its origin is uncertain, but the above passage suggests that its root is *h-y-h,* the verb "to be." Thus, when God says "I am," we are being taught that God exists and that God *is* existence, that "This shall be My name forever. This is My appellation for all eternity."

Moses and the Burning Bush by William Blake, 19th century.

Some five hundred years after Moses, God would be revealed to the prophet Isaiah. The following passages, taken from a section of the Book of Isaiah known as Second Isaiah, were probably written by someone living in the time of the Babylonian exile (586–537 B.C.E.) and not by the eighth-century prophet Isaiah son of Amoz. In these passages we find further traits of God.

> Who created you, Jacob?
> Who formed you, Israel?
> Fear not, for I will redeem you.
> I have singled you out by name,
> You are Mine....
> I am *Adonai* [*Y-H-V-H*] your God,
> The Holy One of Israel, your Savior.
> Isaiah 43:1, 3

The passage above reiterates the bond between Israel and God. God's name is stated; God is referred to as *"Y-H-V-H"* and "The Holy One of Israel," reminding us of God's holiness (see chapter 8). The passage also asserts that God is our Creator and Redeemer. These twin traits are often paired, reminding us of the two major biblical events that shape our religious consciousness: the Creation and the Exodus.

The following passages, also from Second Isaiah, convey similar attributes of God:

> Listen, my servant Jacob, Israel, whom I have chosen.
> This is what *Adonai* [*Y-H-V-H*] who made you,
> who formed you in the womb, and who will help you says:
> Do not be afraid, O Jacob, my servant, Jeshurun, whom I have chosen.
> For I will pour water on the thirsty land, and streams on the dry ground;
> I will pour out My Spirit on your offspring, and My blessing on your descendants.
> They will spring up like grass in a meadow, like poplar trees by flowing streams.
> Isaiah 44:1–4

Creation and chosenness are linked with the promise that God will continue to be with us in the future. The text goes on to assert God's uniqueness, ridiculing the worship of made-up gods:

> Thus said *Adonai,* Israel's King and Redeemer, *Adonai* of Hosts:
> I am the first and I am the last; apart from me there is no God.
> Who then is like Me? Let him proclaim it....

Those who make idols are nothing,

and the things they treasure are worthless.

Those who would speak up for them are blind;

they are ignorant, to their own shame.

Who shapes a god and casts an idol, which can profit him nothing?

Isaiah 44:6–7, 9–10

Attributes of God in Judaism

In the sections that follow, some of the attributes of God as reflected in Jewish text and tradition will be examined in detail.

God Is One

The previous passage, from Isaiah 44, lays out in strong terms the idea that there is only one God and that God cannot be manufactured. Jewish tradition teaches that the idol worship of the nations is wrong. There is but one God, who cannot be represented in wood or stone. God cannot be made, because God is the Maker.

The central prayer of Jewish worship is the *Sh'ma,* said twice a day:

שְׁמַע יִשְׂרָאֵל יְהוָֹה אֱלֹהֵינוּ יְהוָֹה אֶחָד!

Sh'ma Yisrael, Adonai Eloheinu, Adonai Echad!

Listen Israel, *Adonai* is our God, *Adonai* is One!

Deuteronomy 6:4

Sometimes referred to as "the watchword of our faith," the *Sh'ma* makes three assertions: (1) this message is for Israel, the Jewish people; (2) we have a relationship with *Adonai;* and (3) *Adonai* is unique, alone, and supreme. God is unlike anything or anyone else. God, as the German philosopher Rudolph Otto would say, is "Wholly Other," completely outside of anything in our daily physical experience. And this God loves and cares for the people Israel.

The Ten Commandments begins with the preamble "I am *Adonai* your God, who brought you out of the land of Egypt" (Exodus 20:2). It is not a commandment at all, but a statement of introduction. As a prologue to the laws that would follow, God makes a personal introduction. In saying that God brought "you"—the singular second-person pronoun—out of Egypt, God is speaking directly to the reader of whatever age or era. In Jewish tradition, this single verse provides the whole of the first commandment. (In Roman Catholicism, the verse is combined with "You shall have no other gods besides me" [Exodus 20:3].)

The notion of monotheism wasn't always so clear in ancient Israel. In the time of the Patriarchs, there was certainly a tolerance of other gods. The gods of the nations were considered inferior to the Israelite God, and God was thought to have a special relationship with the ancient Israelites. Even during the age of the kingdoms, there was occasional recognition of the existence of other gods. Although the prophets of Israel condemned the worship of any God but *Adonai,* Ahab, a king of Israel (ca. 873–851 B.C.E.), openly worshiped the Canaanite god Baal, making him an adversary of Elijah the prophet.

God Is Creator

According to Babylonian mythology, the world came into existence when Marduk cut open the body of his mother, the great sea serpent Tiamat.

> He turned back to where Tiamat lay bound, he straddled the legs and smashed her skull (for the mace was merciless), he severed the arteries and the blood streamed down the north wind to the unknown ends of the world.
>
> When the gods saw all this they laughed out loud, and they sent him presents. They sent him their thankful tributes. The Lord rested; he gazed at the huge body, pondering how to use it, what to create from the dead carcass. He split it apart like a cockleshell; with the upper half he constructed the arc of sky, he pulled down the bar and set a watch on the waters, so they should never escape.
>
> *Enuma Elish,* tablet 4

In a similar tale from Greek mythology, the father of the world was Cronus, who, when he learned that one of them would eventually kill him, ate all his children. One child, Zeus, was hidden away. When Zeus grew to adulthood, he returned to Olympus, freed his brothers and sisters, and defeated Cronus.

The Israelite Creation story is altogether different. God created the world without intrigue, violence, or vengeance. God was alone before the beginning and called Creation into being with words. In other words, God's Creation was planned, conscientious, and as is repeated seven times in the story in Genesis 1, "it was good."

In the Psalms and elsewhere, the Bible reminds us how Creation occurred and what its implications are:

By the word of *Adonai* the heavens were made,

By the breath of His mouth, all their host.

He heaps ocean waters like a mound,

Stores the deep in their vaults.

Let all the earth fear *Adonai,*

Let all the inhabitants of the world dread Him.

For He spoke, and it was,

He commanded, and it endured.

Psalm 33:6–9

In the Book of Job, after Job suffers devastating personal losses and receives unsatisfying explanations from his wife and friends, God appears to him from a whirlwind. In response to Job's questions, God provides no explanation at all. Rather, God reviews the accomplishments of Creation, asking Job where he was during all those events.

Then *Adonai* answered Job out of the storm. He said:

Who is this that darkens my counsel with words without knowledge?

Brace yourself like a man; I will question you, and you shall answer me.

Where were you when I laid the earth's foundation?

Tell me, if you understand.

Who marked off its dimensions?

Surely you know! Who stretched a measuring line across it?

On what were its footings set, or who laid its cornerstone—

while the morning stars sang together and all the angels shouted for joy?

Job 38:1–7

In confronting the awesomeness of God's creative powers, Job is satisfied with God's response. And so, ideally, is the reader of that passage.

God Is the Redeemer of Israel

As stated earlier, "Creator" and "Redeemer" are the twin traits of God. The single pivotal event that brought the Israelites together as a people was the Exodus from Egypt, an event that, according to our tradition, was orchestrated by God:

I have heard the groaning of the Israelites, whom the Egyptians are enslaving, and

I have remembered My covenant. Therefore, say to the Israelites: I am *Adonai* and

67

I will bring you out from under the yoke of the Egyptians. I will free you from being slaves to them, and I will redeem you with an outstretched arm and with mighty acts of judgment.

I will take you as My own people, and I will be your God. Then you will know that I am *Adonai* your God, who brought you out from under the yoke of the Egyptians.

Exodus 6:5–7

The Exodus was a single event in the history of the Israelites. But God's redemption is eternal and ongoing. The promises of God's salvation for the future will be explored further in chapter 6.

Fear of God

"Fear" is a fine example of how translation has led to more confusion and misunderstanding than clarity. The ancient Germanic word *feraz* meant "danger" or "disaster"—a descriptive word for a situation or condition, and not a name for an emotional state. Today we associate the word "fear" with "fright," the emotion we have in response to threats, whether real or perceived. We can be afraid of pain, death, and loss, as well as have phobias of spiders, snakes, high places, and darkness. Yet the expression "fear of God" is a translation of יִרְאַת־אֱלֹהִים, *yirat Elohim,* found throughout the Hebrew Bible. יָרֵא, *yarei,* can refer to being afraid of dangers or threats, but it also applies to the deep inner experience of awe and trembling that comes from being close to God. This kind of "fear"—a form of profound respect—is linked with love and obedience to God in the following passage:

And now, O Israel, what does *Adonai* your God ask of you but to fear *Adonai* your God, to walk in all His ways, to love Him, to serve *Adonai* your God with all your heart and with all your soul, and to observe *Adonai*'s commands and decrees that I am giving you today for your own good?

Deuteronomy 10:12–13

Yirat Elohim is an emotional experience, but it goes beyond personal emotion. It has practical meaning as it shapes our behavior. We are told to "Serve *Adonai* with fear and rejoice with trembling" (Psalm 2:11). Ethical mitzvot are linked to the experience of God's awe, as in "Do not curse the deaf or put a stumbling block in front of the blind, but fear your God" (Leviticus 19:14). God rewards those who show fear, Jews as well as non-Jews like Rahab of Jericho [Joshua 2] and the midwives of Egypt ("Because the midwives feared God, He gave them families of their own"

[Exodus 1:21]). And cruel behavior, associated with a lack of fear, is punished, as when Moses tells Pharaoh, "I know that you and your officials still do not fear *Adonai* God" (Exodus 9:30).

God as a Shepherd

The Bible is filled with shepherds. Moses and King David both spent time herding sheep. The first murder victim, Cain's brother Abel, was a shepherd. This idyllic, pastoral profession appears in the legends of other religions as well. The Hindu god Krishna spent many an afternoon seducing the shepherd girl Radha. In the Greek story of Oedipus, the fugitive child-king is raised by an old shepherd. The Sumerian goddess Inanna professes her love for her shepherd, the god Dumuzi.

A shepherd is a caretaker, a guide, and a caring guardian. At times of loss, Jews (as well as Christians) recite the Twenty-Third Psalm:

> *Adonai* is my shepherd; I shall not be in want.
> He makes me lie down in green pastures, He leads me beside quiet waters,
> He restores my soul. He guides me in paths of righteousness for His name's sake.
> Even though I walk through the valley of the shadow of death, I will fear no evil, for
> You are with me; Your rod and Your staff, they comfort me. You prepare a table
> before me in the presence of my enemies. You anoint my head with oil; my cup
> overflows. Surely goodness and love will follow me all the days of my life, and I will
> dwell in the house of *Adonai* forever.
>
> Psalm 23

Referring to God as a shepherd is a metaphor. But it is a very rich, potent, and important metaphor, one that has brought strength and support to "God-fearing" people for thousands of years, and continues as a promise to future generations:

> *Adonai* is the strength of His people, a fortress of salvation for His anointed one.
> Save your people and bless your inheritance; be their shepherd and carry them
> forever.
>
> Psalm 28:8–9

God as a Judge

God is concerned with fairness. Well-meaning people who define justice as the opposite of kindness often skew the concept of justice. While justice does at times involve punishment or retribution, justice is nothing more than doing what is fair.

The Torah forbids us from giving deferential treatment to either rich or poor. Rather, we are told to judge each person according to his or her actions. Just as people are to judge based on fairness, so does God promise to act in a fair, ethical manner:

> Let *Adonai* judge the peoples.
> Judge me, O *Adonai,* according to my righteousness,
> According to my integrity, O Most High.
> O righteous God, who searches minds and hearts,
> Bring to an end the violence of the wicked and make the righteous secure.
> My shield is God Most High, who saves the upright in heart.
> God is a righteous judge, a God who expresses His wrath every day.
>
> Psalm 7:9–12

And in the following promise:

> Let the rivers clap their hands, let the mountains sing together for joy;
> Let them sing before *Adonai,* for He comes to judge the earth.
> He will judge the world in righteousness and the peoples with equity.
>
> Psalm 98:8–9

God Desires Ethical Conduct

Linked to God's justice is God's desire and expectation that we should act in a just, kind, and ethical manner:

> He loves righteousness and justice; the earth is full of *Adonai*'s unfailing love.
>
> Psalm 33:5

Examples of ethical conduct provided in the Torah include everything from using accurate weights when selling produce to leaving the corners of your field to the widow and the orphan. God commands us to be fair in all our judgments, giving favor neither to the rich nor the poor. We are commanded to treat our slaves and laborers fairly, and even when we are at war we are forbidden to lay waste to trees.

The prophet Micah exhorted the people to please God through ethical conduct, and not by following empty rituals:

> Will *Adonai* be pleased with thousands of rams, with ten thousand rivers of oil? Shall
> I offer my firstborn for my transgression, the fruit of my body for the sin of my soul?
> He has showed you, O man, what is good. And what does *Adonai* require of you? To
> act justly and to love mercy and to walk humbly with your God.
>
> Micah 6:7–8

To walk the ethical life is no small task. Our Redeemer, Shepherd, and Judge provides us with the toolbox to help us to act justly, love mercy, and walk humbly with God. That toolbox is the Torah.

God as Giver of Torah

The morning service *(Shacharit)* contains a prayer, said just before the *Sh'ma*, that conveys the message that the love God has for us is expressed in teaching:

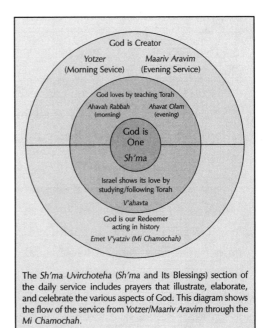

The *Sh'ma Uvirchoteha* (*Sh'ma* and Its Blessings) section of the daily service includes prayers that illustrate, elaborate, and celebrate the various aspects of God. This diagram shows the flow of the service from *Yotzer/Maariv Aravim* through the *Mi Chamochah.*

> With eternal love You have loved us, *Adonai* our God, with great mercy You have been merciful, our Father, our King, for the sake of Your great Name and for the sake of our ancestors who trusted in You and whom You taught the laws of life, to do Your will wholeheartedly. May You be so gracious with us and teach us. Our Father, Merciful Father, acting mercifully, may You have mercy upon us, instilling in our hearts the ability to understand and explain, to listen, learn, teach, keep, perform, and fulfill all the words of Your Torah's teaching with love. Enlighten our eyes with Your Torah. Bind our hearts to Your mitzvot, and unify our hearts to love and revere Your name.
>
> From the *Ahavah Rabbah* prayer

God is the ultimate Teacher. In *Pirkei Avot,* we learn that wherever two people study Torah, God's presence can be found (*Pirkei Avot* 3:3).

Wrestling with God

The relationship to God in Judaism differs from Islam's submission to God and Christianity's unquestioning faith and love of God. While faith, love, and obedience are of course part of the relationship between Israel and God, Jews have an extra charge to wrestle with God. The very name of the Jewish people, "Israel," means "God wrestles" and is derived from the story of Jacob wrestling with an angel at the shores of the Jabbok River:

So Jacob was left alone, and a man wrestled with him till daybreak.

When the man saw that he could not overpower him, he touched the socket of Jacob's hip so that his hip was wrenched as he wrestled with the man. Then the man said, "Let me go, for it is daybreak." But Jacob replied, "I will not let you go unless you bless me."

The man asked him, "What is your name?"

"Jacob," he answered.

Then the man said, "Your name will no longer be Jacob, but Israel, because you have struggled with God and with men and have overcome."

Jacob said, "Please tell me your name."

But he replied, "Why do you ask my name?" Then he blessed him there.

So Jacob called the place Peniel, saying, "It is because I saw God face-to-face, and yet my life was spared."

Genesis 32:25–31

What does this mean for modern Jews? It is first of all an acknowledgment that the idea of God is at times a difficult one to swallow. Jews are not expected to accept belief in God blindly. Rather, we struggle with the ideas, wrestling with God, even after God has blessed us.

The struggle of individuals with ethical dilemmas can be understood as struggling with God. When faced with difficult choices about right and wrong, we often have to weigh possible outcomes, trying to choose the lesser of evils. Wrestling with God then becomes a wrestling with right and wrong, and a struggle within ourselves. For some, wrestling with God is not

Jacob wrestling with the angel by Marc Chagall, 20th century.

about ethics, but rather a challenge of personal fate, as when Job questions God about why he has endured so much suffering, or on a lighter note, how Tevye the Dairyman—in Sholom Aleichem's stories and in the play, *Fiddler on the Roof*—engages in regular debates with God.

While in Jacob's story the patriarch was caught in an all-night fight with a divine being, wrestling "with" God doesn't necessarily make God the opponent. When we wrestle with difficult matters, we can find God fighting on our side.

Conversely, for many modern Jews, wrestling with God is an apt description of the struggle between believing in God's existence and questioning that existence. Modern science, morality, and current events provide many opportunities for one to question whether there is a God. Wrestling, then, is taking on these challenges and finding one's own understanding of God.

Chapter Five

מַלְאָכִים

Malachim

Angels and the Heavenly Hosts

And he dreamed, and behold a ladder set up on the
earth, and the top of it reached to heaven; and behold
the angels of God ascended and descended on it.

Genesis 28:12

People have a tendency to personify natural and cosmic forces—water, sky, love, war, fire, etc.—into beings or personalities that behave and often look like human beings. In most cultures, these beings are called gods and are objects of respect and worship.

Monotheistic religions—Judaism, Christianity, Islam, and to a certain extent Zoroastrianism—are not immune to this. Judaism and other monotheistic religions have no room in their belief system for other deities. Yet the *Tanach,* rabbinic literature, and Jewish legends are filled with angels and other divine beings. This presents a thorny dilemma: while these religions assert the existence of only one God, their traditions are filled with other heavenly beings.

How are these beings different from the gods of polytheistic religions? The difference is sometimes a murky one. Polytheistic gods include supreme deities—like Marduk, Zeus, and Odin—as well as servant gods, second- and third-stringers like the Muses, the Fates, and the Furies. The Greek god Hermes served as messenger of Olympus, delivering messages among the gods and between the gods and men. How different is Hermes from Hebrew angels like Gabriel and Michael?

Angels have become popular in Western society. Hundreds of books, Web sites, even stores are devoted to these gossamer-winged beings that are believed to watch over us. In this chapter, the origins of the belief in angels and how that belief is manifest in Judaism and other religions will be explored. We will also look at the Jewish concept of *satan* and how that idea evolved into the image of the diabolic fallen-angel with horns and tail prevalent in Medieval Christian literature.

Word Histories

Angel. People today tend to think of angels either as cupid-like beings with halos and gossamer wings or as guardian spirits that help people in times of need. In the Hebrew Bible, angels (מַלְאָכִים, *malachim*), which are mentioned some 108 times, are never described with halos or wings, but certainly serve as helpers and messengers. The job of an angel was to guide, provide, protect, deliver, encourage, worship and praise God, and reveal God's plan or will.

Angels in the Bible are generally described as looking human. Abraham's three visitors, the two angels that visited Lot in Sodom, and the angel who fought with Jacob are referred to as angels, but all

---

Key Terms

Angel. Messenger, from the Greek *aggelos*. A celestial being that acts as an intermediary between heaven and earth, as a messenger or servant to God.

Devil. From the Greek *diabolos*, meaning "slanderer." A being, associated with the biblical Satan, that acts as the personification of evil.

Host. An army, a multitude, or a great number. Referring to the heavenly armies of God. Translation of the Hebrew צָבָא *(tzava)*, "army."

מַלְאָךְ *(malach)*. Messenger or servant. Used primarily to describe people or beings who func-tion as heralds, messengers, or interpreters for God. From the same root as מְלָאכָה *(m'lachah)*, "work" or "occupation."

שָׂטָן *(satan)*. Adversary or opponent.

---

appeared as ordinary men. At times the Bible refers to human messengers, prophets, and priests—all flesh and blood men—as angels. But sometimes normally inanimate objects, like the Burning Bush that appeared to Moses, are called angels. In contemporary slang, cute and/or obedient children are sometimes called angels. A person who helps others, both in humanitarian and in business situations, is sometimes called an angel.

Devil. From the Greek *diabolos*, meaning "slanderer." In Christianity, the word "devil" was equated with the Hebrew concept of *satan*. While "Satan" is present in Judaism and Islam, the word "devil" is rarely used in these religions, nor is Satan the force of evil that it represents in Christianity. Christianity expanded the idea of the

Devil, associating it with the serpent in the Garden of Eden and elevating it from being one of God's attendants to being the ultimate spirit of evil and God's opponent in a final battle that would occur at the end of days.

Over the years, the image of devil has acquired horns and sometimes goat feet and a pointed tail. This may be due, in part, to references in the Bible to the worship of goat idols (Leviticus 17:7; Isaiah 34:14; II Chronicles 11:15). It may also be the result of a conscious effort by Church leaders to demonize mythical characters like the Satyrs and the god Pan of Greek mythology. In slang, a child (generally male) who creates mischief is called a "devil." Mischievous behavior is called "devilish." The modern term "devil's advocate"—a person who takes a contrary point of view—is surprisingly close to the original meaning of the Hebrew *satan*.

מַלְאָךְ *(malach)*.   While the word literally means "herald" or "messenger," מַלְאָךְ *(malach)* is used almost exclusively in the Bible in regard to messengers in the service of God. The term can be applied to human as well as nonhuman messengers, as noted above in the definition of "angel."

שָׂטָן *(satan* pronounced "sah-tahn").   Used in the Books of Numbers, Samuel, and Kings to mean human enemies, either individual or national. In the Book of Job and in Zechariah, Satan is a spiritual being, among the angels. In rabbinic writings, Satan is largely an agent of accusation and temptation working alongside God, albeit in a negative manner, rather than being an agent of ultimate evil.

Angels in Judaism?

Judaism, as well as the other monotheistic faiths and Zoroastrianism, is opposed to accepting the existence of gods other than its own. But the desire, perhaps innate in humanity, to identify natural and cultural phenomena with spiritual beings finds an outlet in the belief in angels. An angel in Judaism is a messenger, servant, or functionary of God. Sometimes they look human. Certain biblical texts suggest that some angels are human. Other angelic beings have the appearance of animal or other forms from nature. Whether or not they have wings, or have heads of men or of beasts, whether they are called angels, seraphs, or cherubs, and whether they are real creatures or intended as allegories, these beings exist in the service of God, as messengers, servants, or guardians.

People are sometimes surprised to learn that belief in angels is found in Judaism. The following song, composed by kabbalists in the Middle Ages, has become the quintessential Sabbath evening song:

Shalom aleichem	שָׁלוֹם עֲלֵיכֶם,	Welcome,
Malachei hashareit	מַלְאֲכֵי הַשָּׁרֵת,	Ministering angels,
Malachei Elyon	מַלְאֲכֵי עֶלְיוֹן,	Messengers of the Most High,
MiMelech malchei hamlachim	מִמֶּלֶךְ מַלְכֵי הַמְּלָכִים,	Of the supreme Ruler of rulers,
HaKadosh baruch hu.	הַקָּדוֹשׁ בָּרוּךְ הוּא.	The Holy One, blessed be God.
Bo-achem l'shalom	בּוֹאֲכֶם לְשָׁלוֹם,	Come in peace,
Malachei hashalom	מַלְאֲכֵי הַשָּׁלוֹם,	Messengers of peace,
Malachei Elyon	מַלְאֲכֵי עֶלְיוֹן,	Messengers of the Most High,
MiMelech malchei hamlachim	מִמֶּלֶךְ מַלְכֵי הַמְּלָכִים,	Of the supreme Ruler of rulers,
HaKadosh baruch hu.	הַקָּדוֹשׁ בָּרוּךְ הוּא.	The Holy One, blessed be God.
Barchuni l'shalom	בָּרְכוּנִי לְשָׁלוֹם,	Bless me with peace,
Malachei hashalom	מַלְאֲכֵי הַשָּׁלוֹם,	Messengers of peace,
Malachei Elyon	מַלְאֲכֵי עֶלְיוֹן,	Messengers of the Most High,
MiMelech malchei hamlachim	מִמֶּלֶךְ מַלְכֵי הַמְּלָכִים,	Of the supreme Ruler of rulers,
HaKadosh baruch hu.	הַקָּדוֹשׁ בָּרוּךְ הוּא.	The Holy One, blessed be God.
Tzeitchem l'shalom	צֵאתְכֶם לְשָׁלוֹם,	And may your departure be in peace,
Malachei hashalom	מַלְאֲכֵי הַשָּׁלוֹם,	Messengers of peace,
Malachei Elyon	מַלְאֲכֵי עֶלְיוֹן,	Messengers of the Most High,
MiMelech malchei hamlachim	מִמֶּלֶךְ מַלְכֵי הַמְּלָכִים,	Of the supreme Ruler of rulers,
HaKadosh baruch hu.	הַקָּדוֹשׁ בָּרוּךְ הוּא.	The Holy One, blessed be God.

The origin of the song, according to A. Z. Idelson (*Jewish Liturgy and Its Development*, p. 151), is found in a midrash in the Talmud (*Shabbat* 119b), which describes the two angels, one good and one evil, that accompany every person's return home from synagogue Friday night. When the person arrives at home, if candles are lit and the house prepared for Shabbat, the good angel says, "May it be God's will that it should be like this every Shabbat," to which the evil angel must say, "Amen." If, however, the person returns from synagogue and the house is not prepared for Shabbat, the evil angel says, "May it be God's will that it should be like this every Shabbat," to which the good angel is compelled to say, "Amen."

Angels in the Bible

There are several different kinds of angels portrayed in the Bible. These include humanlike messengers, creatures with physical traits of animals, and members of God's celestial court.

Angels as God's Companions

Jewish teachings on this subject range from an emphatic "yes" to a positive "no." While Jewish philosophy suggests that before the beginning there was nothing but God, our texts suggest that God had company. During the creation of humankind, the Torah tells us:

> God said, "Let us make man in our image, after our likeness."
>
> Genesis 1:26

While this suggests that there were other beings in addition to God, the plural "us" and "our" may be a rhetorical "royal *we*." Later in the text, after Adam and Eve have eaten from the fruit of the tree of knowledge, the plural form is repeated:

> *Adonai* God said, "The man has now become like one of us, knowing good and evil. He must not be allowed to reach out his hand and take also from the tree of life and eat, and live forever."
>
> Genesis 3:22

The consensus of Jewish theologians is that God was alone at the onset of Creation. That belief, coupled with the above passages, can be explained in several possible ways: it is rhetorical language (i.e., the "royal *we*"); God created the angels early on to assist with the rest of Creation; or these phrases may be holdovers from an earlier period in Israelite history before monotheism had been fully realized.

Cherubim, Seraphim, Nephilim, and *B'nei Elohim*

In the next verses, another element is added:

> So *Adonai* God banished him from the Garden of Eden to work the ground from which he had been taken. After God drove the man out, He placed cherubim and a flaming sword flashing back and forth on the east side of the Garden of Eden to guard the path to the tree of life.
>
> Genesis 3:23–24

Who and what are the cherubim? The origin of the Hebrew word כְּרוּב *(k'ruv)* is shrouded in mystery. It is possibly related to the Assyrian word *karabu*, meaning "to be gracious" or "to bless." The tradition may also be derived from the winged bull *(kirubu)* found in Assyrian mythology.

The cherubim of the Bible appear in two contexts: guarding the Garden of Eden (Genesis 3:24) and accompanying the Holy Ark or the throne of God. Of the sixty-eight or so occurrences of "cherubim" in the Bible, most are descriptions of ornamental figures decorating the Tabernacle or Temple. The cherubim were a pair of winged figures that were set on either side of the Ark of the Covenant, with their wings spread out over it.

In the ninth and tenth chapters of the Book of Ezekiel, the prophet has a dream-vision in which he is in a chamber that is at once a depiction of the Holy of Holies in the Jerusalem Temple while also being the heavenly throne of God:

The Vision of Ezekiel by Raphael, 16th century.

I looked, and I saw the likeness of a throne of sapphire above the expanse that was over the heads of the cherubim. . . . Now the cherubim were standing on the south side of the Temple when the man went in, and a cloud filled the inner court.

Then the glory of *Adonai* rose from above the cherubim and moved to the threshold of the Temple. The cloud filled the Temple, and the court was full of the radiance of the glory of *Adonai*. The sound of the wings of the cherubim could be heard as far away as the outer court, like the voice of God Almighty when He speaks.

When God commanded the man dressed in linen, "Take fire from among the wheels, from among the cherubim," the man went in and stood beside a wheel.

Then one of the cherubim reached out his hand to the fire that was among them. He took up some of it and put it into the hands of the man in linen, who took it and went out. The cherubim appeared to have human hands beneath their wings. I looked, and I saw beside the cherubim four wheels, one beside each of the cherubim; the wheels sparkled like beryl stone.

In appearance, the four of them looked the same; each was like a wheel intersecting a wheel. As they moved, they would go in any one of the four directions the cherubim faced; the wheels did not turn about as the cherubim went. The cherubim went in whatever direction the head faced, without turning as they went. Their entire bodies, including their backs, their hands, and their wings, were completely full of eyes, as were their four wheels. I heard the wheels being called "the whirling wheels."

Each of the cherubim had four faces: One face was that of a cherub, the second the face of a man, the third the face of a lion, and the fourth the face of an eagle. Then the cherubim rose upward.

Ezekiel 10:1, 3–15

Compare Ezekiel's vision to the vision of Isaiah. A notable difference is that in the place of the cherubim, Isaiah is faced with beings called seraphim. A seraph (שָׂרָף, *saraf*, from a root meaning "flame") was possibly a fiery dragonlike beast described elsewhere in the Bible. Other than their six wings, we get very little visual description of these beings. In function, however, they perform much like the cherubim in Ezekiel:

In the year that King Uzziah died, I saw the Lord seated on a throne, high and exalted, and the train of God's robe filled the Temple. Above God were seraphs, each with six wings: with two wings they covered their faces, with two they covered their feet, and with two they were flying. And they were calling to one another: "Holy, holy, holy is *Adonai* Almighty; the whole earth is full of God's glory."

At the sound of their voices the doorposts and thresholds shook, and the Temple was filled with smoke. "Woe to me!" I cried. "I am ruined! For I am a man of unclean lips, and I live among a people of unclean lips, and my eyes have seen the King, *Adonai* Almighty."

Then one of the seraphs flew to me with a live coal in his hand, which he had taken with tongs from the altar. With it he touched my mouth and said, "See, this has touched your lips; your guilt is taken away and your sin atoned for."

Isaiah 6:1–7

The cherubim and seraphim aren't the only spiritual creatures found in the Bible. The story of Noah begins with a prologue that might seem to fit better in Greek mythology than in the Bible:

When men began to increase in number on the earth and daughters were born to them,

Seraphim, detail from The Last Judgment by Pietro Cavallini, 13th century.

the sons of God *(B'nei Elohim)* saw that the daughters of men were beautiful, and they married any of them they chose. *Adonai* said, "My Spirit will not remain in man forever, for he is mortal; his days will be a hundred and twenty years."

The Nephilim were on the earth in those days—and also afterward—when the sons of God went to the daughters of men and had children by them. They were the heroes of old, men of renown.

Genesis 6:1–4

Who were these sons of God, and what were the Nephilim? According to legend, the Nephilim are giants. The Israelites encountered more of these when they scouted out the land of Canaan:

"The country that we crossed and scouted is one that devours its settlers. All the people that we saw in it are men of great size. We saw Nephilim there—the Anakites are part of the Nephilim—and we were like grasshoppers compared to them."

Numbers 13:32–33

The identity of the "sons of God" is also problematic. In the Book of Job (e.g., 1:6), the expression represents an angelic court that meets with God. But whether the expression refers to angels or some other god-like beings is not clear.

Angels as Messengers

The earliest angels in the Bible come from the stories of the Patriarchs and Matriarchs, whom angels frequently visit for divine purposes. Twice, an angel appears to Sarah's handmaid Hagar, first giving her reassurance that she will bear a son (Genesis 16:7–12), and then after she and her son Ishmael are expelled from Abraham's camp, to guide her to water:

God heard the boy crying, and the angel of God called to Hagar from heaven and said to her, "What is the matter, Hagar? Do not be afraid; God has heard the boy crying as he lies there. Lift the boy up and take him by the hand, for I will make him into a great nation." Then God opened her eyes and she saw a well of water.

Genesis 21:17–19

Before Sarah became pregnant with Isaac, Abraham was visited by three men, whom he served a meal and who promised him that his wife would conceive:

Adonai appeared to Abraham near the great trees of Mamre while he was sitting at the entrance to his tent in the heat of the day. Abraham looked up and saw three men standing nearby. When he saw them, he hurried from the entrance of his tent to meet them and bowed low to the ground.

Genesis 18:1–2

While the three men were not explicitly called angels, their task was one of bringing a message from God. In the very next chapter, two more men (according to midrash, in the Babylonian Talmud, *Bava M'tzia* 86b, one of the men may have been the angel Gabriel) come to Sodom to warn Lot to leave that city. This time the men are called angels, although they appear to be human.

The two angels arrived at Sodom in the evening, and Lot was sitting in the gateway of the city. When Lot saw them, he got up to meet them and bowed down with his face to the ground.

"My lords," he said, "please turn aside to your servant's house. You can wash your feet and spend the night and then go on your way early in the morning." "No," they answered, "we will spend the night in the square."

But he insisted so strongly that they did go with him and entered his house. He prepared a meal for them, baking bread without yeast, and they ate.

Before they had gone to bed, all the men from every part of the city of Sodom—both young and old—surrounded the house.

They called to Lot, "Where are the men who came to you tonight? Bring them out to us so that we can have sex with them."

Genesis 19:1–5

The desire on the part of the men of Sodom to have sexual relations with the angels (which, by the way, is the source of the term "sodomy" to describe sex between men) suggests that the angels were human in appearance. But angels didn't always look like people. The angel that first approached Moses in the hills of Midian took on the distinctly nonhuman appearance of a burning bush:

Moses was tending the flock of Jethro his father-in-law, the priest of Midian, and he led the flock to the far side of the desert and came to Horeb, the mountain of God. There the angel of *Adonai* appeared to him in flames of fire from within a bush. Moses saw that though the bush was on fire it did not burn up. So Moses thought, "I will go over and see this strange sight—why the bush does not burn up."

Exodus 3:1–3

One of the more fanciful stories of angels comes from the Book of Numbers, in which God sends an angel to stop the prophet Balaam. The Moabite king, Balak, has enlisted Balaam—a non-Israelite prophet—to curse the Israelites. As Balaam set out to the Israelite encampment, an angel who was invisible to him, but visible to his donkey, blocked his path.

> When the donkey saw the angel of *Adonai* standing in the road with a drawn sword in his hand, she turned off the road into a field. Balaam beat her to get her back on the road.
>
> Numbers 22:23

Three times the donkey veered off the path to avoid the angel, and each time Balaam beat her. After the third beating, God "opened the donkey's mouth" and she spoke to Balaam, complaining about her mistreatment when all she was doing was trying to avoid the angel.

> Then *Adonai* opened Balaam's eyes, and he saw the angel of *Adonai* standing in the road with his sword drawn. So he bowed low and fell facedown. The angel of *Adonai* asked him, "Why have you beaten your donkey these three times? I have come here to oppose you because your path is a reckless one before me. The donkey saw me and turned away from me these three times. If she had not turned away, I would certainly have killed you by now, but I would have spared her."
>
> Balaam said to the angel of *Adonai*, "I have sinned. I did not realize you were standing in the road to oppose me. Now if you are displeased, I will go back."
>
> The angel of *Adonai* said to Balaam, "Go with the men, but speak only what I tell you."
>
> Numbers 22:31–35

In the Bible, angels are especially common as guardians and protectors of travelers. When Abraham sent his servant to find a wife for Isaac, God sent an angel to help assure his success (Genesis 24:40). Jacob encountered angels at two important junctures of his life, as he was leaving Canaan (Genesis 28:12, the dream of the angels on the ladder) and again upon his return to Canaan (Genesis 32:3). Similarly, angels accompanied the Israelites during the Exodus from Egypt:

> See, I am sending an angel ahead of you to guard you along the way and to bring you to the place I have prepared. Pay attention to him and listen to what he says. Do not rebel against him; he will not forgive your rebellion, since My Name is in him.

If you listen carefully to what he says and do all that I say, I will be an enemy to your enemies and will oppose those who oppose you. My angel will go ahead of you and bring you into the land of the Amorites, Hittites, Perizzites, Canaanites, Hivites, and Jebusites, and I will wipe them out.

Exodus 23:20–23

These examples of biblical angels serve to convey messages, to protect, to minister, and to guide. Some angels have very specific tasks that they perform for God. Two such angels are Michael and Gabriel.

Gabriel and Michael

The two most famous angels, the only angels whose names are given in the Hebrew Bible, are Gabriel and Michael. "Gabriel" (גַּבְרִיאֵל) means "Man of God" or "Mighty One of God." Daniel's second encounter with Gabriel is described:

While I was still in prayer, Gabriel, the man I had seen in the earlier vision, came to me in swift flight about the time of the evening sacrifice.

He instructed me and said to me, "Daniel, I have now come to give you insight and understanding."

Daniel 9:21–22

"Michael" (מִיכָאֵל) means "Who is like God." It was as common a name in biblical times as it is

Gabriel, England, 14th century.

today. In nine of the ten places it appears in the Bible, it is the name of a human being. In the Book of Daniel, however, a great prince named Michael, mentioned three times (Daniel 10:13; 10:21; 12:1), is sent by God to guide the Israelites during the end of days:

"At that time Michael, the great prince who protects your people, will arise. There will be a time of distress such as has not happened from the beginning of nations until then. But at that time your people—everyone whose name is found written in the book—will be delivered."

Daniel 12:1

In one midrash, Michael was the angel who held back Abraham's hand when he was about to sacrifice Isaac (Bialik, *The Book of Legends* 41:45); in another, he is the one who wrestled with Jacob (ibid., 49:83, from Babylonian Talmud, *Sotah* 41b).

Satan

In the Hebrew Bible, the word *satan* is used more often to describe human adversaries than superhuman ones. King Solomon's various military opponents are referred to as *satan* (I Kings 5:18; 11:14, 23, 25). Even in the passage quoted previously, in which an angel blocks Balaam's donkey, the angel served as a *satan* to the donkey (Numbers 22:32). Where *satan* appears as something other than human, he serves as an interrogator or prosecuting attorney serving God. In one of the dream-visions of the prophet Zechariah, Satan is challenging the authority of Joshua son of Jehozadak, a survivor of the Babylonian exile who in Zechariah's time was High Priest:

> Then he showed me Joshua the High Priest standing before the angel of *Adonai,* and Satan standing at his right side to accuse him. *Adonai* said to Satan, "*Adonai* rebuke you, Satan! *Adonai,* who has chosen Jerusalem, rebuke you! Is not this man a burning stick snatched from the fire?"
>
> Zechariah 3:1–2

The Book of Chronicles is a retelling of the history of Israel from Adam and Eve through the end of the Babylonian exile. It often paraphrases stories from elsewhere in the Bible, while providing subtle nuances and retellings. Look at these parallel passages. The verse from I Chronicles is a paraphrase of the verse from II Samuel. Note how the phrase "anger of *Adonai*" is replaced with "Satan."

The anger of *Adonai* again flared up against Israel, and He incited David against them, saying, "Go and count Israel and Judah." II Samuel 24:1	Satan arose against Israel and incited David to count Israel. I Chronicles 21:1

These parallel passages suggest that sometime between the writing of Samuel and the writing of Chronicles, God's anger became personified as Satan.

The most noted appearance of Satan in the Hebrew Bible is in the Book of Job, where Satan suggests that God test Job's loyalty:

> One day the angels presented themselves before *Adonai,* and Satan came with them. *Adonai* said to Satan, "Where have you come from?"

Satan answered *Adonai,* "From roaming through the earth and going back and forth in it."

Then *Adonai* said to Satan, "Have you noticed My servant Job? There is no one on earth like him; he is blameless and upright, a man who fears God and shuns evil."

"Does Job fear God for nothing?" Satan replied. "Have You not put a hedge around him and his household and everything he has? You have blessed the work of his hands, so that his flocks and herds are spread throughout the land. But stretch out Your hand and strike everything he has, and he will surely curse You to Your face."

Adonai said to Satan, "Very well, then, everything he has is in your hands, but on the man himself do not lay a finger." Then Satan went out from the presence of *Adonai.*

Job 1:6–12

In this story, Satan is doing the job of a "devil's advocate." While his function is contrary and, in Job's case, certainly malicious, Satan is not the agent of evil that he would become in Christian tradition.

Angels and Demons in Islam and Christianity

Angels are far more prevalent in the Christian Bible and the Quran than they are in the Hebrew Bible. Christianity teaches that angels are composed of pure spirit and were created by God. Christianity distinguishes nine classes of angels: seraphim, cherubim, thrones, dominions, virtues, powers, principalities, archangels, and regular angels. In addition to the angelic functions elaborated in the Hebrew Bible, Christianity has a notion of "fallen angels"—creatures that have been weighted down by pride—principal among them being Satan.

In Christianity, the role of Satan or the Devil was elevated from being an accusing messenger of God to being a spirit of ultimate evil. Satan took on many other names, among them Prince of Evil, Beelzebub (from the Hebrew *Baal Z'vuv,* "Master of Flies"), and Lucifer (which, ironically, means "Morning Star"). In the Gospels, Jesus at times uses these names as though they refer to different beings, but elsewhere in the Christian Bible and throughout most of Christianity, the names Satan, Lucifer, and the Devil, are used for the same being.

The main task of Satan is that of tempter. Christianity proposes that Satan was responsible for the "Fall of Man" by tempting Eve in the Garden of Eden. Similar to Ahriman of the Zoroastrian religion, Satan is in a constant battle with God and will engage God in a final battle at the end of time, a battle that God will win, banishing evil for all time.

Angels are similarly important in Islam. The Quran and Hadith literature teach that angels—*mala'ikah*—are real beings, not illusions, metaphysical abstractions, or figments of human imagination. They are beings created by Allah from light. Belief in angels is an integral part of *iman* (faith). Disbelief in angels, according to Muslim law, is tantamount to disbelief in God.

Guardian angels play an important role in Islam. Their task, rather than merely being protective spirits, is to keep the believer on Allah's path:

> For each person, there are angels in succession, before and behind him. They guard him by the command of Allah. Truly, Allah will not change the good condition of people as long as they do not change their state of goodness themselves by committing sins and by being ungrateful and disobedient to Allah. But when Allah wills a people's punishment, there can be no turning back of it, and they will find no protector beside Him.
>
> Quran 13:11

As with Christianity, Islam identifies numerous classes of angels. Among the angels named in the Quran and Sunna writings are Jibreel ("Gabriel," in charge of delivering revelation), Mika'il ("Michael," responsible for nature, knowledge, and bringing rain), Israfil (the blower of the horn on Judgment Day), Izra'il (also known as Malik-ul-Maut, the "Angel of Death"), the four Throne Bearers of Allah, Ridhwan (Guardian of Paradise), and Malik (Guardian of Hell).

In addition to the angels *(mala'ikah),* Islam acknowledges the existence of other beings, including *ghuls,* jinn, *ifrit,* and shaitan. A jinni (singular form of "jinn," source of the anglicized word "genie") is similar to an angel, except that being made of fire (rather than light), a jinni is capable of sin. Related to the jinn are *ifrit,* huge winged creatures made of smoke who live in ruins and underground caverns. Shaitan (related to the Hebrew *satan*) are dark, disbelieving jinn. While not totally evil in nature, shaitan work in the service of Iblis (the Devil, also called *ash-shaitan*—the Shaitan), the enemy of Allah.

In a story repeated several times in the Quran, Allah explains to Muhammad how Iblis refused to pay homage to man:

> We created you, then We fashioned you, them We said to the angels, "Make obeisance to Adam." So they all made obeisance, except Iblis. He did not make obeisance.

He [Allah] said, "What hindered you so that you did not make obeisance when I commanded you?"

He [Iblis] said: "I am better than him. You created me of fire, while you created him from dust."

He [Allah] said: "Get out of this place, for it does not befit you to behave proudly here. Go on, then, for you are surely hopeless."

Quran 7:11–13

As in Christianity, it was the Devil (Iblis—in this passage referred to as "the Shaitan") that tempted Adam in the Garden:

The Shaitan made an evil suggestion. He said, "Adam, shall I guide you to the tree of immortality and a kingdom that does not decay?" Then they are of it, so their evil inclinations became manifest to them, and they both began to cover themselves with leaves from the garden, and Adam disobeyed his Lord, so his life became evil.

Quran 20:120–121

Angels in Later Jewish Tradition

In the Talmud, as in the Bible, angels serve as God's messengers to human beings. While in the Bible angels are often portrayed as resembling people and at times are actually of flesh and blood, in the Talmud they are purely spiritual beings, spirits that fly from world to world, do not require food or drink, are incapable of procreation, and do not die unless by God's explicit direction.

In addition to Gabriel and Michael, the Talmud mentions Samael, the angel of death, and Raphael, the angel of healing. Angels assisted God at the time of Creation and continue to help guide the stars and the seas.

Worship of angels is strictly forbidden. In the Jerusalem Talmud, we are told:

If a man is in distress, let him not call on Michael or Gabriel, but let him call directly on Me, and I will hearken to him straightaway.

Jerusalem Talmud, *B'rachot* 9:1

According to Maimonides, the angels described in the Bible are forces in nature. Correlating Greek philosophy with Judaism, Maimonides explains that when Aristotle "speaks of separate intellects, we speak of angels" (*Guide of the Perplexed* 2:6). For Maimonides, angels are the forces that guide the stars in their path, maintain the laws of nature, and guide the biological processes that develop an egg and sperm into a human being.

Kabbalistic writings are filled with references to angels including Metatron, who guards God's Throne of Glory; Raphael (God Heals), who protects the spirits of humanity; and Uriel (God's Light). The names of these angels were used on amulets and blessings in Jewish folk tradition, especially during the Middle Ages.

Today, the belief in angels in Judaism is a smorgasbord of ideas, where one can pick and choose from the various ideas: Are angels a reality or a fantasy like the tooth fairy? Are they made out of energy or light, or are they flesh-and-blood people? Are they a metaphor for the many tasks and functions that God fulfills, or are they a holdover from polytheistic beliefs?

Perhaps the safest conclusion is to recognize that a belief in angels exists in Judaism, but that this belief is more of a footnote than a major aspect of Jewish religion. Whether or not angels play a role in human life, they play little or no role in the religious life of most Jews.

Chapter Six

מָשִׁיחַ

Mashiach

The Messiah,
an Image of Hope and Salvation

> The days are coming when I will fulfill the promise that
> I made concerning the House of Israel and the House of
> Judah. In those days and at that time I will make a true
> branch sprout from David's line, and he will do what is
> just and right in the land. In those days Judah will be
> saved and Israel will live in safety.
>
> Jeremiah 33:14–16

Messiah is a Jewish concept. In fact, it was among the prophets of biblical Israel
that the concept first arose. The word itself is based on the Hebrew term מָשִׁיחַ
mashiach. Yet the Jewish and Christian ideas of messiah are so dissimilar that it is
bewildering that the same word is used to represent both.

Messiah is also the single most important concept in Christianity. The very word
"Christianity"—from the Greek word *kristos* (messiah)—means messianism, the
religion of the messiah. If the idea of messiah were taken out of Christianity, the
content that remained would no longer be Christianity.

This chapter will trace the development of the messianic idea in Judaism and
Christianity and look at similar concepts in Buddhism, Native American religion, and
Rastafarianism. Our discussion of messiah in Judaism and world religions will have to
take into account two very different sets of ideas: messiah as a political and military
champion, and messiah as a spiritual abstraction for the perfection of the world at the
end of time.

Word Histories

Messiah. From the Hebrew מָשִׁיחַ (*mashiach;* see below), which in turn comes from the verb מָשַׁח (*mashach*), meaning "to dab with oil." In the ancient Near East, smearing a person or item with oil was a means of consecrating, or dedicating, the person or item for a special, sacred purpose. Jeremiah used מָשַׁח to describe the painting of palace walls (Jeremiah 22:14). The verb is used elsewhere in the Bible to describe dabbing or polishing food or weapons with oil (Exodus 29:2; Leviticus 2:4; II Samuel 1:21). Anointing with oil served to consecrate prophets (I Kings 19:16), priests (Exodus 28:41; Leviticus 7:36), sacred objects such as the vessels used in the Tabernacle (Exodus 29:36), and kings (I Samuel 10:1).

Christ. From the Greek work *kristos,* "Christ" means "Anointed," and is thus, to Christians, a synonym for "Messiah." The word occurs 514 times in the Christian Bible, always referring to Jesus of Nazareth. Jesus, believed by Christians to be the anointed redeemer, prophet, priest, and king of his followers, is usually called Jesus Christ—"Jesus the Messiah." Transcending the idea of a human savior, Christ in Christianity is a divine being, a god, the Son of God.

מָשִׁיחַ *(mashiach)*. Anointed one; a person chosen or consecrated by God for a special purpose, as symbolized by the ceremony of anointing with oil. The High Priest was sometimes referred to as הַכֹּהֵן הַמָּשִׁיחַ (*HaKohein HaMashiach*), "the Anointed Priest" (Leviticus 4:3; 6:15). By and large, the word מָשִׁיחַ was used as a synonym for the kings of Israel (I Samuel 12:3; 16:6), in particular King David (Psalm 132:10, 17). The term מָשִׁיחַ is also used in Isaiah to refer to a non-Israelite king, Cyrus of Persia (Isaiah 45:1), whom God commissioned to free Israel from the Babylonians. In the Book of Daniel, מָשִׁיחַ refers to a future prince who will usher in "eternal righteousness" (Daniel 9:24–26).

Key Terms

Messiah. One who is anointed. May refer to a king, a prophet, or a priest appointed by God and anointed with oil.

Christ. From the Greek *kristos,* meaning "anointed with oil."

Messianic age. A period of peace and bliss alluded to by the prophets in which the kingdom of God will exist on earth.

Eschatology. The branch of philosophy concerned with human destiny after death or with the last days, the final judgment, and the end of history. From the Greek *eskatos,* meaning "last."

Apocalypse. From the Greek *apokalupsis,* literally "uncovering" or "revealing." Used in Christianity as a synonym for doom, final destruction, and the end of time.

Armageddon. From the Hebrew *Har M'giddo,* a term used in Christianity for the setting of final battle between God and Satan.

מָשִׁיחַ *(mashiach).* Anointed one, from the Hebrew מָשַׁח (*mashach*), "daubed in oil," a ceremony used to mark kings and other offices in the ancient Near East.

Apocalypse.   From the Greek *apokalupsis,* literally "uncovering" or "revealing." The expression originally referred to Jewish and Christian writings containing prophetic visions, meaning "that which was revealed." It was later associated specifically with the Revelations of John the Apostle, called the Book of Revelations in the Christian Bible. Since the Book of Revelations deals with the End of Days, "apocalypse" has come to mean "doom," "final destruction," and "the end of time."

Armageddon.   From the Hebrew הַר מְגִדּוֹ *(Har M'giddo)* referring to Mount Megiddo, the site of an ancient town in the Jezreel Valley, eighteen miles southeast of Haifa. In ancient times, Megiddo was the site of many battles, and it is mentioned once in the Christian Bible (Revelations 16:16) as the place where the final battle between God and the forces of evil would begin. "Armageddon" has become a term used in Christianity as another synonym for the End of Days or the Apocalypse.

Human Saviors

Judaism has had its share of saviors. In the early years after the Exodus and before the reign of kings, Israel had a long string of leaders called judges who rallied the troops and strengthened the community. The stories of Joshua, Deborah, Gideon, and Samson are filled with miracles and acts of bravery. Joshua led the Israelites to bring the walls of Jericho down (Joshua 6) and called on the sun to stand still in the sky until his armies could defeat the Amorites (Joshua 10:12–13). Deborah was a prophet and political leader who led a military campaign against the Canaanites. The hero Samson was a Nazirite and a judge, whose strength was superhuman. Gideon led an army of 300 men to confuse Midianite and Amalekite troops with the sound of trumpets (Judges 7:19–22).

Heroism is a theme that runs through the legends and stories of nearly every human culture. The ancient Mesopotamian book of *Gilgamesh* tells the story of a young king who tries to free his friend from the realm of the dead. When that fails, he goes to the ends of

Gilgamesh, relief from Palace of Sargon II, 8th century B.C.E.

the earth to try (also unsuccessfully) to find the secret of immortality. Hindu mythology is filled with stories of avatars—gods who have taken human form to help those on the human plane of existence. In Buddhism, a bodhisattva is an enlightened person—a Buddha—who foregoes reward in order to help others to reach enlightenment. In addition, Judaism and Christianity are filled with stories of *tzaddikim* and saints whose brave acts of goodness and kindness help others.

In the following section, the biblical idea of God's anointed one is superimposed in the hero motif, evolving into the notion of messiah familiar today.

The Idea of Messiah in Biblical Times

The Jewish concept of messiah has its seed in the history of the Israelite kingdom under the rule of King David. David was the middle of three kings that ruled under a commonwealth that united two rival nations: Judah and Israel. David's monarchy, despite the various scandals that it suffered, was seen as a Golden Age of Jewish nationhood.

Why was David's reign so highly romanticized? Like King Arthur of English legend, David was glorified far beyond what he may have deserved. When Jews for thousands of years have looked back in Jewish history, it is the kingdom of David that produces the strongest nostalgic pangs. Yet why are the kingdoms of Saul or Solomon overlooked? Saul was the first king of Israel, but according to the Bible, he quickly lost God's favor because of his greed, jealousy, paranoia, and mismanagement. Solomon, David's son, was a peaceful ruler under whose reign the Temple was built in Jerusalem. He was considered a wise and just king. But perhaps because the union between Israel and Judah fell apart so quickly after his reign, Solomon is not remembered as fondly as David. Therefore, we associate David and his line with the Messiah.

David ruled in Judah from around 1013 until 1006 B.C.E. and then in a united Judah and Israel until 973 B.C.E. After his death, his son Solomon succeeded him. King Solomon ruled in Jerusalem for approximately forty years, 973–933 B.C.E. When King Solomon died in 933 B.C.E., the union of Judah and Israel fell apart. Jeroboam, a man with no hereditary claim to the throne, became ruler of the Northern Kingdom, while Solomon's son, Rehoboam, ruled Judah in the south. Neither nation, Judah or Israel, achieved the glory that they knew under David and Solomon.

David became connected with the concept of messiah when, around 760 B.C.E., a sheep breeder from Tekoa, to the south of Jerusalem, moved from Judah to the

Northern Kingdom of Israel and began preaching warnings that the opulence of the ruling class, and general disobedience to God, would lead to the destruction of Israel. The man's name was Amos, and he was the first of the prophets to have a biblical book named for him. Amos criticized the people in the Northern Kingdom for worshiping at the old sanctuaries of Bethel, Shechem, and Gilgal:

> Hear this word, O house of Israel, this lament I take up concerning you:
> "Fallen is Virgin Israel, never to rise again, deserted in her own land, with no one to lift her up." This is what my Lord *Adonai* says: "The city that marches out a thousand strong for Israel will have only a hundred left; the town that marches out a hundred strong will have only ten left." This is what *Adonai* says to the House of Israel: "Seek Me and live; do not seek Bethel, do not go to Gilgal, do not journey to Beersheba. For Gilgal will surely go into exile, and Bethel will be reduced to nothing."
>
> Amos 5:1–5

Amos's message of doom was tempered by a positive promise that Israel would be restored and would again be a part of a Davidic kingdom:

> "In that day I will restore David's fallen tent. I will repair its broken places, restore its ruins, and build it as it used to be, so that they may possess the remnant of Edom and all the nations that bear my name," declares *Adonai,* who will do these things.
> "The days are coming," declares *Adonai,* "when the reaper will be overtaken by the plowman and the planter by the one treading grapes. New wine will drip from the mountains and flow from all the hills. I will bring back My exiled people Israel; they will rebuild the ruined cities and live in them. They will plant vineyards and drink their wine; they will make gardens and eat their fruit. I will plant Israel in their own land, never again to be uprooted from the land I have given them," says *Adonai* your God.
>
> Amos 9:11–15

Isaiah son of Amoz (no relation to the prophet Amos) belonged to the next generation of prophets. Like Amos, Isaiah stressed that Jerusalem was the appropriate place for Israelites to worship their God, as opposed to the mountains and high places of the north. He emphasized that, in the end, all would return to Jerusalem, people would be guided by Torah, and nations would rule in peace:

> This is what Isaiah son of Amoz saw concerning Judah and Jerusalem:
> In the last days the mountain of *Adonai*'s Temple will be established as chief among the mountains; it will be raised above the hills, and all nations will stream to it.

Many peoples will come and say, "Come, let us go up to the mountain of *Adonai*, to the House of the God of Jacob. God will teach us God's ways, so that we may walk in God's paths." The law will go out from Zion, the word of *Adonai* from Jerusalem.

God will judge between the nations and will settle disputes for many peoples. They will beat their swords into plowshares and their spears into pruning hooks. Nation will not take up sword against nation, nor will they train for war anymore.

Isaiah 2:1–4

Isaiah also began using highly creative and spiritual language to describe the coming Messiah. He spoke of the descendant of King David—often referred to as a shoot, branch, or sprout from the line of David or Jesse (David's father)—who would lead with such fairness that even wild beasts would behave in a just and gentle manner:

A shoot will come up from the stump of Jesse; from his roots a Branch will bear fruit.

The Spirit of *Adonai* will rest on him—the Spirit of wisdom and of understanding, the Spirit of counsel and of power, the Spirit of knowledge and of the fear of *Adonai*—and he will delight in the fear of *Adonai*. He will not judge by what he sees with his eyes, or decide by what he hears with his ears; but with righteousness he will judge the needy, with justice he will give decisions for the poor of the earth. He will strike the earth with the rod of his mouth; with the breath of his lips he will slay the wicked. Righteousness will be his belt, and faithfulness the sash around his waist. The wolf will live with the lamb, the leopard will lie down with the goat, the calf and the lion and the yearling together; and a little child will lead them. The cow will feed with the bear, their young will lie down together, and the lion will eat straw like the ox. The infant will play near the hole of the cobra, and the young child put his hand into the viper's nest.

They will neither harm nor destroy on all my holy mountain, for the earth will be full of the knowledge of *Adonai* as the waters cover the sea. In that day the Root of Jesse will stand as a banner for the peoples; the nations will rally to him, and his place of rest will be glorious.

Isaiah 11:1–10

In 722 B.C.E., as predicted by Amos, Isaiah, and others, Israel fell. The Assyrians attacked the Northern Kingdom, driving it into exile. The ten tribes that comprised the Northern Kingdom were scattered (hence the ten lost tribes), leaving Judah as the only surviving Israelite nation. Despite their rivalries, the people of Judah must have felt sadness at the destruction of their cousins to the north. During this period, prophets like Jeremiah and Zephaniah began writing about the cataclysm that they expected would fall upon Judah. In the writings of these prophets, the cataclysmic events were often described on a global scale, affecting the entire planet, and not merely on the national level, affecting the people of Israel and Judah. It is uncertain whether the prophets saw global cataclysm as a real possibility or whether such descriptions were hyperbole, symbolic exaggeration. Regardless, out of these descriptions would arise an entire body of literature about the end of the world.

The reason for this cataclysmic imagery may have been the influence that the Zoroastrian religion of Persia was already having on the people of Judah. As in Zoroastrianism, the prophets described a major event that would mark the end of the world as we know it:

> "I will sweep away everything from the face of the earth," declares *Adonai*.
>
> "I will sweep away both men and animals; I will sweep away the birds of the air and the fish of the sea. The wicked will have only heaps of rubble when I cut off man from the face of the earth," declares *Adonai*. "I will stretch out My hand against Judah and against all who live in Jerusalem. I will cut off from this place every remnant of Baal, the names of the pagan and the idolatrous priests—those who bow down on the roofs to worship the starry host, those who bow down and swear by *Adonai* and who also swear by Molech, those who turn back from following *Adonai* and neither seek *Adonai* nor inquire of him."
>
> Zephaniah 1:2–6

For the prophets, as for the Persians, the end was not a final one. The struggle at the end of the world would result in God and goodness winning out, and the beginning of a new age of perfect, ongoing peace. For Zephaniah, this final day—known later as the Day of Judgment or the Day of the Lord—would be a testing period for all the nations:

> "Wait for Me," declares *Adonai*, "for the day I will stand up to testify. I have decided to assemble the nations, to gather the kingdoms and to pour out my wrath on them—all My fierce anger. The whole world will be consumed by the fire of My jealous anger. Then will I purify the lips of the peoples, that all of them may call on the name of *Adonai* and serve Him shoulder to shoulder. From beyond the rivers of Cush My worshipers, My scattered people, will bring Me offerings. On that day you

will not be put to shame for all the wrongs you have done to Me, because I will remove from this city those who rejoice in their pride. Never again will you be haughty on My holy hill. But I will leave within you the meek and humble, who trust in the name of *Adonai*. The remnant of Israel will do no wrong; they will speak no lies, nor will deceit be found in their mouths. They will eat and lie down and no one will make them afraid....

"At that time I will deal with all who oppressed you; I will rescue the lame and gather those who have been scattered. I will give them praise and honor in every land where they were put to shame. At that time I will gather you; at that time I will bring you home. I will give you honor and praise among all the peoples of the earth when I restore your fortunes before your very eyes," says *Adonai*.

Zephaniah 3:8–13, 19–20

The Babylonian Exile

The great cataclysm came for the people of Judah at the beginning of the sixth century B.C.E. The Babylonians, under King Nebuchadnezzar, attacked Jerusalem in March of 597 B.C.E. Nebuchadnezzar shut down the Temple and confiscated its vessels, arrested government officials, and replaced them with his own puppet king. Finding that he was still unable to dominate the Judean people who fought for independence, Nebuchadnezzar returned in 586 B.C.E. and laid waste to Jerusalem and the Temple, taking much more of the population into exile.

During this period, known as the Babylonian exile, prophecy grew. Jeremiah, whose career as a prophet spanned from just prior to the 597 B.C.E. exile until the final exile in 586 B.C.E., writes about the return of a united Israelite kingdom in Jerusalem:

"The days are coming," declares *Adonai*, "when I will fulfill the promise I made to the House of Israel and to the House of Judah. In those days and at that time I will make a true branch sprout from David's line; he will do what is just and right in the land. In those days Judah will be saved and Jerusalem will live in safety. This is the name by which it will be called: *Adonai* Our Righteousness." For this is what *Adonai* says: "David will never fail to have a man to sit on the throne of the House of Israel, nor will the priests, who are Levites, ever fail to have a man to stand before me continually to offer burnt offerings, to burn grain offerings, and to present sacrifices."

Jeremiah 33:14–18

Jeremiah continues, reiterating that the line of David would continue into the future, as will the priestly class. Jeremiah then reassures the people that God's mercy and the covenantal relationship established with Abraham would return to the Jewish people:

> This is what *Adonai* says: "As surely as I established My covenant with day and night and the laws of heaven and earth, I will never reject the descendants of Jacob and David My servant and will choose one of his sons to rule over the descendants of Abraham, Isaac, and Jacob. For I will restore their fortunes and have compassion on them."
>
> Jeremiah 33:25–26

Another prophet, Ezekiel, was among the Judeans removed to Babylon in 597 B.C.E. Out of his experience in exile came the following prophecy about the restoration of David's kingdom:

> "My servant David will be king over them,
> And they will all have one shepherd.
> They will follow My laws and be careful to keep My decrees.
> They will live in the land I gave to My servant Jacob,
> The land where your fathers lived.
> They and their children and their children's children will live there forever,
> And David My servant will be their prince forever.
> I will make a covenant of peace with them;
> It will be an everlasting covenant.
> I will establish them and increase their numbers,
> And I will put My Sanctuary among them forever.
> My Dwelling Place will be with them;
> I will be their God, and they will be My people.
> Then the nations will know that I *Adonai* make Israel holy,
> When My Sanctuary is among them forever."
>
> Ezekiel 37:24–28

The End of Time

The "Day of Judgment" first appeared in Hebrew writings during the eighth and seventh centuries B.C.E. This idea—which in Christianity would evolve into the themes of Armageddon, Apocalypse, and the Second Coming—was viewed not simply as the end of existence, but as an end followed by a new beginning. After the final cataclysm, the world would be re-created as a new world with eternal peace, security, and happiness. In this new age, David's kingdom would be reestablished, God would be closer to the human realm, and war and disease would disappear. Since previous notions of time and history would no longer be meaningful, the transition into this age was sometimes called "the End of Days" or "the End of Time."

During the period of Babylonian exile, a prophet (sometimes referred to as Second Isaiah because his writings appear later in the Book of Isaiah) promises:

> "Behold, I will create new heavens and a new earth."
> Isaiah 65:17

The prophecy continues with the promise of longevity and political independence:

> "Never again will there be in it an infant who lives but a few days, or an old man who does not live out his years. He who dies at a hundred will be thought a mere youth; he who fails to reach a hundred will be considered accursed. They will build houses and dwell in them; they will plant vineyards and eat their fruit. No longer will they build houses and others live in them, or plant and others eat."
> Isaiah 65:20–22

The prophecy ends with a metaphoric vision of peacefulness:

> "The wolf and the lamb will feed together, and the lion will eat straw like the ox, but dust will be the serpent's food. They will neither harm nor destroy on all My holy mountain."
> Isaiah 65:25

The prophet Joel, who wrote sometime around 400 B.C.E., used many of the metaphors and images found in the Book of Amos. In Joel, together with the ideas of the earlier prophets, are descriptions of a final battle that may have been introduced through the Jews' close relationship with Persia:

> Blow the trumpet in Zion; sound the alarm on My holy hill. Let all who live in the land tremble, for the day of *Adonai* is coming. It is close at hand—a day of darkness and gloom, a day of clouds and blackness. Like dawn spreading across the mountains a large and mighty army comes, such as never was of old nor ever will be in ages to come. Before them fire devours, behind them a flame blazes. Before them the land is like the Garden of Eden, behind them, a desert waste—nothing escapes them.
> Joel 2:1–3

In a later chapter, Joel describes what will occur after the cataclysmic final event:

In those days and at that time, when I restore the fortunes of Judah and Jerusalem,
I will gather all nations and bring them down to the Valley of Jehoshaphat. There
I will enter into judgment against them concerning My inheritance, My people Israel,
for they scattered My people among the nations and divided up My land.

Joel 4:1–2

As we will see below, these Hebrew notions of messiah and the messianic age will influence Christianity where it will be developed into the idea of Christ.

Messianism during the Roman Empire

Just as the idea of a messiah developed while Israel and Judah were oppressed under the dominion of Assyria and Babylonia, messianism blossomed under the tyranny of Roman authority. In the years since the Babylonian exile, the nation of Judea (as Judah came to be called after the exile) existed under the friendly authority of Persia (539–332 B.C.E.) and Alexander the Great (332–323 B.C.E.). After Alexander, Judea was controlled by two Greek dynasties, first under the Ptolemies (Egyptian Greeks, 323–200 B.C.E.), and then under the Seleucids (Syrian Greeks, 200–64 B.C.E.). (It was early in the Seleucid period that the Maccabees revolted against Antiochus Epiphanes in 168 B.C.E.)

Around 63 B.C.E., the Seleucid empire was defeated by the Roman Emperor Pompey the Great. Under Roman control, the Jews had limited control over their own land. Roman governors oversaw the region and imposed severe taxes. The descendants of the Maccabees, who were given religious authority, were often more Roman than Jewish in outlook and affiliation.

Jesus of Nazareth

It was at this time (around 7–6 B.C.E.) that Joshua son of Joseph and Miriam was born in Roman-occupied Judea. The boy, who would be called by the Latin pronunciation of his name, Jesus, was to become the most important messianic figure in history.

Jesus' career as a leader of a religious cult spanned from approximately 27 C.E. until his execution in 30 C.E. Jesus taught messages of purity through baptism (based on the Jewish tradition of *mikveh* bathing) and preparing for the coming Kingdom of God. The core ideas of Jesus' ministry were that the Kingdom of God is approaching and that his followers should prepare themselves through repentance and by surrendering all connections with family and work.

Jesus was asked numerous times in the Gospels whether he was the Messiah, but he carefully avoided answering this question. Upon his arrest and execution under the Romans in 30 C.E., his followers declared him to be the Messiah.

During his lifetime, Jesus taught that the Kingdom of God was at hand, that the prophecies of the Hebrew Bible would soon be fulfilled, and that redemption was imminent. At the time of Jesus' death, these messianic missions of reestablishing the Kingdom of David and establishing universal peace had not occurred. The writers of the Christian Bible explained that the messianic promise would be fulfilled when Jesus returned, an event later Christians called the "Second Coming."

Simeon bar Kochba

Another man believed by many to be the Messiah was Simeon bar Koziva (also spelled Bar Kosba and Ben Koziva), a Jewish leader who led a revolt against Roman authority between 132 and 135 C.E. Rabbi Akiva renamed the military hero Bar Kochba—"Son of a Star":

> How great was the strength of Ben Koziva? He would intercept the stones shot by Roman catapults with one of his knees, heave them back, and thus slay ever so many Roman soldiers. When Rabbi Akiva beheld Ben Koziva, he exclaimed, "A star [kochav] has risen out of Jacob—Koziva has risen out of Jacob! He is the king Messiah!"
>
> <div align="right"><i>Eichah Rabbah</i> 2:2 #4; Jerusalem Talmud, <i>Taanit</i> 4:5, 68:d;
Babylonian Talmud, <i>Gittin</i> 57–58 (from Bialik, <i>The Book of Legends</i> 194:8)</div>

While many Jews followed Akiva's belief that Bar Kochba (as he was thereafter called) was the Messiah, other rabbis were less certain:

> Rabbi Yochanan ben Torta responded, "Akiva, grass will be growing out of your cheeks and David's son the Messiah will still not have come."
>
> Ibid.

In 135 C.E., Hadrian's armies defeated the Jewish troops. Bar Kochba and Rabbi Akiva were among those captured and executed by the Romans. As valiant and heroic a leader as Bar Kochba was, and as much as both he and Rabbi Akiva died as martyrs, history ultimately recognizes that Bar Kochba was not the Messiah.

False Messiah Movements

Born in Smyrna, Turkey, in 1626, Shabbetai Zvi raised the eyebrows of any who witnessed his religious services. Zvi's behavior was erratic and bizarre—sometimes wildly self-indulgent, while at other times painfully ascetic—and led him to be expelled from the community by the rabbinate of Smyrna. In 1665, a young man named Nathan of Gaza declared himself to be a prophet and announced that Shabbetai Zvi was the Messiah. The two men traveled together and accumulated a huge number of followers. They declared that the Kingdom of God would arrive in 1666. The movement was extremely popular throughout the Jewish communities of Europe and North Africa. People saw in Zvi's message a hope for the end of persecution and an ecstatic reunion with God. Then, in September 1666, after arriving in Constantinople and declaring the Kingdom of God, he was arrested. Faced with the threat of torture, Zvi converted to Islam, to the disappointment of thousands of his followers.

About a century later, in 1751, a Polish Jew called Jacob Frank declared himself to be the reincarnation of Shabbetai Zvi, returned to fulfill Zvi's promise. Frank rejected all rabbinic authority, saying that a higher Torah made him exempt from moral law. He led wild, orgiastic ceremonies. Probably more of a charlatan than a madman or true visionary, Frank openly sought money and sex, while gaining favor from the Catholic Church by promising to provide converts. Supported financially by his many followers, he declared himself a baron. He died in Germany in 1791.

Modern Attitudes about Messianism

The stories of false messiahs Shabbetai Zvi and Jacob Frank support the Jewish view that all messianic claims be approached with skepticism. It's certainly appropriate for Jews to hope for the coming of the Messiah and to conduct their lives in a way that lays the groundwork for the messianic age. The Jewish value of *tikkun olam* (fixing the world) suggests that humanity is in partnership with God to bring the Kingdom of God to earth.

The Chabad Chasidic movement, the largest Chasidic sect in the world, has been at the forefront of modern Jewish messianic fervor, with songs, chants, and banners proclaiming "We Want Moshiach Now!" Chabad followers looked to their spiritual leader, the Rebbe Menachem Mendel Schneerson, to be the Messiah. When Schneerson died in 1994, having left no heir to become the next Rebbe, many of his followers were convinced that the time of the Messiah had come. Only time will tell.

Messiahs in Non-Western Religions

The Buddha

While differing greatly from Jewish and Christian ideas of messiah, a survey of the heroes and saviors of other religions can provide a broader understanding of messiah.

The man who came to be called "the Buddha" was born in the early sixth or late seventh century B.C.E. (623 B.C.E. according to Theravada tradition and 565 B.C.E. according to Mahayana tradition). Born a prince of the Sakya nation, near the present-day Indian border with Nepal, his name, in Sanskrit, was Siddhartha Gautama. While searching for the meaning of human suffering, he came to the realization, while sitting in the shade of a bodhi tree, that desire is the cause of all suffering, and by removing desire, one can eliminate suffering. Gautama's philosophy was not a theological one. Ideas of God or gods were irrelevant to his teachings. He

Great Buddha, from Todai-ji Temple, Nara, Japan, 745–752 C.E.

forbade his followers from making or worshiping any likenesses of him. In many ways, the career of the Buddha—both during his life and after his death—parallels that of Jesus.

For several hundred years after the death of the Buddha, his followers kept his instructions and avoided making pictures or statues of their teacher. Early Buddhist carvings and paintings portrayed scenes from the life of the Buddha, but substituted symbols such as a footprint, a throne, or a "wheel of dharma" to represent the Buddha. By 100 C.E., images of the Buddha in human form were being widely produced in India. As Buddhism was introduced into China (37 C.E.) and Korea (350 C.E.), statues and paintings of the Buddha became important artforms and objects of worship. In Japan, which was introduced to Buddhism in the sixth century C.E., a huge statue of a figure called the Vairocana Buddha was completed in 752 C.E. at the Todai-ji Temple in Nara. It contains an estimated one million pounds of copper, tin, and lead and stretches over fifty-two feet high.

In addition to Siddhartha Gautama, there have been many other historical and mythical figures that have been called Buddha. Among these are beings known as bodhisattvas. A bodhisattva is a person who has achieved enlightenment but postpones personal nirvana in order to help others to achieve enlightenment. Bodhisattvas are revered throughout Buddhist countries as saints, saviors, and celestial teachers. As with the Buddha himself, bodhisattvas over time became mythical, celestial beings while reports of their human origins diminished. Today Buddhists continue to call on statues of Amitaba, Avalokitesvera (Kuan Yin), Manjusri, and Maitreya to help them in times of need.

Native American: Ghost Dance

Toward the end of the nineteenth century, North American Indian culture seemed doomed. Land was being seized by the White Man. The animals that the Indians relied on were becoming scarce. Alcohol abuse was epidemic. Military conflicts with the U.S. Army were common.

In 1869–1870 in Nevada, a Paiute Indian named Tävibo began preaching the message that he said he had received in a vision: An earthquake would occur soon that would destroy all non-Indians living in North America. At that point, all dead Indians would rise from their graves and rejoin their families, food would be plentiful, peace and happiness would reign, and the old ways would return. Indians, he said, should prepare themselves through a ceremony called the Ghost Dance. The earthquake never took place, and when Tävibo died in 1972, the movement faded.

In 1889, an Indian named Wovoka—another Paiute and possibly Tävibo's son or other relation—had a vision during a solar eclipse. The Great Spirit that the Indians called Grandfather told him that the Ghost Dance was to be revived. Wovoka's vision is filled with Christian imagery and, most notably, mention of Jesus. This is perhaps due to influence on Wovoka by Mormons, the Indian Shaker Church, and the Presbyterian family who owned the ranch where he worked.

> Grandfather says, when your friends die you must not cry. You must not hurt anybody or do harm to anyone. You must not fight. Do right always. It will give you satisfaction in life. . . . Do not tell the white people about this. Jesus is now upon the earth. He appears like a cloud. The dead are still alive again. I do not know when they will be here; maybe this fall or in the spring. When the time comes there will be no more sickness and everyone will be young again. . . .

I want you to dance every six weeks. Make a feast at the dance and have food that everybody may eat. Then bathe in the water. That is all. You will receive good words again from me some time. Do not tell lies.

James Mooney, 14th Annual Report of the Bureau of American Ethnology, part 2 (1896)

This message took hold among the Utes, Bannocks, and Shoshone, as well as Northern Plains tribes likes the Arapaho, Northern Cheyenne, and Oglala Sioux. The message turned to one of hope mixed with resistance. In the tragic events of Wounded Knee, South Dakota, hundreds of Sioux warriors, dressed in costumes called Ghost Shirts that they believed would protect them from bullets, left the reservation and stood opposed to U.S. Army troops. Driven by fear based on rumors about the Ghost Dance rituals, the U.S. soldiers massacred the Sioux. The massacre at Wounded Knee marked the official end of the Ghost Dance cult. But elements of this belief have been adopted and adapted by many Indian communities up to the present.

Rastafarianism

The Rastafarian movement, which developed among the Black population of Jamaica in the early 1950s, is based on the life of Ethiopian king Haile Selassie and influenced by the political ideas of Marcus Garvey. Celebrating African pride, reggae music, marijuana, and hair styled in uncombed "dreadlocks," the Rastafarian religion teaches that modern Blacks are the reincarnated souls of the ancient Israelites, expelled from their homeland. They await the time when the Messiah will usher them back to Africa.

The Messiah, for Rastafarians, was Haile Selassie, emperor of Ethiopia from 1930 to 1974. Selassie, born Tafari Makonnen in 1892, was named *ras* (prince) and heir apparent to the Ethiopian throne in 1917. Selassie was a progressive leader and a devout Christian opposed to what he saw as a Muslim stranglehold on African culture. Selassie was not a Rastafarian himself. In fact, when a group of Rastafarians visited Ethiopia to honor him, a palace official told them to go away and not upset the king.

Haile Selassie by William H. Johnson, 1945.

Despite Selassie's own rebuff of Rastafarianism, Rastafarians believe that Selassie (or "Ras Tafari") is the living God prophesied in the Bible, the Jesus of the Christian Bible, and the Messiah who would bring them all back to Africa. Rastafarian music is filled with imagery from the Hebrew prophets, and followers refer to God by the name of Jah, from the Hebrew *Yah*.

Waiting for God

Messianic movements have historically led to disappointment or, worse, disaster. When the world is ready for the Messiah, then the Messiah will come. But like chasing a butterfly, actively bringing about the messianic age, or trying to predict when it will come, will undoubtedly make it go further away. The Talmud teaches: "Three things cannot be predicted: the Messiah, finding a lost item, or a scorpion" (Babylonian Talmud, *Sanhedrin* 97a).

What should we do if we are told that the Messiah is coming? We should probably go about our business. The news is probably false. But even if it were true, the Messiah would rather see us striving for good in our own lives than chasing after empty or premature hopes. When the world is at peace and all live in justice, truth, kindness, and security—only then will we know that the Messiah has truly come.

According to another midrash, "'Yochanan ben Zakkai used to say, 'If you are planting a tree and you hear that the Messiah has come, finish planting the tree, and then go and greet the Messiah.'" (*Avot D'Rabbi Natan* B, 31).

Chapter Seven

חַיִּים

Chayim

Life, Death, and Afterlife

I put before you life and death, blessing and curse.
Choose life—that you and your offspring should live—by
loving *Adonai* your God and heeding His commands,
and holding fast to Him.

Deuteronomy 30:19–20

Judaism is a religion of life.

Some religions offer methods to escape the suffering and the limitations of physical existence. Some religions provide hope for a better existence that will come after physical bodies expire. Judaism, by contrast, emphasizes *this* life, the world of physical existence.

The Jewish toast *L'chayim!*—"To life!"—is a small but indicative token of the Jewish joy and appreciation of life. The word חַי (*chai*, meaning "life" or "alive") is a popular design in jewelry.

Through the observance of mitzvot—life-affirming rituals, blessings, celebrations, and interpersonal conduct—Jews find and create holiness in everyday life. In later chapters, we will look at how mitzvot celebrate and give meaning to life. In this chapter, we will look briefly at the Jewish attitude toward physical life—*olam hazeh*—and then, paradoxically, spend the bulk of the chapter examining the attitudes and theories in Judaism and other religions about death and what happens to us afterwards.

Word Histories

Heaven. The origins of the word "heaven" are uncertain. It seems to be parallel to the German *himmel* and may be related to the English word "heave" or from a root meaning "to cover." In English translations of the Bible, it is commonly used in place of the Hebrew *shamayim* (שָׁמַיִם, sky) and *marom* (מָרוֹם, hill, high place). When the ancients looked up, they saw a blueness that resembled the color of water. And since the sky was the source of rain, it seemed logical that the sky was a body of water. To them, the sky was a clear dome stretched out over the earth that kept the "waters above" separated from the "waters below." The Hebrew word for this dome was *rakia* (רָקִיעַ), often translated as "firmament."

The heavens were often seen as multilayered, with the lowest level containing birds and insects, the next level containing the spheres of the stars and planets, and the topmost being the realm of God. In medieval English, the word "heaven" referred to the sky and not necessarily to the domain of God. In the twelfth or thirteenth century, the word "sky" (from a root meaning "cover") came into common usage. Today, most often the word "heaven" refers to the domain of God as well as of angels and the souls of the dead.

Hell. Ironically, while "heaven" and "hell" are seen as diametric opposites, their origins, as well as the origins of related words, are very similar. Specifically,"hell" comes from a Germanic root meaning, "to cover, hide, or conceal" and is related to the English "hall," "hole," "hollow," and "helmet." As a place, hell is a hidden, unseen realm, related in meaning to the Hebrew *Sheol*.

Key Terms

Life. The interval between birth and death; an organism's experiences of growth, reproduction, and response to stimuli. From a Germanic root, *lieb*, meaning "body."

Heaven. Unknown origin, but with probable original meaning "cover." Heaven—like the Hebrew *rakia*—is the expanse of space spread out over the world. Also refers to the abode of God, the angels, and in some traditions, human souls.

Hell. Also from a Germanic root. Hell originally referred to a place that was hidden and, in Norse mythology, to the goddess Hel.

Purgatory. The state or place in which, according to Roman Catholic belief, a soul must be cleansed or purged of sins before entering heaven.

עוֹלָם הַזֶּה *(olam hazeh)*. Hebrew for "this world," i.e., the world of physical existence.

עוֹלָם הַבָּא *(olam haba)*. Hebrew for "the coming world" or "the world-to-come," i.e., a plane of existence after death and/or after the coming of the Messiah.

שְׁאוֹל *(Sheol)*. "Underworld" or "hollow place." The gloomy realm where people descend to after death.

Hell also appears to come from the name of the Norse goddess Hel, daughter of Loki, goddess of death and the underworld. For the Norse, the realm of Hel was extremely cold, in contrast to the contemporary view of hell as a burning pit. It has also been suggested that "hell" is related to the Greek *helios* or "sun." Evidence for this connection is scant, but if true, it deepens the paradox of hell being understood as a dark place.

Purgatory. The word "purgatory" comes from the Latin for "cleanse," hence "purge." In Roman Catholic tradition, purgatory is an intermediate period between death and admission into heaven in order to give the soul an opportunity to be purified. Purgatory is often used as a synonym for "hell."

שְׁאוֹל *(Sheol)*. There are a number of theories about the origin of this word, among them: (1) *Sheol* comes from the root שָׁאַל *(shaal)*, "to ask," hence *Sheol* is the place of inquiry; (2) *Sheol* comes from the root שָׁעַל *(shaal)*, "hollow," thus *Sheol* is the hollow place or pit. *Sheol* is often translated as "underworld" or "netherworld" and is generally depicted as a place set underground, a dark, gloomy place where the dead reside.

Hades. In Greek mythology, Hades was the brother of Zeus who abducted Zeus's daughter Persephone and took her to his realm, the underworld, as his wife. With Persephone separated from her mother, Demeter, the two women were distraught. The mother eventually rescued Persephone from the underground realm of Hades, which had the effect of making the whole earth barren. Zeus intervened and arranged for Persephone to spend half the year above ground with her mother and the remaining half-year below ground with her husband Hades. The name "Hades" is associated both with the god and with his realm. The word "Hades" is used frequently in the Christian Bible to signify the Hebrew idea of *Sheol*.

גֵּיהִנוֹם *(Geihinom/Gehenna)*. The word *gehenna* is a contraction of *Gei-hinnom*, the Hinnom Valley, a deep glen to the south of Jerusalem. In several biblical references (Jeremiah 7:31; 19:2–6; II Chronicles 28:3; 33:6), this was the site where idolatrous and unfaithful Israelites sacrificed their children to the god Molech. In later biblical years, the Hinnom Valley was used as a landfill, a waste dump for the city of Jerusalem, which was perpetually kept on fire to prevent spread of disease. The place was associated with idolatry and with waste disposal, with disease and perpetual fire, and later with the idea of afterlife. In the Christian Bible, the term "Gehenna" is used as a synonym for "hell."

Afterlife in World Religions

Mesopotamia

In ancient Sumeria, Babylonia, and Assyria—the closest neighbors and most direct influences on Judaism—the realm of the dead was dark, damp, and gloomy. Upon death, a person was thought to go to an underworld. In a very real sense, the dead *did* go to dark, damp, and gloomy places, namely, burial caves. The following passage from Genesis, describing Abraham's purchase of a burial cave, is illustrative of Mesopotamian culture:

> Then Abraham rose from beside his dead wife and spoke to the Hittites. He said, "I am an alien and a stranger among you. Sell me some property for a burial site here so I can bury my dead."
>
> Genesis 23:3–4

And a few verses later:

> Abraham agreed to Ephron's terms and weighed out for him the price he had named in the hearing of the Hittites: four hundred shekels of silver, according to the weight current among the merchants.
>
> So Ephron's field in Machpelah near Mamre—both the field and the cave in it, and all the trees within the borders of the field—was deeded to Abraham as his property in the presence of all the Hittites who had come to the gate of the city. Afterward Abraham buried his wife Sarah in the cave in the field of Machpelah near Mamre (which is at Hebron) in the land of Canaan. So the field and the cave in it were deeded to Abraham by the Hittites as a burial site.
>
> Genesis 23:16–20

Mesopotamian people did not have strong or explicit views of afterlife. For them, for the most part, death was the final resting place. In the *Epic of Gilgamesh*, the warrior Enkidu describes a dream predicting his own death, in which he describes the "House of Dust":

> The house where the dead dwell in total darkness,
> Where they drink dirt and eat stone,
> Where they wear feathers like birds,
> Where no light ever invades their everlasting darkness,
> Where the door and the lock of the netherworld is coated with thick dust.
>
> *Gilgamesh,* tablet 7, column 4

There was an acknowledgment in Mesopotamian cultures that human beings are composed of "dust" and that death has no return. In the following Babylonian myth, Ishtar (Sumerian Inanna), the goddess of love and war, descends through seven gates of the netherworld in an attempt to rescue her lover, Tammuz (Sumerian Dumuzi), from death:

To the Land of No Return, the realm of Ereshkigal,
Ishtar, the daughter of the Moon, set her mind.
To the dark house, the abode of Irkalla,
To the house which none leave who have entered it,
To the road from which there is no way back,
To the house wherein the entrants are bereft of light,
Where dust is their fare and clay their food,
Where they see no light, residing in darkness,
Where they are clothed like birds, with wings
    for garments,
And where over door and bolt is spread dust.

Descent of Ishtar, in *Ancient Near Eastern Texts*,
trans. E. A. Speiser (Princeton, 1950), p. 106

Ishtar, Babylon, 4th century B.C.E.

For the ancient Mesopotamians, afterlife was a real possibility, but one that was filled with dust, darkness, and regret. The many stories of heroic descent into the netherworld underscores the Mesopotamian attention to death and the normally futile attempts to escape it.

Egypt

While ancient Mesopotamians saw death as a dark and dusty eternal rest, to ancient Egyptians, the idea that life would go on after death was as real as the regular flow of the Nile. Afterlife was believed to be a real and physical existence, albeit one invisible to those still alive.

Egyptian beliefs and rituals surrounding death and afterlife were indelibly tied to the myth of Osiris. The son of Nuit and Geb, Osiris was both a god and a human who married his sister, Isis. His lifelong rivalry with his brother Set led to his eventual murder. When Osiris was celebrating his twenty-third birthday, Set gave him a beautiful, gold-inlaid chest. When Set tricked his brother into climbing inside the chest, it was locked and tossed into the Nile. Hearing news of the murder, Isis went in search for Osiris in the hopes of bringing him back to life. She eventually found that a tree

113

had grown around the chest bearing Osiris's body. Osiris became a symbol of resurrection in ancient Egyptian thought, and his name was invoked in nearly all tombs and funeral rites.

According to Egyptian beliefs, the human soul is comprised of several components, including *ba,* the soul that goes on living after death, remaining close to the body to assure its preservation; and *ka,* a person's abstract or double, sort of an astral body able to separate itself from physical form, able to live apart from the body, and able to enjoy an ongoing existence after death.

Preparing for life after death was as important to ancient Egyptians as retirement planning is in modern Western culture. This was particularly true of royalty, for whom extravagant tombs were often built as lavish condominiums for the dead, containing every convenience one might need in the afterlife: pottery, utensils, food, drink, boats, clothing, weapons, and even servants. That the afterlife was seen as a physical existence is reflected in the care Egyptians took in preserving the bodies of the dead. Since it was impossible to imagine life without a body, great care was taken to prevent decay of the body and its vital organs.

In the following passage, inscribed on linen wrappings found on the mummy of Thutmose III (died 1426 B.C.E.), the dead king praises Osiris in order to emulate the god's immortality. The mortal body—*khat*—is transformed into Khepera, the beetle-headed god of the "rising sun," ready to burst forth into a new life:

> Homage to thee, O my father Osiris, thy flesh suffered no decay, there were no worms in thee, thou didst not crumble away, thou didst not wither away, thou didst not become corruption and worms; and I myself am Khepera, I shall possess my flesh for ever and ever, I shall not decay, I shall not crumble away, I shall not wither away, I shall not become corruption.
>
> E.A. Wallis Budge, *The Egyptian Book of the Dead:* *(The Papyrus of Ani) Egyptian Text, Transliteration and* *Translation* (Dover Publications, 1967), p. lix

Osiris, Tomb of Sennutem, Thebes, Egypt, ca. 14th century B.C.E.

The journey into the next life was not a neat, simple experience for Egyptian rulers. Each soul, or *ka,* had to pass a variety of tests and trials, including a courtroom-like hearing before a jury of forty-two gods. The heart of the dead man is placed on a scale and weighed against the feather of *maat* (truth):

> O ye who open the way and lay open the paths to perfected souls in the Hall of Osiris, open ye the way and lay open the paths to the soul of Osiris, the scribe and steward of all the divine offerings, Ani who is triumphant with you. May he enter in with a bold heart and may he come forth in peace from the house of Osiris. May he not be rejected, may he not be turned back, may he enter in [as he] pleaseth, may he come forth [as he] desireth, may he be victorious. May his bidding be done in the house of Osiris; may he walk, and may he speak with you, and may he be a glorified soul among you. He hath not been found wanting there, and the Balance is rid of [his] trial.
>
> Ibid., p. 273

Greek (Plato)

As we discussed in chapter 2, the Greek philosopher Plato held a strong and elaborate belief in a soul. The world of ideas was far more important to Plato than was the physical world, which represented but a portion of reality. The soul, or psyche, embodied the permanence of ideas. The final book of Plato's *Republic* contains a description of the near-death experience of a soldier named Er, son of Armenias, who apparently died in battle, but who recovered on the day he was to be cremated:

> And on the twelfth day, as he was lying on the funeral pyre, he returned to life and told them what he had seen in the other world. He said that when his soul left the body he went on a journey with a great company, and that they came to a mysterious place at which there were two openings in the earth; they were near together, and over against them were two other openings in the heaven above. In the intermediate space there were judges seated, who commanded the just, after they had given judgment on them and had bound their sentences in front of them, to ascend by the heavenly way on the right hand; and in like manner the unjust were bidden by them to descend by the lower way on the left hand; these also bore the symbols of their deeds, but fastened on their backs.
>
> He said that for every wrong which they had done to anyone they suffered tenfold; or once in a hundred years—such being reckoned to be the length of man's life, and the penalty being thus paid ten times in a thousand years. If, for example,

there were any who had been the cause of many deaths, or had betrayed or enslaved cities or armies, or been guilty of any other evil behavior, for each and all of their offenses they received punishment ten times over, and the rewards of beneficence and justice and holiness were in the same proportion. I need hardly repeat what he said concerning young children dying almost as soon as they were born. Of piety and impiety to gods and parents, and of murderers, there were retributions other and greater far which he described.

Plato, *The Republic,* book 10:614

Er's account of the afterlife went on to describe how each soul is given a choice of who or what they will be in the next life. The souls of several great heroes—Ajax, Agamemnon, and Orpheus—all chose to be animals in their next lives because of disappointments in their human incarnations. As the final book of *The Republic* comes to a close, Plato renders Socrates' discussion with his student Glaucon on the meaning of the story of Er:

But in what manner or by what means he returned to the body he could not say; only, in the morning, awaking suddenly, he found himself lying on the pyre.

And thus, Glaucon, the tale has been saved and has not perished, and will save us if we are obedient to the word spoken; and we shall pass safely over the river of Forgetfulness, and our soul will not be defiled. Wherefore my counsel is that we hold fast ever to the heavenly way and follow after justice and virtue always, considering that the soul is immortal and able to endure every sort of good and every sort of evil. Thus shall we live dear to one another and to the gods, both while remaining here and when, like conquerors in the games who go round to gather gifts, we receive our reward. And it shall be well with us both in this life and in the pilgrimage of a thousand years which we have been describing.

Plato, *The Republic,* book 10:621

Hindu

While Hinduism shares with Judaism an attention to ritual, wisdom, and worship, the two religions are as far apart from each other as two thought systems can be regarding the meaning of life, death, afterlife, and the physical world. To the Hindu, the soul, or atman, is trapped in the world of *samsara,* the physical world. The world of action (karma) has us bound to an endless, ongoing cycle of life, death, and rebirth. It's interesting to note that in Hinduism, reincarnation is not seen as a positive, exotic experience that it has taken on in Western New Age culture; rather, since physical life is seen as suffering, each rebirth is viewed as a burden.

The following passage, from the Katha Upanishad (around 1400 B.C.E.), illustrates how the endless cycle of rebirth is seen as undesirable, while the goal is to cease being reborn:

> But he who knows not how to discriminate,
>
> Mindless, never pure
>
> He reaches not that [highest] state *(pada)*, returns
>
> To this round of never-ending birth and death *(samsara)*.
>
> But he who does not know how to discriminate,
>
> Mindful, always pure,
>
> He gains [indeed] that [highest] state
>
> From which he's never born again.
>
> Katha Upanishad 3:7–8

The goal of the Hindu is to escape the world of *samsara* and its cycle of rebirths by achieving *moksha* or nirvana, breaking the wheel of karma and becoming one with Brahman (the Universal Godhead), the only true reality. Thus, although it seems surprising to Westerners, Hindus do not desire immortality. Eternal life is seen as a curse that the individual must strive to escape, to break the wheel of karma. *Moksha* or nirvana only occurs with the complete cessation of individuality.

Zoroastrian/Mithraism

Although almost unheard of today, Mithraism, with its powerful rituals promising resurrection, was once a powerful faith spreading from Persia all the way across Asia, Europe, and northern Africa. Based on the Hindu god of the sun, Mithras, Mithraism was a mystery religion that shared its inner secrets with only its adherents as they arose through seven grades of initiation. Mithraism involved a bull-sacrifice to Mithras, whom worshipers saw as a god of justice, war, and contact with the next world. They held a strong belief in heaven and hell as reward and punishment in the world-to-come for our actions in this world. They looked forward to a Day of Judgment that would destroy the world as we know it, bringing about a lasting triumph of light over darkness, and bringing back the dead.

Mithraism was popular throughout the Roman Empire, especially among soldiers, and was the dominant religion for a time until Emperor Constantine declared

Christianity the official religion in 324 C.E. Mithraist practice involved a form of water purification similar to baptism, as well as taking of wine and bread to symbolize the body and blood of Mithras, who experienced his own resurrection from death, according to myth. Historians have suggested that Mithraism powerfully influenced Christianity during the early centuries of the Christian Church.

Zoroastrianism was in a sense a rebellion against the corrupt bull-sacrifices of Mithraism. But what the two Persian religions had in common was a strong, vivid, and hopeful vision of resurrection at the end of days.

The dualism of good versus bad, light versus darkness is a theme that runs throughout Zoroastrianism. For three days after a person's death, the soul remains at the head of the body, during which time a sort of angelic accountant makes a ledger of all the person's good and evil deeds. The judgment of a soul is described in Menok I Khrat, a Zoroastrian catechism:

> Put not your trust in life, for at the last death must overtake you; and dog and bird will rend your corpse and your bones will be tumbled on the earth. For three days and nights the soul sits beside the pillow of the body. And on the fourth day at dawn (the soul) accompanied by the blessed Srosh, the good Vay, and the mighty Vahram, and opposed by Astvihat (the demon of death), the evil Vay, the demon Frehzisht and the demon Vizisht, and pursued by the active ill-will of Wrath, the evil-doer who bears a bloody spear, (will reach) the lofty and awful Bridge of the Requiter to which every man whose soul is saved and every man whose soul is damned must come. Here does many an enemy lie in wait.
>
> Menok I Khrat 71–74

If the person weighs in as "good," then he or she passes across a bridge to the next level of heaven. If the person is evil, he or she falls off the bridge and tumbles into a dismal hell.

> And when the soul of the saved passes over that bridge, the breadth of the bridge appears to be one parasang broad. And the soul of the saved passes on accompanied by the blessed Srosh. And his own good deeds come to meet him in the form of a young girl, more beautiful and fair than any girl on earth. And the soul of the saved says, "Who art thou, for I have never seen a young girl on earth more beautiful or fair than thee." In answer the form of the young girl replies, "I am no girl but thy own good deeds, O young man whose thoughts and words, deeds and religion were good."
>
> Menok I Khrat 79–83

118

And finally, at the end of time—following the final battle in which Ahuramazda will defeat Ahriman—all the good souls will rise from the dead and live an eternal existence on earth.

Christianity

Christianity is as "next world" centered as Judaism is based in "this world." The promise of eternal life is central to Christian belief. Death is a direct result of sin, and through the death of Jesus, all sin and death will be eliminated:

Jesus Christ by Jovan Vasilievic, 18th century.

> Therefore, just as sin entered the world through one man, and death through sin, and in this way death came to all men, because all sinned—for before the law was given, sin was in the world. But sin is not taken into account when there is no law. Nevertheless, death reigned from the time of Adam to the time of Moses, even over those who did not sin by breaking a command, as did Adam, who was a pattern of the one to come.
>
> Romans 5:12–14

In a direct rejection of Jewish beliefs, Paul, in his letter to the Romans, explained that Torah was unable to eliminate sin or death. These can only be achieved through accepting Jesus as the Messiah:

> The law was added so that the transgression might increase. But where sin increased, grace increased all the more, so that, just as sin reigned in death, so also grace might reign through righteousness to bring eternal life through Jesus Christ our Lord.
>
> Romans 5:20–21

True eternal life would not come until Christ's return, in the Second Coming. Until that time, there have been various views within Christianity as to what happens to the souls of the faithful. According to some, the dead will sleep pending resurrection. Other views suggest that the soul resides in heaven or in purgatory until Christ returns and gathers the faithful.

Islam

In Islam, Allah is the ultimate truth and ultimate perfection. Everything that exists, good or evil, comes from Allah and is under Allah's control. Death is neither an accident nor a punishment, but is part of Allah's plan. No one dies except when Allah ordains it. This does not suggest that there is no free will in Islam. Rather, a believer will live according to God's will and accept the path set by God. One has the choice not to submit to Allah, but in so doing, one guarantees punishment in the world-to-come:

> To those who disbelieve, for them are cut out garments of fire; boiling water shall be poured over their heads. With it shall be melted what is in their bellies and skins as well. And for them are whips of iron. Whenever, in their anguish, they wish to get away from it, they will be forced back, and taste the penalty of burning.
>
> Quran 22:19–22

For faithful Muslims, paradise awaits after death:

> Surely Allah will make those who believe and do good deeds enter gardens beneath which rivers flow; they shall be adorned therein with bracelets of gold and pearls, and their garments therein shall be of silk.
>
> Quran 22:23

Paradise is described in great detail in the Quran as well as in Hadith literature, the teachings and sayings attributed to Muhammad. The rewards are graphically and elaborately described:

> Surely those who guard shall be in gardens and bliss, rejoicing because of what their Lord gave them, and their Lord saved them from the punishment of the burning fire. Eat and drink pleasantly for what you did. Reclining on thrones set in lines, and we will provide them with large-eyed virgins.
>
> Quran 52:17–20

Belief in an afterlife is a mandatory tenet in Islam. The rewards and punishments one receives in this life are, at best, a hint of what is to come. This belief in the reward of paradise helps encourage Muslims to lead good, ethical lives. But history has also shown that these beliefs can be misused to justify violent acts of terror.

What Do Jews Believe about Afterlife?

Judaism doesn't claim a single view of death and afterlife. Instead, Jews hold a variety of different views. Jews hold high regard the sanctity of life and an emphasis on the importance of the physical world—עוֹלָם הַזֶּה *(olam hazeh)*—as well as the importance of ethical conduct. These ideas have remained consistent throughout mainstream Judaism. These constants aside, Jews have held a wide range of evolving views of life after death. The foundations of the Jewish afterlife experience grew out of Mesopotamian and Egyptian beliefs. The biblical view of *Sheol* resembles the dark, musty netherworld of Mesopotamian myths. Jewish death and burial customs are a response to, and a reaction against, what Israelites saw as the excesses of Egyptian funerary customs. Along the long path of history, Jews have adopted and incorporated ideas drawn from Persian, Greek, and even Hindu beliefs.

Early Judaism—the religion of the biblical Israelites—offered very little information about an afterlife. Jews then, as now, placed far more emphasis on physical existence than on afterlife. Like the surrounding Babylonians, Assyrians, and Akkadians, the Israelites conceived of a netherworld, a dark, clammy, dreary realm where the dead sleep eternally. As Job says:

> But man dies and is laid low; he breathes his last and is no more.
> As water disappears from the sea or a riverbed becomes parched and dry,
> So man lies down and does not rise; till the heavens are no more,
> Men will not awake or be roused from their sleep.
>
> Job 14:10–12

Surprisingly, the Bible is ambiguous about the rewards of the world-to-come. The twelfth-century philosopher Maimonides listed the "belief in divine reward and retribution" as one of the Thirteen Principles of Faith. Yet the Book of Ecclesiastes provides stark and seemingly unfair images of death and reward. The first passage suggests that man and beast may all suffer the same end, and what happens after that is not knowable:

> For what happens to the sons of men also happens to animals; one thing befalls them: as one dies, so dies the other. Surely, they all have one breath; man has no advantage over animals, for all is vanity. All go to one place: all are from the dust, and all return to dust. Who knows the spirit of the sons of men, which goes upward, and the spirit of the animal, which goes down to the earth? So I perceived that

nothing is better than that a man should rejoice in his own works, for that is his heritage. For who can bring him to see what will happen after him?

Ecclesiastes 3:19–22

This passage asserts that there is no reward in death:

For the living know that they will die;
But the dead know nothing,
And they have no more reward,
For the memory of them is forgotten.

Ecclesiastes 9:5

In the Bible, "heaven" (or שָׁמַיִם, *shamayim,* in Hebrew) refers to the skies or celestial regions, or sometimes to the abode of God and angels. But the Bible never uses "heaven" as a realm for the souls of the dead. Rather, in the Bible, the dead are said to be "gathered to their people" (Genesis 25:8; Deuteronomy 32:50) or to "rest with ancestors" (Deuteronomy 31:16; II Samuel 7:12; I Kings 1:21). The final resting place of the dead was understood as an underground place, not with the negative implication of the Christian concept of hell, but with the practical observation that underground—whether in caves or in graves—was where bodies were laid to rest.

By the second century B.C.E., the idea of the resurrection of the dead was appearing in Jewish writings, perhaps, in part, an influence of Persian Zoroastrian beliefs. As messianic ideas of the prophets crystallized, one of the events that was agreed would occur in the messianic age was the rising of the dead. This resurrection was thought to be a physical one, in which our whole bodies would live again, and not merely our discorporate souls. Judaism generally rejects the Greek belief that body and soul, like matter and form, are separate entities. Flesh and spirit are intermingled and interdependent aspects that are inseparable and indivisible. The Jewish tradition that bodies are buried whole and the prohibition against cremation are meant as safeguards to bodily resurrection at the time of the Messiah.

The Talmud is filled with references to paradise, *Gan Eden* (Garden of Eden), and *olam haba* (world-to-come) as afterlife rewards. While the Rabbis of the Talmud stressed that the reward in fulfilling a mitzvah was the mitzvah itself, the Rabbis also pointed out that our conduct in this world is directly related to our reception in the world-to-come:

Rabbi Shmuel bar Nachmani said in the name of Rabbi Yonatan: When a man performs a mitzvah in this world, it precedes him—goes ahead of him—in the world-to-come. And when a man commits a transgression in this world, it clings to him and goes before him on the Day of Judgment. Rabbi Elazar said it attaches itself to him like a dog.

Babylonian Talmud, Sotah 3b

The reward and punishment that the Rabbis describe is reminiscent of the Hindu idea of karma. The imagery of actions clinging to a person is identical to that found in Hindu teachings, which refer to karma (action) as a substance that clings to the individual.

There are numerous descriptions of the world-to-come found in the Talmud and other rabbinic writings. In the following passage, *olam hazeh* (this life) is viewed as a mere prologue to the *olam haba* (world-to-come):

Rabbi Yaakov said: This world is like an entrance hall before the world-to-come. Prepare yourself in the entrance hall so that you may enter the banquet hall.

Pirkei Avot 4:21

Y'hudah HaNasi (called Rav in the Talmud) describes a differing view of the afterlife, suggesting that it is totally different from this world:

Rav has a favorite saying: The world-to-come is not at all like this world. In the world-to-come, there is no eating, no drinking, no procreation, no commerce, no envy, no hatred, no rivalry; the righteous sit with crowns on their heads and enjoy the radiance of the Presence.

Babylonian Talmud, B'rachot 17a

It's worth noting that Judaism is perhaps the only religion that asserts not only that there is a place for the righteous of all nations in the world-to-come, that Jews are not favored over non-Jews, but rather that it's actually more difficult for a Jew to achieve reward than a non-Jew. "The righteous of the nations of the world have a portion in the world-to-come" (*Tosefta Sanhedrin* 13:2). While Jews are obligated to observe the 613 laws of Torah, a non-Jew need only follow the seven laws of Noah to be considered righteous.

The expression "Garden of Eden" is often used to describe the abode of the righteous in the messianic age. Is this the same garden that was the home of Adam and Eve in the early chapters of Genesis? Probably not. While this region of reward may be very real, the name Garden of Eden is used metaphorically, just as *Geihinom* refers to *Sheol,* and not to the geographical Hinnom Valley.

Regarding *Sheol* and *Geihinom,* while the terms appear throughout rabbinic writings, they are never understood as the severe or permanent punishments that they represent in Christianity:

> Rabbi Akiva used to say, the punishment of the wicked in *Geihinom* lasts no more than twelve months.
>
> *Mishnah Eduyot 2:10*

In kabbalistic writings and in Chasidic tales, reincarnation is frequently described as the experience of the soul after death. The Hebrew term for reincarnation is *gilgul* (from the Hebrew for "wheel" or "circle"). According to the sixteenth-century kabbalist Rabbi Isaac Luria, in a teaching that is amazingly similar to the Hindu notions of karma and *samsara,* we are expected to fulfill the 613 mitzvot during our lifetime before going on to the next plane of existence. Most of us return numerous times to fulfill what we missed in previous births.

In a similar vein, many Jewish stories and folktales propose that reincarnation is God's way of helping people to fulfill their destinies. Common motifs in Chasidic stories include the following:

- A wealthy man who visits his rebbe, who tells the man a story of someone who commits some injustice. At the end of the story, the wealthy man exclaims, "That was me!" meaning that he recognizes his mistake from a previous life, and he vows to atone and make recompense for his mistakes.
- A man and a woman are destined to be together, but circumstances prevent it from being so. In the next life, they are finally joined in marriage.
- At the moment of a man's death, he realizes that, despite his pious lifestyle, he was guilty of the sin of pride. His soul returns to earth in a new body, and without the benefit of the memory of his previous life, he learns the lesson of humility.

In this chapter, we have learned that Judaism offers a variety of beliefs about death and afterlife that in many ways parallel and in many others ways contrast the views and beliefs of other religions. Above all, Judaism emphasizes that holiness can be found in this life rather than in the next life.

Chapter Eight

K'dushah

Holiness

You shall be holy for I, *Adonai* your God, am holy.

Leviticus 19:2

"Holy, holy, holy is *Adonai* of Hosts! The whole earth
is filled with God's glory."

Isaiah 6:3

What is a religious experience? What does it feel like to be in the presence of God? How can we know what the presence of God is? When we say that a person or thing is religious or spiritual, what are we talking about?

Many Native American groups have the belief in a sacred energy that can be found in places, people, and things. This energy is called *wakan* or *wakanda* and is best described by the Lakota Sioux holy man John Fire Lame Deer:

> You can't explain it except by going to the circles within circles idea, the spirit splitting itself up into stones, trees, tiny insects even, making them all *wakan* by his ever presence. And in turn all these myriad of things which make up the universe flowing back to their source, united in the one Grandfather spirit.
>
> John Fire Lame Deer, *Lame Deer Seeker of Visions* (Simon and Schuster, 1972), p. 114.

This description portrays *wakan,* or holiness, as ever present and manifest in many different things, but representing a single, unified force. Any attempts to define the holy will not be fully adequate. The sacred is ultimately unnameable and unknowable.

Religious experience most often happens when we don't expect it. We can plan and prepare to encounter the holy, but in the end we are surprised by when, where, and how the encounter occurs. The life of Jewish philosopher Franz Rosenzweig is a case in point. Rosenzweig was born on December 25, 1886, in Kessel, Germany. He grew up in a secular, upper-class family with very little background or connection to his Jewish heritage. At the University of Berlin, he studied existentialism and early on was noted as an expert on Hegelian philosophy. His professors saw promise in Rosenzweig's future in the academic world. Because tenured positions were not available for Jews though, they encouraged him to convert to Christianity.

For Rosenzweig, conversion to Christianity might have been easy. He saw Judaism as a relic of ancient times that held little meaning. Christianity offered a more immediate approach to God. In the fall of 1913 he announced his plan to be baptized in the Lutheran Church. Like Jesus and the Apostles, he wanted to come to Christianity by way of Judaism. As a final nod to the religion of his ancestors, he attended *Kol Nidrei* services on Erev Yom Kippur, with the intention of being baptized the following day.

Instead, during *Kol Nidrei* services, the young Rosenzweig had an emotional and spiritual insight, an awareness of the Oneness of God and the grandeur of God's presence. What he had thought was a useless relic—an empty museum piece of a religion—became the focus of the rest of his life. He began studying Judaism and Jewish texts with some of Germany's great Jewish philosophers, such as Hermann Cohen and Martin Buber, and wound up becoming one of the most important Jewish thinkers of the twentieth century.

When World War I broke out in 1914, Rosenzweig signed up to serve in the Red Cross and later in the regular German army. While crouching in the trenches at the Macedonian front line, he escaped the horrors of battle by writing his religious thoughts on postcards and whatever other scraps of paper he could find. He mailed these back to his mother, and what he wrote became the basis for his most important work, *The Star of Redemption.*

After the war, Rosenzweig married Edith Hahn and became director of the Freies Judisches Lehrhaus (Free Jewish Study-House) in Frankfurt am Main. Then, in 1922, Rosenzweig began suffering muscular weaknesses and lack of coordination, which was diagnosed as amyotrophic lateral sclerosis (ALS, later called Lou Gehrig's Disease). Within a year Rosenzweig was unable to speak, eat, dress, or wash without assistance. Yet he continued his work writing Jewish philosophical works and translations by dictating to his wife using eye movements and blinks to spell out each word. He died in 1929, just before his forty-third birthday.

Rosenzweig found God and holiness in surprising places:

1. At synagogue on the eve of his planned conversion *from* Judaism
2. In the trenches of World War I
3. While suffering a debilitating and terminal disease

By his own life's example, Rosenzweig shows how the experience of holiness can be wrapped in paradox. The holy can be simultaneously beautiful and frightening, fascinatingly attractive and repulsive. When we call something "holy," we are often describing a human experience, yet it is also something totally outside of the day-to-day realm.

Word Histories

Holy. Derived from an ancient Germanic root, *khailag,* meaning "whole," the word "holy" originally described things that were complete, unimpaired, and inviolate. It is closely related to the word "hallow." "Holy" shares the same source of such diverse words as "hollyhock," "Halloween," and "halibut" (a fish traditionally eaten on holy days)—and possibly "hail," "health," and "heal." "Holy" is the standard English translation for *kadosh* (קָדוֹשׁ) and is commonly used as an adjective to describe God, as well as places, objects, and people associated with God.

Sacred. From the Latin root *sacer,*

> ### Key Terms
>
> **Holy.** Special, sacred; that which belongs to or is imbued with divine power.
>
> **Sacred.** Special, reserved for religious purpose or function.
>
> **Profane.** Not sacred. Literally "before/outside of the Temple." Used in this context, "profane" does not mean evil or offensive, but merely that which isn't sacred.
>
> **Numinous.** The experience evoked by being in the presence of the holy. Term was coined by German philosopher Rudolph Otto.
>
> קְדֻשָּׁה *(k'dushah).* Holiness. Set apart, consecrated, separate. Refers to places, people, and things dedicated to God. Akin to the adjective קָדוֹשׁ *(kadosh),* "holy."

which paradoxically meant "criminal" and "infamous" as well as "devoted to a deity for destruction." The Latin verb *sacrare* meant "to set apart, dedicate, or devote," as well as "to doom or curse." The Latin noun *sacrum* applied to holy places, objects, and rituals. "Sacred" shares the same root as "consecrate" and "sacrifice," as well as "saint," "sanctify," and "sanctuary." The adjective "sacred" typically applies to books, music, or objects dedicated to religious purposes, such as sacred texts, sacred music, and sacred vessels.

The word "profane" is often used as an antonym for "sacred," hence the common dichotomy "sacred and profane." Today the word "profane" usually refers to vulgar and offensive words or blasphemous action, though "profane" (from *pro-fanum*) originally meant simply "outside the Temple" and referred to anything that was not devoted to religious use.

קְדֻשָׁה *(k'dushah)*. The Hebrew root ק-ד-שׁ *(k-d-sh)* occurs in numerous words throughout the Hebrew Bible, including *kodesh, kadosh, kadeish, kadash,* and *mikdash*. The noun *kodesh* can refer to the separateness/sacredness of God, as well as of places, people, and things set aside for God. The adjective *kadosh* means "sacred" or "holy" and refers to God as well as holy

The Sacred Root ק-ד-שׁ *(k-d-sh)*	
kadosh	holy (adj.)
kodesh	sanctity (n.)
k'dushah	holiness (n.)
mikdash	sanctuary (n.)
m'kadeish	to make holy (v.)
kiddush	sanctification (n.)
kaddish	holy (Aramaic, adj.)
kiddushin	marriage engagement (n.)

people, angels, places, times, and objects. The common form of the verb *m'kadeish* means "to consecrate, make holy, set apart, or devote."

The Temple of Jerusalem, as well as the desert Tabernacle, old Israelite sanctuaries, and non-Israelite holy sites were referred to as *mikdash*. The term *Beit HaMikdash* (House of the Holy) continues to be used today to refer to the Jerusalem Temple. One of the more common appellations for God is *HaKadosh Baruch Hu*, "The Holy One Praised Be He."

The Idea of the Holy:
Rudolph Otto and Mircea Eliade

Any discussion of holiness in world religions would be remiss without a brief discussion of the works of Rudolph Otto and Mircea Eliade. Neither men were Jewish but presented broad, historical views of religion that included and expounded upon basic Jewish ideas of holiness.

Until the late 1800s, the study of religion was generally conducted by members of specific religions for the purpose of broadening the faith of those religions. In other words, the only reason to study Christianity was for a Christian to gain deeper faith in Christianity. The idea of comparing one religion to another was often forbidden. But in the universities of Europe, primarily in Germany, a new science was emerging called *Religionswissenschaft,* "the science of religion" which involved studying many religions, with an objective, nonjudgmental approach. Initially, most such studies dealt with religious texts, myths, and rituals. But in 1917, German scholar Rudolph Otto approached the science of religion in a new way. His study analyzed the mystical experiences of human beings from many different religions and identified the common elements of those experiences.

Otto distinguished between the holy as an ultimate, unfathomable reality and the human experiece of the holy, which he called the numinous. His term "numinous" came from the Latin word *numen* ("spirit," "divine power," or "nod of the head"). The numinous is what happens to people when faced with God or ultimate reality. To describe the numinous experience, Otto used the following Latin axiom:

Mysterium tremendum et fascinans.
A mystery frightening and fascinating.

The three elements of his axiom described the three essential aspects of the experience of the holy that Otto saw in all religious traditions:

Mysterium—mysterious. The holy is beyond conception and cannot be adequately described in human terms.
Tremendum—frightening. Being confronted by the holy is a terrifying experience, causing the person to be stricken with awe, repelled, and shaken by fear.
Fascinans—fascinating. In contrast to *tremendum,* the holy is attractive, alluring, and beautiful.

Otto used other terms when describing the numinous experience, such as:

Majestas—majestic. The awareness of the glory, grandeur, and awesome beauty of the holy; the sense of humility and "creature feeling" one gets in the face of the supremely sublime.
Ganz andere—"totally other" or "wholly other." As mentioned above, the recognition that the holy is unlike anything else. As Otto put it: "The wholly other, that which is quite beyond the sphere of the usual, the intelligible, and the familiar."

Prior to World War II, Romanian-born writer and historian Mircea Eliade had made a name for himself with his research in Sanskrit, Hindu philosophy, and yoga. He continued his studies in Europe and the United States, becoming a professor of religion at the University of Chicago in 1956. In his 1957 book, *The Sacred and the Profane,* Eliade described the experience of the sacred as "the manifestation of something of a wholly different order, a reality that does not belong to our world, in objects that are an integral part of our natural 'profane' world." Thus, everything in our natural world—trees, rocks, words, and human interactions—is profane, not in the sense of being vulgar or offensive, but in the sense that they are of our world. Eliade then looks at four realms—space, time, nature, and human existence—and provides examples of how the profane is made sacred through myth and ritual.

Rather than looking at cases of holiness in individual religions, we will follow the lead of Mircea Eliade and look briefly at how holiness is manifest in time, space, books, and people in various religions. First, we will examine how people have experienced the holy when faced with ultimate reality, and finally we will look at how Judaism expresses the idea of holiness in text, law, sanctuaries, prophecy, and prayer.

Holiness in the Presence of the Ultimate

Whether it is a real, objective thing outside of human experience or created out of our own action and perceptions, the holy exists. As we learn from Otto and Eliade, there are startling similarities in people's descriptions of their encounters with the holy, despite the differences of the religious traditions from which they come. Later in this chapter we will look at records of the Hebrew prophets Moses, Isaiah, and Ezekiel as they faced the holy in the presence of God. For now, other descriptions of the holy that reflect elements of Otto's and Eliade's interpretations will be examined.

Lao Tzu, Chinese scroll painting.

The word *Tao* (pronounced "dow") literally means "way" or "path." The Chinese expression of ultimate truth parallels that of holiness in the West. The philosophy of Taoism is probably best presented in the poetic writings of the semi-historical teacher Lao Tzu (who may have lived and written around 300 B.C.E.) in his collection Tao Te Ching (The Way of Power), which opens with the following passage:

> The Tao that can be told is not the eternal Tao.
> The name that can be named is not the eternal name.
> The nameless is the beginning of heaven and earth.
> The named is the mother of ten thousand things.

Ever desireless, one can see the mystery.

Ever desiring, one can see the manifestations.

These two spring from the same source but differ in name;

   this appears as darkness.

Darkness within darkness.

The gate to all mystery.

Lao Tzu, Tao Te Ching, trans. Gia-fu Feng and Jane English
(Vintage Books, 1972), p. 2

Note how this description of Tao expresses a sense of mystery by avoiding description altogether. It is only the profane world that can be named. This notion of ultimate truth, filled with paradoxes, is unnameable, unknowable, and totally other—*ganz andere.*

The paradoxical nature of the holy is expressed in the following description of one woman's encounter with an angel. The seventeenth-century Catholic nun Saint Teresa of Avila recorded her own revelation in an experience that is both violently painful *(tremendum)* and beautifully attractive *(fascinans):*

> In his hands I saw a long golden spear and at the end of the iron tip I seemed to see a point of fire. With this he seemed to pierce my heart several times so that it penetrated to my entrails. When he drew it out, I thought he was drawing them out with it, and he left me completely afire with a great love for God. The pain was so sharp that it made me utter several moans; and so excessive was the sweetness caused me by this intense pain that one can never wish to lose it, nor will one's soul be content with anything less than God. It is not bodily pain, but spiritual, though the body has a share in it—indeed a great share.

Saint Teresa's experience is both physical and spiritual, in that she uses worldly (profane) descriptions that are more than what they seem. Intense pain is coupled with a sense of sweetness and love, leaving her with an entirely new sense of herself and the universe.

Sacred Space

In *The Sacred and the Profane,* Mircea Eliade suggests that holy places—shrines, temples, rocks, trees, and high places—are symbolic centers, or navels, of the earth. Examples of such places are India's Ganges River, the Kaaba in Mecca, Mount Fuji in Japan, and the Temple Mount in Jerusalem.

It's difficult for modern readers to grasp this idea of a center of the world. What Eliade means is not a geometrical center, but a spiritual one. It is myths and rituals that identify this center, not a compass or measuring stick. For example, the Kwakiutl Indians of British Columbia erect a cedar pole in the center of their ceremonial houses. This pole represents the link between the underworld, the earth, and the sky. During various rituals and ceremonies, celebrants proclaim: "I am at the center of the world."

Sacred spaces represent important memories—personal or mythological. Eliade gives examples of individual sacred space: "There are, for example, privileged places, qualitatively different from all other—a man's birthplace, or the scenes of his first love, or certain places in the first foreign city he visited in his youth." One of the most powerful biblical images of a center of the world is the site in Haran where Jacob laid down a rock as a pillow and then dreamed of a ladder reaching to heaven with angels climbing up and down. In the morning, Jacob announced: "How awesome is this place. This is none other than the House of God, and this is the gate of heaven" (Genesis 28:17).

The Ganges River in India is probably the most sacred body of water on earth. Each year, hundreds of thousands of Hindus make pilgrimage to special beaches along the Ganges—Allahabad, Benares, Kasi, and Haridwar—to immerse themselves in the waters of the river. It is also traditional for the ashes of the dead to be cast out over the Ganges, making cities like Benares popular funeral sites.

For Muslims, one of the Five Pillars of their religion (similar to the Ten Commandments of Judaism) is to make pilgrimage—or hajj—to Mecca at some point during their life, and to walk around the ancient Kaaba shrine seven times before kissing the Black Stone of Mecca, set in a corner wall of the Kaaba. It is believed that the stone was given to Adam to absorb his sins after his expulsion from paradise. When Muslims anywhere in the world pray during their five daily services, they orient themselves toward the Kaaba in Mecca.

Japan's Mount Fuji is a dormant volcano stretching 12,388 feet high, with a circumference of 78 miles. Its name means "everlasting life," and surrounded by temples and shrines, it has long been a site for pilgrimage. More than 100,000 people visit Fuji each year.

Fuji from the Mountains of Izu by Ando Hiroshige, 19th century.

In Australia, Ayers Rock—or Uluru as the Aborigine population calls it—is one of the world's most unusual rock formations. This mound of magnetized sandstone forms a 1,000-foot-high monolith that changes its color depending on time of day and atmospheric conditions. According to Aboriginal belief, the space beneath Uluru contains a connection to Dream Time, a sacred, eternal realm where the mythic ancestors dwell and which is the source of all matter and activity in our world.

Christianity has also honored many pilgrimage sites over the centuries: Saint Mary Major Basilica and the Vatican; the Grotto of Our Lady of Lourdes, known for miraculous cures; and Bethlehem and Jerusalem, the sites where Jesus was born, bore the cross, and was buried. Latin America is filled with destinations for pilgrims seeking to witness miracles alleged to have occurred there.

Sacred space, then, is a physical place bound up in mythic events and which is the object of pilgrimage. In Judaism, various tombs and monuments have taken on a sacred dimension, but none more so than the site of the Temple in Jerusalem, of which only the retaining western wall remains to this day. The Jerusalem Temple will be looked at more closely later in this chapter.

Sacred Time

Normal ("profane") time moves in a linear path from past to present to future. Sacred time operates more like a spiral, connecting the now to the primordial past by remembering and reenacting mythical events. The Hebrew Sabbath is a good illustration of sacred time: it occurs every seven days, but when it occurs, we recall and repeat the events of Creation.

By observing holidays and life-cycle events, we reenact age-old myths and rituals in ways that raise human experience to the holy. During Pesach we are asked to remember when "we" were liberated from Egypt. The liturgy is very clear: celebrants are not remembering the Exodus of their ancestors, but are reenacting the Exodus as though they themselves are going through it.

Sacred Texts

Sacred texts are books, scrolls, or tablets containing poems, prayers, laws, stories, or philosophical and religious teachings. Sacred texts are often "revealed" texts because they are believed to have been given through some divine medium. For example, it is believed that the Torah was given by God to Moses at Sinai, and the Quran given to Muhammad by the angel Gabriel.

133

What all sacred texts have in common is that they convey a spiritual or magical power over those who read—or hear—the words of the text. Like being in a sacred place or participating in a ritual within sacred time, reading or listening to sacred words has the effect of raising one to a higher level of consciousness, to a sacred plane of awareness.

Sacred Texts of the World

	Place/Dates	Content	Significance
The Vedas	India/before 1000 B.C.E.	Ritual hymns	One of the oldest writings in the world; the Vedas serve to link the individual Hindu with the gods through chanting these hymns and performing sacrifices.
Upanishads	India/1000 B.C.E. to 600 B.C.E.	Philosophical teachings	These writings help the student (of Hinduism) to understand his relationship with Brahman (ultimate truth) through attaining wisdom.
Torah	Israel/before 622 B.C.E.	Stories and laws	Contains 613 mitzvot believed to have been given by God to Moses to help the Israelite people live ethical and holy lives.
Tripitaka	India/500–1 B.C.E.	Three collections of rules and discourses	Believed to be the earliest Buddhist texts, many of which are attributed to the Buddha. These form the canon of Theravada Buddhism.
Tao Te Ching	China/around 500 B.C.E.	Poetic wisdom about nature and holiness	These verses teach the Taoist to celebrate the way of nature and to imitate that way in human society.
New Testament	Roman Near East/ before 400 C.E.	Gospels and Acts (narratives of the life of Christ and of the early days of the Church), Epistles (letters between Church leaders), and Revelations (an apocalyptic vision)	Provides numerous links with prophetic works of the Hebrew Bible (Old Testament) to serve as proof texts to validate the divinity of Jesus. Contains many lessons, sermons, and teachings attributed to Jesus.
Quran	Arabia/600–630 C.E.	Revelations given to Muhammad	This collection of 114 chapters of revelation are considered by Muslims to be the exhaustive word of God. Apart from these words, nothing else is needed.
Book of Mormon	America/1830 C.E.	Contains stories and revelations describing the migration of Israelite tribes to North America around 600 B.C.E.	Believed to have been discovered and translated by the prophet Joseph Smith, founder of the Church of Jesus Christ of Latter Day Saints, it is thought by Mormons to be the newest and fullest revelation of God.

As with most religions, Judaism has many different sacred texts, each with different levels of sacredness. The most sacred of Jewish texts is the Torah—the Five Books of Moses—which forms the beginning of the Hebrew Bible. The Torah, according to Jewish tradition, is the word of God given to Moses at Sinai. It is the core set of myths, laws, and values at the center of all other Jewish thought and writings.

The Bible (Hebrew, *Tanach*) is a set of twenty-four books that includes the Five Books of the Torah, as well as eight prophetic collections (Prophets) and eleven Wisdom books (Writings). The Prophets and Writings are sacred texts but do not have the same power or significance to Jews as does the Torah.

Rabbinic writings—which include commentary on the Bible, the Talmud, and the *siddur* (prayer book)—are also considered sacred texts in Judaism. The Talmud and law codes constitute a body of literature called Oral Torah *(Torah Shebal Peh).* According to Jewish tradition, God dictated the entire Written Torah (the Five Books) to Moses. At that same time, God gave many instructions to Moses that were not written down. These instructions were passed orally from generation to generation. During the second century C.E., the great rabbi Y'hudah HaNasi began the effort of transcribing these oral traditions, a process that would take more than a thousand years. The Mishnah tractate *Avot* (known as *Pirkei Avot,* part of this Oral Torah) opens:

> Moses received the Torah at Sinai and handed it down to Joshua; Joshua to the elders; the elders to the prophets; and the prophets handed it down to the men of the Great Assembly. The latter said three things: be careful in judgment, develop many students, and make a fence around the Torah.
>
> *Pirkei Avot 1:1*

How was it decided which books would be included in the Bible and which not? The twenty-four books of the Hebrew Bible were gradually selected over a period of centuries, beginning with the official recognition of the Five Books of Moses as the Torah under King Josiah in 622 B.C.E.

The officially selected list of books is called the canon, from the Greek word for "measuring stick" (hence the English word "cane"). The process of selecting the canon is called canonization. Many books that were not canonized have survived and are considered to have varying degrees of sacredness. These books are called Apocrypha, which are considered sacred by Catholics. (While all Christians recognize the sacredness of the *Tanach* as their Old Testament, most do not recognize the Apocrypha as being sacred). The word "canon" can be applied to any officially sanctioned ("made holy") set of texts, including the Hebrew Bible and the New Testament, as well as Hindu, Buddhist, and Muslim sacred texts.

Sacred People

In many nations and cultures, there are individuals and groups that are regarded as holy. These include

- people who have experienced revelations or spiritual transformations (shamans, mystics, prophets, the Buddha, Zoroaster, Muhammad);
- people who have accepted certain vows (Nazirites and nuns, as well as Hindu, Buddhist, and Catholic priests); and
- people who have undergone special training, initiation, or ordination (rabbis and ministers, as well as priests and nuns).

Of the various classes of holy people that appear in world religions, two types occur on every continent and in nearly every culture: priests and shamans. While there is some overlap in the function and style of priests and shamans, and while cultural differences make definition difficult, these two roles represent very different approaches to holiness.

A shaman is a specialist in religious ecstasy: teaching, healing, performing magic, and communicating with the spirit world through wild, emotional behavior. The term "shaman" applies to medicine men and women, healers, diviners, prophets, witches, and sorcerers, from the Inuit *angakoq* to the Aborigine medicine men, in every area of Africa and the Americas. Japan has many different types of shamans, including the *Itako,* who achieve ecstasy through music, and the primarily female *Yuta* living on the island of Okinawa. The word "shaman" is derived from an ancient Tungus (Siberia) word meaning "one who knows."

Are shamans real? They appear to experience things and act in ways different from normal "profane" people. But are they actually able to leave their bodies and be visited by spirits? It is doubtful that it can be proven one way or the other. There have been many accounts of

Robes and equipment of a shaman, Canada.

136

survivors of near-death experiences who have become shamans. Shamans often experience hallucinations and sometimes display behavior characteristic of epilepsy or psychotic episodes.

While they both represent holiness, shamans and priests are outwardly opposites. Shamans are independent, alone, and nonconforming. Priests often belong to monastic orders, pray in groups, and conform to specific rules and lifestyle patterns. While a shaman receives insight from the spirit world, a priest receives his knowledge from study, practice, and discipline. The word "priest" is a contraction of the Greek word *presyteros* (elder). Its Latin parallel is *sacerdos* (from the same root as "sacred"). A priest, traditionally, is an expert in worship, sacrifices, and rituals.

The nature of priesthood differs from culture to culture. In some cases, the priesthood is limited to certain groups. In Hinduism, one must be born into the Brahmin caste, and in Judaism, one must be a descendant of Aaron. In Buddhism and Christianity, the priesthood is open to any male (and in some cases female). Different rules apply to priests of various faiths. Roman Catholic priests must take a vow of celibacy, while priests of the Episcopal and Eastern Orthodox churches may be married.

Until the destruction of the Jerusalem Temple by the Romans in 70 C.E., there were practicing Jewish priests, too. According to tradition, these priests (*kohanim* in Hebrew) are direct descendants of Moses' brother Aaron. Even though the temple no longer exists, some Jews are still considered *kohanim* in traditional communities. A Jewish priest *(kohein)* is prohibited from coming in contact with corpses or from marrying a divorcée. *Kohanim* are called on to perform certain special rituals, including giving the Priestly Benediction, being called for the first *aliyah,* and participating in *pidyon haben* (redemption of a firstborn).

Buddhist priests take an eight-part vow, to be kept as long as they remain in the priesthood (see Chapter Ten, page 178). This vow includes promising not to take a life, not to take what is not theirs, not to get drunk, and to act in a way in keeping with their role.

With their daily life structured by study, worship, and reflection, it is the duty of the community to feed them. Buddhist priests and monks traditionally do not prepare their own food, but can eat only what is placed in their rice bowls by community members.

The Idea of K'dushah

The concept of *k'dushah* (קְדֻשָׁה) is prevalent throughout Judaism. Two of the best known Hebrew prayers—*Kiddush* (קִדּוּשׁ, sanctification of wine) and *Kaddish* (קַדִּישׁ, sanctification of God's name, also used as a mourner's prayer)—both take their names from the root ק-ד-שׁ *(k-d-sh)*. The Hebrew word for "sanctuary" is *mikdash* (מִקְדָּשׁ). The word for a nuptial engagement is *kiddushin* (קִדּוּשִׁין), suggesting both that the future bride and groom are "set apart" for each other and that the institution of marriage is a sacred one.

The Hebrew Bible is filled with accounts of individual revelations—instances when God or a divine agent confronts a person and calls on that person with a special assignment or promise. (The one notable group revelation is the giving of the Ten Commandments at Sinai, when God spoke from the mountain to the entire people of Israel.) As we learned from Rudolph Otto's delineation of the numinous experience, holiness typically arouses a sense of mystery, fear, fascination, majesty, and the "totally other." This sense of awe and strangeness is expressed in Moses' first encounter with God in the Midianite hills:

> Moses was tending the flock of Jethro his father-in-law, the priest of Midian, and he led the flock to the far side of the desert and came to Horeb, the mountain of God. There the angel of *Adonai* appeared to him in flames of fire from within a bush. Moses saw that though the bush was on fire it did not burn up. So Moses thought, "I will go over and see this strange sight—why the bush does not burn up."
>
> When *Adonai* saw that he had gone over to look, God called to him from within the bush, "Moses! Moses!" And Moses said, "Here I am."
>
> "Do not come any closer," God said. "Take off your sandals, for the place where you are standing is holy ground." Then he said, "I am the God of your father, the God of Abraham, the God of Isaac, and the God of Jacob." At this, Moses hid his face, because he was afraid to look at God.
>
> Exodus 3:1–6

This story of Moses' encounter with God is filled with examples of holiness: the Burning Bush was holy in that it was on fire but did not burn up; God commanded Moses to do a special action (remove his shoes) because the ground on which he was standing was special; and Moses' reaction to God was one of fear, like the *mysterium tremendum* of Otto.

The books of the Literary Prophets (Isaiah, Jeremiah, Ezekiel, and the Twelve Minor Prophets) are comprised primarily of revelations. The prophets are repeating to the people what they have been told by God. At times, the prophets provide graphic descriptions of their encounters with God, as in Isaiah 6, which is included in chapter 5 of this book. Ezekiel wrote several similar accounts, such as the following:

> I saw a windstorm coming out of the north—a great cloud with flashing fire surrounded by bright light.... In the fire was what looked like four living creatures.... The creatures sped back and forth like flashes of lightening.... Spread out above the heads of the living creatures was what looked like an expanse, sparkling awesomely like ice.... When the creatures moved, I heard the sound of their wings, like the roar of rushing waters, like the voice of the Almighty, like the tumult of an army.... Above the expanse over their heads was what looked like a throne of sapphire, and high above on the throne was a figure like that of a man. I saw that from what appeared to be his waist up he looked like glowing metal, as if full of fire, and that from there down he looked like fire; and brilliant light surrounded him. Like the appearance of a rainbow in the clouds on a rainy day, so was the radiance around him.
>
> That was the appearance of the glory of *Adonai*. When I saw it, I fell facedown, and I heard the voice speaking.... "Son of man, stand up on your feet and I will speak to you."
>
> Ezekiel 1:4–5, 14, 22, 24, 26–28; 2:1

In this account, we again find all the attributes Otto gave for the holy experience: frightening and fascinating contradictions, fire and ice, a violent windstorm, burning metal and flying creatures, a sapphire throne, and sounds like the "roar of rushing waters" and "the tumult of an army." Upon seeing this vision, Ezekiel—out of humility and possibly fright—fell facedown until the voice commanded him to rise.

The Temple in Jerusalem and the presiding priesthood are important parts of ancient Jewish holiness. The Temple and the priesthood were tightly interdependent manifestations of the holy in ancient Israel.

There were actually two priestly classes among the people of Israel: the Levites (*L'vi-im;* tribe of Levi) and the *kohanim* (descendants of Aaron, who were a subset of the Levites). While the Israelites were in their period of wandering, God instructed Moses:

Appoint the Levites over the Tabernacle of the Testimony, and over all its furnishing, and over all that belongs to it; they are to carry the Tabernacle and all its furnishings and they shall tend it, and they shall encamp around the Tabernacle.

Numbers 1:50

The Levites served in ministerial roles, as guards, musicians, craftsmen, and other official Temple-related roles. The Levites were a priestly tribe, but within the Levite tribe were a special subgroup, the *kohanim*, descendants of Moses' brother Aaron who held the responsibility to govern over all sacrifices and other Temple functions. In addition to their sacrificial duties, the *kohanim* served as teachers and decision makers, roles that were later taken on by the Rabbis. The diagram below shows how the holiness of the priests functioned as a series of spheres within spheres. While all humanity is holy, the people of Israel are especially holy, and the tribe of Levi the holiest of Israel. The holiest members of the tribe of Levi are the *kohanim*, and the holiest *kohein* is the *Kohein Gadol*, the High Priest.

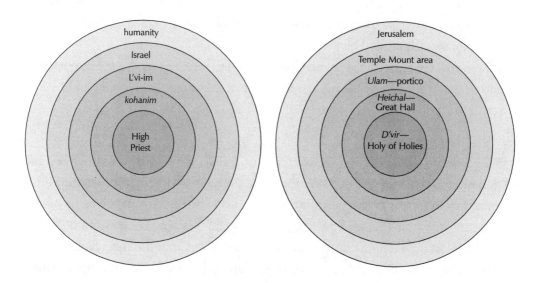

As the diagram also indicates, the Temple had increasing levels of holiness the closer one came to the center. The Temple Mount area is traditionally believed to be Mount Moriah, the very spot where Abraham brought his son Isaac to sacrifice to God.

Model of the Temple in Jerusalem.

In the four hundred and eightieth year after the Israelites had come out of Egypt, in the fourth year of Solomon's reign over Israel, in the month of Ziv, the second month, he began to build the Temple of *Adonai*. The Temple that King Solomon built for *Adonai* was sixty cubits long, twenty wide, and thirty high. The portico at the front of the Great Hall of the Temple extended the width of the Temple, that is, twenty cubits, and projected ten cubits from the front of the Temple. He made narrow windows in the Temple. Against the walls of the Great Hall and Holy of Holies, he built a structure around the building, in which there were side rooms. The lowest floor was five cubits wide, the middle floor six cubits, and the third floor seven. He made offset ledges around the outside of the Temple so that nothing would be inserted into the Temple walls.

I Kings 6:1–6

Holiness was expressed in the very architecture of the Temple (called *Beit HaMikdash*, "House of the Holy"). At the front of the Temple was an altar and a large fountain called the *Yam* (sea). People entered through the *Ulam* (portico), which served as a foyer or entryway.

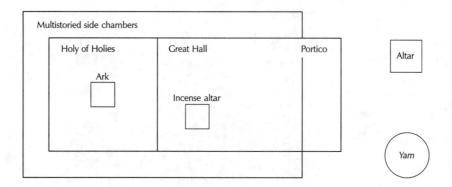

From the *Ulam,* one passed into the *Heichal* (palace)—or Great Hall—which was the main sanctuary and was as far as anyone would normally go. Past the Great Hall was a special room, perfectly cubic in shape, which contained the Ark of the Covenant and was "guarded" by two statues of cherubim. This inner sanctuary was called the *D'vir* (back chamber) or *Kodesh HaKodashim* (Holy of Holies). Its preparation (under King Solomon's supervision) is described below:

> He partitioned off twenty cubits at the rear of the Temple with cedar boards from floor to ceiling to form within the Temple an inner sanctuary, the Holy of Holies.... He prepared the Holy of Holies within the Temple to set the Ark of the Covenant of *Adonai* there.
>
> The Holy of Holies was twenty cubits long, twenty wide, and twenty high. He overlaid the inside with pure gold, and he also overlaid the altar of cedar....
>
> In the Holy of Holies he made a pair of cherubim of olive wood, each ten cubits high. One wing of the first cherub was five cubits long, and the other wing five cubits—ten cubits from wing tip to wing tip. The second cherub also measured ten cubits, for the two cherubim were identical in size and shape. The height of each cherub was ten cubits.
>
> He placed the cherubim inside the innermost room of the Temple, with their wings spread out. The wing of one cherub touched one wall, while the wing of the other touched the other wall, and their wings touched each other in the middle of the room. He overlaid the cherubim with gold.
>
> I Kings 6:16, 19–20, 23–28

The Holy of Holies—this innermost chamber of the Temple—was entered only once a year, on Yom Kippur. And even then it was only one man, the High Priest, who entered and proclaimed God's name.

Jews attain holiness through observance of mitzvot (plural for "mitzvah"). The mitzvot, which will be explored in detail in chapter 10, are the many varied and various laws, observances, and prohibitions laid out in the Torah and its interpretations. Mitzvot include ethical statutes like caring for the poor and using accurate scales in commerce, as well as spiritual observances like the recitation of blessings and fasting on Yom Kippur. According to traditional counting, there are 613 mitzvot contained in the Torah, the most famous of which are the Ten Commandments. Another set of mitzvot found in the Torah is called the Holiness Code, which begins:

> *Adonai* said to Moses, "Speak to the entire assembly of Israel and say to them: 'Be holy because I, *Adonai* your God, am holy. Each of you must respect his mother and father, and you must observe My Sabbaths. I am *Adonai* your God. Do not turn to idols or make gods of cast metal for yourselves. I am *Adonai* your God.'"
>
> Leviticus 19:1–4

The Holiness Code contains numerous laws of every type, ranging from how to eat sacrifices, to ethical farming practices. Each of the Ten Commandments can be found in the Holiness Code in some form or another, together with the Golden Rule: "Love your neighbor as yourself" (Leviticus 19:18).

In ancient times as well as today, Jews create holiness in their lives through the observance of mitzvot. Much of the mystery and awe of the world seems to have been tamed by modernity, allowing the modern Jew fewer opportunities to experience the holiness. What are the ways we can share in *k'dushah,* in the *mysterium tremendum et fascinans?* Where can we go that will give us a sense that we're standing on holy ground?

Chapter Nine

אַגָּדָה

Aggadah

How Stories, Myths, and Legends Shape Our Lives

These are the generations of the heavens and the earth
when they were created.

Genesis 2:4

Among the characteristics that separate our ancient ancestors from the rest of the animal kingdom is their ability to tell stories. Many animals communicate, but only human beings, from Cro-Magnon to modern Homo sapiens, have demonstrated the ability to recount events and give meaning to them.

Storytellers do not merely retell events; they put an overlay on those events, giving them meaning.

This chapter will explore how stories and myths are used in religion, how they shape our lives, and how we can better understand them. Also explored will be the way in which Jews traditionally interpret text through midrash, as well as the two great myths of Jewish literature: Creation and the Exodus.

Word Histories

Story.   The word "story" began its life as a distant ancestor of the Indo-European root *wid,* meaning "to know or see." (*Wid* is the root of such words as "wit," "wise," "vision," and "video".) Along the way, it evolved into the Greek form, *histor* (wise, learned), and eventually to *historia* (knowledge, inquiry). The Romans borrowed the word *historia* and used it to mean a tale or story. The Latin *historia* evolved into the French *estoire* and the English "story." The words "story" and "history" meant the same thing until recent centuries. In modern usage "history" has come to mean "an account of what actually happened," while "story" came to be "something that is made up, a fiction."

Myth. A highly misunderstood and misused word. According to the *Oxford English Dictionary*, a myth is "a traditional story, especially one concerning the early history of a people or explaining some natural or social phenomenon, and typically involving supernatural beings or

---

Key Terms

Story. Any account of an event or series of events.

Myth. A story, often containing supernatural elements, that serves to explain the worldview of a people by giving explanation and meaning to aspects of nature, customs, values, and/or human psychology. NOTE: In the context of this book, the word "myth" does *not* mean "false belief," even though that is a common usage of the word.

Legend. A story passed down through generations that may have some basis in historical events or characters.

אַגָּדָה *(aggadah)*. Tale, story, or lesson; rabbinic writings that interpret the Bible.

מִדְרָשׁ *(midrash)*. Explanation or interpretation; the process of interpreting biblical text.

מַעֲשֶׂה *(maaseh)*. "Account" or "story"; from the root ע-שׂ-ה, "to do or make."

---

events." According to the *American Heritage Dictionary,* a myth "serves as a fundamental type in the worldview of a people, as by explaining aspects of the natural world or delineating the psychology, customs, or ideals of society."

The word "mythology" derives from the Greek *muthologia,* meaning "storytelling," and has come to encompass all the tales of gods and heroes found in Homer, Hesiod, Aeschylus, and Pindar, as well as the stories of the various gods of Mesopotamia, Rome, and everywhere stories of heroes and pantheons abound. The purpose of myths is to present higher truth through stories. However, because myths tend to tell of supernatural events, people use "myth" in modern usage as a synonym for "falsehood" or "misconception": "That's just a myth," "You don't believe that old myth, do you?"

Legend. From the Latin root *legere* (to read), "legend" originally meant "for reading" or "to be read" and referred to lessons, symbols, or interpretive devices. The first usage of "legend" in English was in the fourteenth century, when it was used in reference to the accounts of the lives of saints, written works used as moral lesson books. Before long the word referred to any old stories, especially those about great lives. Today we refer to great accomplishments, such as those in sports, as legendary.

אַגָּדָה *(aggadah)*.   From the root נ-ג-ד *(n-g-d,* "to be conspicuous, apparent"). The word נֶגֶד *(neged)* means "in front of," "corresponding to," or "straightforward." The causative verb לְהַגִּיד *(l'hagid)* means "to make apparent," "to present," or more simply, "to tell, announce, declare, or inform." The word אַגָּדָה *(aggadah)* began to occur in rabbinic literature with the meaning "tale, story, or lesson," used primarily to describe nonlegalistic interpretations of the Bible.

The word הַגָּדָה *(haggadah)* is sometimes synonymous with אַגָּדָה *(aggadah),* but it has two additional meanings: it refers to evidence or witnessed testimony brought forth in a court of law, and to the Passover Haggadah, the prayer book used during the seder to retell the story of the Exodus. The term מַגִּיד *(magid,* "speaker, preacher") is used both in the Talmud and in Chasidic tradition to apply to a person expert in explaining Torah, as in the great teacher the Maggid of Mezrich.

מִדְרָשׁ *(midrash)*.   From the root ד-ר-שׁ *(d-r-sh),* meaning "to seek or inquire," a midrash is an explanation. The Hebrew word *midrash* appears twice in the Bible, both times in Chronicles (II Chronicles 13:22; 24:27), referring to specific books or to interpretations of specific books.

In the rabbinic period, *midrash* came to be used for the explanation by a specific Rabbi of a specific biblical passage or to refer to the broader process or study of textual interpretation. In modern usage, *midrash* can also refer to the various books that collect interpretations and discourses on the Bible.

מַעֲשֶׂה *(maaseh)*.   This word for "story" comes from the root ע-שׂ-ה, "to do or make." Thus, *maaseh* generally refers to an account of some action or activity, as in *Maaseh B'reishit*—the Account of Creation. In rabbinic and kabbalistic writings, *maaseh* often refers to the miraculous acts of saints or to the Account of the Chariot (*Maaseh Merkavah*—the description of God's chariot in Isaiah 66, Zechariah 6, and interpretations of Ezekiel 1–4).

In Yiddish, a *meise* is any story, fable, or anecdote used in teaching, and a *bubbemeise* is an "old wives' tale." A more common word for "story" in Hebrew is סִפּוּר *(sipur),* from the root ס-פ-ר *(s-p-r),* meaning "to count, measure, recount, or relate." ס-פ-ר *(s-p-r)* is the root of סֵפֶר *(sefer,* "book") and סוֹפֵר *(sofer,* "scribe"), as well as the English word "cipher."

Understanding Myths

Myths are a unique form in the world of literature. Myths are related to and share certain characteristics with fables, legends, allegories, fairy tales, and epics. Yet they have other characteristics that, taken together, set them apart from other types of stories. Myths are stories set in the distant past, told in vivid detail, and containing a universal set of archetypal characters and situations. Despite being set in the distant past, myths have a timeless reality that makes them as much alive and meaningful today as in any age. Myths have the power of bringing about spiritual, "numinous" experiences through the reading and reliving of them.

Mythology is an integral part of culture and is probably bound up in our genetic code. Myths and mythmaking are the nervous system of human nature. As anthropologist Claude Levi-Strauss said, "myths operate in men's minds without their being aware of the fact." In the mid-1970s, when filmmaker George Lucas was composing his epic *Star Wars* trilogy, he turned to the works of mythology expert Joseph Campbell, and in particular *The Hero with a Thousand Faces*. In an interview for the PBS series *American Masters,* Lucas lamented that his generation had lost that sense of myth. "There was no modern mythology to give kids a sense of values, to give them a strong mythological fantasy life. Westerns were the last of that genre for Americans. Nothing was being done for young people with real psychological underpinnings."

Armed with an understanding of Campbell's theories of mythology as well as a lifetime of popular culture, George Lucas weaved his space epic using universal archetypes into a classic tale of a hero's journey. While mythic characteristics ran through the initial *Star Wars* trilogy, all the elements are set in place in the 1977 film *Star Wars: A New Hope:* Luke Skywalker was born the son of a princess and a great knight, but was raised in secret on a remote farm, his identity a secret even to himself. While fiddling with a droid, he receives a mysterious call (holographic projection) for help from a beautiful girl. Luke tries to ignore the call, but when tragedy strikes the farm, he sets out to find his destiny. Along the way he meets a wise teacher (Obi-Wan Kenobi), a beautiful princess (Leia Organa), and a rogue (Han Solo). Luke survives being swallowed in the belly of a whale (the trash compactor scene as well as his attack on the Death Star), learns the skills of a Jedi Knight, and is tempted by the Dark Side (Darth Vader). In the end, Luke successfully leads a rebellion against the Empire and is victorious.

We find in the story of *Star Wars: A New Hope* all the mythic elements identified by Joseph Campbell. Campbell's outline, along with several examples, can be found in the table below:

Joseph Campbell's Stages of the Hero's Quest

I. Departure

1. Call	The point in a hero's life when he or she is called on and given a special task or mission.
2. Refusal	As is the case with Moses and most of the prophets of Israel, after the call is given, the would-be hero refuses or tries to explain that he/she is inadequate for the task.
3. Supernatural aid	A magical guide or helper often appears. In Hebrew myths, this generally refers to the involvement of God or angels.
4. First threshold	The hero departs on the adventure.
5. Belly of the whale	Campbell uses the whale as a metaphor for the unknown and frightening transition from the old life to the new one.

II. Initiation

6. Road of trials	A series of tests, tasks, or ordeals, which often occur in threes.
7. Meeting with goddess	The hero encounters unconditional love, often represented by a woman.
8. Temptation	The hero is tempted to act in a way that would reject the task or mission. The tempter is often portrayed as a woman.
9. Atonement with father	The hero confronts a father or father figure with great power.
10. Apotheosis	The hero nearly dies but is, in a sense, reborn. ("Apotheosis" means "to become a god or godlike.")
11. Ultimate boon	A great goal is achieved, a secret is discovered, or a treasure is found.

III. Return

12. Refusal to return	The hero often does not want to return to home and normal life.
13. Magic flight	An adventurous and dangerous escape, as when the Israelites crossed the sea.
14. Rescue from without	Outside helper or guide assists in the hero's return.
15. Return threshold	The hero crosses back into "normal life" while retaining new wisdom.
16. Master of two worlds	The hero often achieves a balance between the physical and spiritual realms of existence.
17. Freedom	The hero has become a master of his/her destiny, without fear or regret of death.

Myths express a culture's notion of the truth using story elements as building blocks. Levi-Strauss used the analogies of music and language, suggesting that just as phonemes (simple speech sounds) are combined to make words and sentences, the individual elements of a myth—what he called "mythemes"—are combined to form a symphony of meaning. Archeologist Henri Frankfort wrote:

> Myth is a form of poetry which transcends poetry in that it proclaims a truth; a form of reasoning which transcends reasoning in that it wants to bring about the truth it proclaims; a form of action, of ritual behavior, which does not find its fulfillment in the act but must proclaim and elaborate a poetic form of truth.
>
> H. and H. A. Frankfort, "Myth and Reality," in *The Intellectual Adventure of Ancient Man*
> (University of Chicago Press, 1946), p. 8

In other words, a myth is truth told in poetic form. Mythology is a form of logic, or reasoning, that cries out for people to act on it and bring about the truth inherent in it.

Types and Functions of Myths

Myths fit into various patterns, categories, and styles. While definitions vary, folktales, fairy tales, legends, and fables are related to myths. Following are some of the categories in which myths can often be found:

- **Myths of origin,** which include:
  o Cosmogony myths—stories of the birth of the world
  o Etiology myths—stories that explain the origin of rain, corn, customs, psychological characteristics, etc.
- **Hero myths,** which portray an individual's transformation as he/she confronts challenges to achieve a goal
- **Myths of rebirth/renewal,** such as the Egyptian Osiris myth, as well as reincarnation mythologies of India and Australia
- **God/pantheon myths,** which explore the hierarchy and interrelations among the gods
- **Religious founders myths,** such as the stories of the Buddha, Zoroaster, Muhammad, and Moses

These categories are not mutually exclusive. Many of the pantheon myths contain cosmogonies and etiologies; many hero myths involve gods of the pantheons and stories of rebirth and renewal; many religious founder myths are also hero myths.

A motif is a pattern, theme, or image that is found recurrently in works of art and literature. Many classic stories—Collodi's *Pinocchio,* the Grimm brothers' "Cinderella" and "Snow White," Lewis Carroll's *Alice's Adventures in Wonderland,* and T. H. White's *The Sword in the Stone*—have been popularized on film by Disney. Contrary to the view that these stories are "fluff" and "just for children," they each, in their own way, address the core human issues found in classical mythology. Some of the motifs that appear in these stories include:

- Cosmic parents: Typically the father-god represents the sky and the mother-god represents the earth, and the union of the two often results in the rest of the gods, the universe, and/or humanity.

- Flood: The best known flood myths are the story of Noah from the Bible, and the Assyrian story of Utnapishtim from the *Gilgamesh Epic.* But flood myths can be found in every part of the world including the Pacific Islands, the Far East, the Americas, and Africa. (One list has been compiled containing 198 flood myths, of which 78 are of North and Central American origin.)

- Swallowed by a whale: In the Bible, Jonah is swallowed by a "big fish." In a Pacific Northwest Indian *(Tlingit)* myth, a raven is swallowed by a whale. In the popular Italian tale *Pinocchio,* the puppet and his father are swallowed by a whale. As we saw in Joseph Campbell's "Stages of the Hero's Quest," this motif figuratively represents passage through any dark and seemingly hopeless condition.

- Secret identity: Moses and Oedipus are two classic examples of heroes who were raised away from their natural families and whose true identities were, up to a point, unknown even to themselves. In fairy tales and popular literature we find secret identities in "Sleeping Beauty," as well as in the "Superman" story.

- Three tests: Heroes are frequently subjected to a sequence of three tests or ordeals: the Buddha faced three realities; Ruth was rejected by Naomi three times; the prophet/judge Samuel was called by God three times when he was a child. In fairy tales we have the stories of the "Three Billy Goats Gruff," "Goldilocks and the Three Bears," and Jack climbing the beanstalk to retrieve three treasures, just to name a few of the many examples.

The table below lists many of the significant myths of the world along with their characteristics:

Great Myths of the World

Myth	Type	Story
Isis and Osiris (Egypt)	Pantheon; rebirth/renewal	The god Set kills his brother Osiris and puts the body in a chest that he sets adrift. Isis retrieves the chest, but before she can revive her lover/brother, the body is again taken by Set, who cuts it into eighteen pieces. Isis gathers all the pieces and with magical aid brings Osiris back to life.
Enuma Elish (Mesopotamia)	Creation	In the beginning all is a watery chaos. Apsu, god of underground streams, merges his waters with Tiamat, goddess of the seas. Their progeny include various gods. When Apsu is killed by Ea, Tiamat imprisons all the other young gods. Marduk escapes and slays Tiamat, whose body and entrails form the world and its inhabitants.
Gilgamesh (Mesopotamia)	Epic; hero	Gilgamesh, the king of Uruk, was a harsh ruler until the creation of the wild man Enkidu. At first Gilgamesh and Enkidu are rivals, then best friends. Together they battle against the demon Huwuwa, whom they defeat. Seeing the bravery of Gilgamesh, the goddess Ishtar asks Gilgamesh to marry her. When Gilgamesh refuses, the Bull of Heaven is sent to punish him. Enkidu kills the Bull of Heaven but is then punished by death. Grieving over the death of his friend, Gilgamesh goes on a journey to find the secret to immortality. His journey leads him to Utnapishtim, a man who (like Noah) survived a great flood. Eventually Utnapishtim reveals the secret of a plant at the bottom of the sea that will provide immortality. Gilgamesh dives to the bottom of the sea, retrieves the plant, but before he has a chance to eat it, a serpent steals it away. Empty-handed, but accepting his own mortality, Gilgamesh returns to Uruk to rule.
Oedipus Rex (Greece— Sophocles)	Hero; tragedy	After hearing an oracle that predicts he will be murdered by his own son, Laius, the king of Thebes, arranges to have his baby son, Oedipus, killed. But the baby is saved by a shepherd and raised in Corinth. As an adult, Oedipus returns to Thebes where he encounters Laius—not knowing that Laius is his father. The men argue, and Laius is killed. Oedipus marries Jocasta, not realizing that she is his mother. When the truth comes out, Jocasta kills herself, and Oedipus pokes out his own eyes.
Accounts of the Life of Buddha Shakyamuni (India)	Religious founder; hero	Siddhartha Gautama, the prince of the Shakya tribe, has been protected from the ugliness of reality all his life. As a young man, he observes for the first time a person suffering from old age. On another occasion, he witnesses a person suffering from sickness. On a third occasion, he witnesses a funeral procession. The prince is tormented by these three signs of suffering until he sees a wandering monk, and he decides to leave the palace and become a monk himself. After several attempts to understand the meaning of suffering, he sits beneath a banyan tree and is tempted by the evil tempter Mara. After withstanding the temptation of Mara, the prince meditates at the tree until he is enlightened, understanding the Four Noble Truths of the nature of suffering and its eradication.

Jewish Storytelling

Jewish tradition is rich in stories and folktales. Storytelling is so important in Judaism that it becomes a ritual act. There is, for example, a mitzvah prescribing that parents must tell the Exodus story to their children. In Chasidic communities, one of the primary roles of a rabbi is as storyteller. Perhaps this emphasis on stories is one of the reasons that a disproportionately high number of authors, actors, and comedians are Jewish, and why Jews—as a group—purchase more books than most other ethnic groups.

One unique characteristic of Jewish stories is their almost humiliating honesty. Going back to the Bible, Israelite heroes all came from modest beginnings, and the storytellers describe them without shying from their weaknesses, mistakes, and losses. From Moses and King David, on through the fools of Chelm and Tevye the Dairyman, there is a humble, sometimes self-effacing quality to Jewish heroes.

Reading of Torah

The cornerstone of Jewish storytelling is the reading and interpretation of the Torah. The Five Books of Moses are read all the way through— from the start of Genesis to the end of Deuteronomy—each year in the annual reading cycle. On Mondays, Thursdays, and Shabbat the weekly Torah portion is read as a part of the daily worship service.

Ezra the Scribe, 8th century.

The study of Torah was institutionalized around 400 B.C.E. under the leadership of Ezra, a man referred to both as a priest and a scribe. Ezra was an important force for rallying the Jewish people after the return from the Babylonian exile. The first public Torah reading is described in the Book of Nehemiah:

> On the first day of the seventh month, Ezra the priest brought the Torah before the assembly that included men and women and anyone able to understand. And he read from it facing the square before the Water Gate from early morning until midday, in the presence of the men and the women and those who

could understand; and the ears of all the people were attentive to the book of the Torah.

And Ezra the scribe stood on a wooden pulpit that they had made for the purpose . . . and he opened the book in the sight of all the people, for he was raised up above everyone. When he opened it all the people stood. Ezra blessed *Adonai,* the great God, and all the people answered, ''Amen, Amen,'' lifting up their hands; and they bowed their heads and worshiped *Adonai* with their faces to the ground. . . .

The Levites helped the people to understand the law, while the people remained in their places. And they read from the book—from the Torah of God—clearly, giving its sense so that the people understood the reading.

Nehemiah 8:2–8

This passage is interesting from a liturgical standpoint. It describes many of the Torah reading customs that remain today: reading from a raised platform *(bimah),* rising when the Torah is taken out, and saying a blessing to which the congregation responds. More important for our purposes, the text tells us that the Torah was not merely read; it was explained and interpreted. The process by which Jews explain and interpret Torah is through midrash.

Midrash: The Process of Interpreting Text

Why are explanations necessary? Why is interpretation of sacred texts such a key element in Judaism? Part of the answer lies in the age of the texts. Most of our holy books are so ancient that attempting to read a passage or chapter without special knowledge may leave a reader baffled, confused, or with an incorrect impression. The Torah is filled with apparent problems: contradictions, repetitions, unusual spellings or grammar, and missing details.

According to Jewish tradition, God dictated every word of the Five Books of the Torah to Moses on Sinai. The text of the Torah that we have today, then, is quite literally (again, according to traditional belief) the word of God and is therefore perfect. Since, according to this belief, there are no mistakes in the Torah, *every word has a purpose,* and true meaning can be found within the text.

To the Levites of Ezra's time—as well as to the Rabbis of the Talmud and the commentators of the Middle Ages—difficulties in the text (the Rabbis used the Aramaic word קוּשְׁיָא [*kushya*], meaning "difficulty, question, or problem") were a ripe opportunity to explore deeper meaning. The Talmud is filled with brief explanations and interpretations of biblical passages. In addition, there have been numerous collections of midrash such as *B'reishit Rabbah, Midrash Tanchuma,* and *P'sikta D'Rav Kahana.*

The process of making midrash involves identifying a textual problem or difficulty and explaining (solving) the problem using stories, other biblical texts, inner textual connections, and precedent opinions. The end result is that the midrash provides a deeper meaning or lesson that wasn't immediately apparent in the original text.

As an example, look at this brief passage, from the beginning of the *Akeidah* (Binding of Isaac) story:

> Some time later God tested Abraham. He said to him, "Abraham!" "Here I am," he replied. Then God said, "Take your son, your only son, Isaac, whom you love, and go to the region of Moriah. Sacrifice him there as a burnt offering on one of the mountains I will tell you about."
>
> Early the next morning Abraham got up and saddled his donkey. He took with him two of his servants and his son Isaac. When he had cut enough wood for the burnt offering, he set out for the place God had told him about.
>
> On the third day Abraham looked up and saw the place from afar. He said to his servants, "Stay here with the donkey while I and the boy go over there. We will worship, and then we will come back to you."
>
> Genesis 22:1–5

The text leaves many questions in the minds of its readers, both ancient and modern. Among the questions that arise from the text, the Rabbis ponder:

1. To which mountain was Abraham instructed to go?
2. How will Abraham know the right place?
3. Where is Sarah during all of this? Did she have a say?
4. Why does the text emphasize "early the next morning"?
5. Why did it take three days to find the right place?
6. How could Abraham see the place "from afar"?
7. Why didn't the servants accompany Abraham and Isaac to the place? Why did Abraham tell them to stay with the donkey?

To answer these *kushyot* (plural for *kushya,* "difficulties"), the Rabbis repeat each passage containing the difficulty and then explain or fill in the details that solve the difficulty. In the following example, the Rabbis explain Genesis 22:1–5 (the sections that are being interpreted are printed here in bold):

"Sacrifice him there as a burnt offering on one of the mountains" (Genesis 22:2). Abraham asked, "Which mountain?" God said, "Wherever you see My glory standing and waiting for you."

H. A. Bialik and Y. H. Ravnitzky, *The Book of Legends,* trans. William Braude (Schocken Books, 1992), pp. 40–41

The Rabbis then begin explaining Sarah's role in the *Akeidah:*

Abraham meditated in his heart, saying: What am I to do? Shall I tell Sarah? Women tend to think lightly of God's commands. If I do not tell her and simply take off with him—afterward, when she does not see him, she will strangle herself. What did he do? He said to Sarah, "Prepare food and drink for us, and we will rejoice today." She asked, "Why today more than other days? Besides, what is the rejoicing about?" Abraham: "Old people like ourselves, to whom a son was born in our old age—have we not cause to rejoice?" So she went and prepared the food. During the meal, Abraham said to Sarah, "You know, when I was only three years old, I became aware of my Maker, but this lad, growing up, has not yet been taught [about his Creator]. Now, there is a place far away where youngsters are taught [about Him]. Let me take him there." Sarah: "Take him in peace."

"Early the next morning Abraham got up" (Genesis 22:3). Why early in the morning? Because he said: It may be that Sarah will reconsider what she said yesterday and refuse to let Isaac go. So I'll get up early and go while she is still asleep. Moreover, it is best that no one see us.

"On the third day Abraham looked up and saw" (Genesis 22:4). Why on the third day? Why not on the first, or on the second? That the nations of the world might not say: God deranged Abraham so that he cut his son's throat.

"And saw the place from afar" (Genesis 22:4). [But since the place was hollowed out], how could it have been seen from afar? The place was originally hollowed out. But when the Holy One decided to cause His Presence to dwell there and to make it His sanctuary, He said: It is not fitting for a king to dwell in a valley, but only on a high and lofty mountain, resplendent in beauty and visible to all. So He beckoned the valley's environs to come together and provide a suitable place for the Presence.

Then Abraham asked Isaac, "Do you see what I see?" Isaac replied, "I see a mountain, radiant in majesty, with a [mysterious] cloud hovering over it." Abraham asked the two lads, "Do you see anything?" They replied, "We see nothing other than stretches of wilderness." Abraham: "Some people are like donkeys! As the donkey sees but does not comprehend, so it is with you. **Stay here with the donkey"** (Genesis 22:5).

ibid.

This is just one set of answers that the Rabbis provide to explain the passage from Genesis 22. Every passage of Torah may suggest many questions, and each question may offer many different answers.

Many midrashim answer problems in a text by providing additional text—called proof texts—to fill in details. In Genesis 29, Jacob has just left his home and is traveling through Bethel to Haran, where he will meet Leah and

Torah scrolls, Prague.

Rachel and will begin his own family. The opening verse of the chapter is translated: "Jacob continued on his journey and came to the land of the eastern peoples." The actual Hebrew of the text reads וַיִּשָּׂא יַעֲקֹב רַגְלָיו *(vayisa Yaakov raglav),* which literally translates as "And Jacob lifted up his feet." The Rabbis explain this odd choice of words in this way:

> **"And Jacob lifted up his feet"** (Genesis 29:1). Rabbi Acha said: "Exhilarating news gives healing to the (weary) heart" (quoting Proverbs 15:30). As soon as Jacob received the exhilarating news (of God's promise to his progeny), his heart lifted up his feet, causing them to move (at great speed).
>
> *B'reishit Rabbah 70*

In this midrash, Rabbi Acha explains the unusual choice of words using a passage from elsewhere in the Bible, in this case from the Book of Proverbs. In the process, he not only explains the initial problem, but draws attention to the pleasure Jacob might have felt after hearing the news that his descendants would be "like the dust of the earth," that "all peoples on earth will be blessed through you and your offspring," and that God would give Jacob and his descendants "the land on which you are lying" (Genesis 28:13–14). The midrash also provides a linking story that bridges Jacob's revelation of the ladder (Genesis 28) with his meeting with the daughters of Laban (Genesis 29).

Below is another example of a midrash. The focus of this is not so much on solving a *kushya,* but on establishing a link between two great teachers separated by more than a thousand years. The frame for this story is Moses' question to God about the meaning of the crowns (stylistic patterns) found on certain letters in a Torah scroll (as shown below):

God answers Moses by first telling about Rabbi Akiva and then taking him forward in time to witness Rabbi Akiva teaching:

> R. Y'hudah said in the name of Rav: When Moses ascended on high, he found the Holy One affixing crowns to letters. Moses asked, "Lord of the universe, why use crowns to intimate what You wish? Who hinders Your hand from writing out in full all of Torah's precepts?" God replied, "At the end of many generations there will arise a man, Akiva ben Yosef by name, who will infer heaps and heaps of laws from each notch on these crowns."
>
> "Lord of the universe," said Moses, "permit me to see him." God replied, "Turn around." Moses went and sat down behind eight rows of Rabbi Akiva's disciples and listened to their discourses on law. Not being able to follow what they were saying, he was so distressed that he grew faint. But when they came to a certain subject and the disciples asked Rabbi Akiva, "Master, where did you learn this?" and Rabbi Akiva replied, "It is a law given to Moses at Sinai," Moses was reassured. He returned to the Holy One and said, "Lord of the universe, You have such a man, yet You give the Torah [not by his hand] but by mine?" God replied, "Be silent—thus has it come to My mind." Then Moses said, "Lord of the universe, You have shown me his Torah—now show me his reward." "Turn around," said God. Moses turned around and saw Rabbi Akiva's flesh being weighed out in a meat market. [He was arrested and executed by the Romans.] "Lord of the universe," Moses cried out in protest, "such Torah, and such its reward?" God replied, "Be silent—thus has it come to My mind."
>
> Babylonian Talmud, *M'nachot* 29b

This story yields a variety of meanings, including an explanation of the calligraphy style of the Torah scroll and drawing a parallel between Moses and Akiva. But the overarching meaning of the midrash is to remind the reader that God's plan and God's will are ultimately unknowable. Moses doesn't understand the meaning of the crowns on the letters, the meaning of Akiva's discourse, or the reason for Akiva's martyrdom.

Creation and Exodus: The Two Great Hebrew Myths

Of the thousands of stories that comprise the Jewish experience, two are repeated again and again as being the defining stories of the Jewish religion. These are the stories of the Creation of the universe and the Exodus from Egypt. As a reminder, the term "myth" is not used to suggest that a story or belief is false or incorrect, but to emphasize that the story tells a truth through "mythemes" and poetic imagery. When a story is called a "myth," it means that it is a story that helps define a worldview and is capable of enhancing human experience.

When the Ten Commandments are repeated in Deuteronomy, the Shabbat commandment is worded differently than in the Exodus version. While the one version emphasizes Creation, the other emphasizes the Exodus. As you read both versions, note the differences that have been highlighted.

In Exodus we are told:	The Deuteronomy version reads:
Remember the Sabbath day by keeping it holy.	**Observe** the Sabbath day by keeping it holy, **as *Adonai* your God has commanded you**.
Six days you shall labor and do all your work, but the seventh day is a Sabbath to *Adonai* your God. On it you shall not do any work, neither you, nor your son or daughter, nor your manservant or maidservant, nor your animals, nor the alien within your gates.	Six days you shall labor and do all your work, but the seventh day is a Sabbath to *Adonai* your God. On it you shall not do any work, neither you, nor your son or daughter, nor your manservant or maidservant, nor **your ox, your donkey, or any of** your animals, nor the alien within your gates, **so that your manservant and maidservant may rest, as you do.**
For in six days *Adonai* made the heavens and the earth, the sea, and all that is in them, but He rested on the seventh day.	**Remember that you were slaves in Egypt and that *Adonai* your God brought you out of there with a mighty hand and an outstretched arm.**
Therefore *Adonai* **blessed** the Sabbath day **and made it holy.** Exodus 20:8–11	Therefore *Adonai* **your God has commanded you to observe** the Sabbath day. Deuteronomy 5:12–15

During the Friday night *Kiddush* (wine blessing), Shabbat is called a remembrance of Creation *(zikaron l'maaseih V'reishit)* as well as being a reminder of the Exodus from Egypt *(zeicher litziat Mitzrayim)*.

The daily prayer service also acknowledges the dual importance of these two myths. The *Sh'ma* section of the service has as its bookends a prayer about Creation and a prayer about the Exodus. In the daily morning *(Shacharit)* service, the *Sh'ma Uvirchoteha* (*Sh'ma* and Its Blessings) section begins with the *Yotzer Or* prayer, which praises God "who forms light and creates darkness, who makes peace and creates everything." A similar prayer, *Maariv Aravim,* is said at this point in the evening service. The *Sh'ma Uvirchoteha* is concluded with the *Emet V'yatziv* prayer, which praises God for redeeming Israel and culminates in the *Mi Chamochah,* which celebrates the crossing of the Sea of Reeds. (The subject of prayer will be explored in depth in chapter 12.)

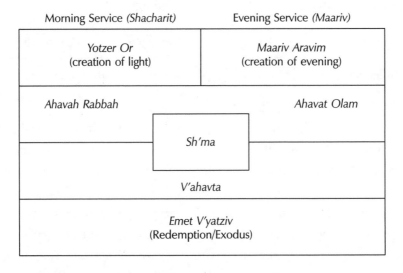

Morning Service (Shacharit)		Evening Service (Maariv)
Yotzer Or (creation of light)		Maariv Aravim (creation of evening)
Ahavah Rabbah	Sh'ma	Ahavat Olam
	V'ahavta	
Emet V'yatziv (Redemption/Exodus)		

The High Holy Days—as a time of renewal and new beginning—call to mind Creation. Rosh HaShanah is often referred to as "the birthday of the world." By contrast, the Three Pilgrimage Festivals (Pesach, Sukkot, and Shavuot) commemorate the Exodus, with Pesach recalling the Exodus itself, Sukkot representing the protection God provided for the Israelites while wandering in the wilderness, and Shavuot celebrating the receiving of the Torah at Sinai.

Creation and the Exodus are key myths in the Jewish religion, providing Jews with ritual, morality, and a life-enhancing worldview. They demonstrate how all myths are intended not only to be told from one generation to the next, but to be lived, reenacted, and celebrated, providing meaning for each generation.

Myths give shape to—and reinforce—the very identity and worldview of a people. For Jews, the stories of the Patriarchs and Matriarchs, of Moses and the Exodus, provide a vision of the Jews as a unified people. The story of Creation provides affirmation that the earth is an orderly and good world. The chronicle of the revelation at Sinai gives meaning and significance to the very notions of mitzvah and ethical monotheism. Without these stories, the values they convey are mere statements or slogans. With the stories, they become part of our very consciousness.

Chapter Ten

מִצְווֹת

Mitzvot

Commandments

These are the commands, decrees, and laws *Adonai* your God directed me to teach you to observe in the land that you are crossing the Jordan to possess, so that you, your children, and their children after them may fear *Adonai* your God as long as you live by keeping all His decrees and commands that I give you, and so that you may enjoy long life.

Deuteronomy 6:1–2

Most religions place a greater emphasis on what a person believes than on what a person does. Yet every religion has some set of behavior standards and rituals. This chapter will explore how various religions view human action and interaction. The behaviors that will be studied fit roughly into two categories: ethical behavior and rituals. We will examine law codes, precepts, and rituals in various world religions.

A ritual is a procedure or set of procedures regarding how to perform ceremonies. These include rites of passage (birth, marriage, death), as well as holiday observances and rituals pertaining to everyday activities such as eating.

Ethics, by contrast, are the rules and standards that characterize desirable conduct between people. Ethics play a role in the realms of business and commerce, justice, and family, as well as in war and crime.

Word Histories

Ritual. A repeated set of actions; a procedure for a religious ceremony; a gesture, action, or ceremony performed for religious reasons. The word "ritual" is derived from "rite," which has an interesting origin. The Latin *ritus* means "ceremony," which in turn comes from the Sanskrit *rti,* meaning "a small river or stream," hence "flow," hence "the way things go." Thus, a ritual, like a stream, flows regularly and in a specific order.

Sin. The word "sin" comes from the Latin *sons,* "guilty." The Old English form *synn* evolved into the Middle English *sinne*. The meaning has changed little over time. While early on it referred to any offense or violation of law, it is largely limited to transgressions of religious law. In Christianity, the term "original sin" refers to humanity's collective guilt, its evil nature, resulting from Adam and Eve's disobedience in the Garden of Eden. The ideas of original sin and humankind's evil nature are absent in Jewish belief.

> ## Key Terms
>
> **Ritual**. A repeated set of actions; a procedure for a religious ceremony; a gesture, action, or ceremony performed for religious reasons.
>
> **Sin**. To willfully violate a religious law.
>
> **Moral**. Goodness or badness in human character and behavior. Good or correct action.
>
> **Ethical**. In accordance with principles of right and wrong. "Ethics" and "morals" are usually used interchangeably.
>
> **Virtue**. Goodness, moral character, merit, courage.
>
> **Sacrament**. A religious act, especially in Christianity, believed to bring God's grace. Also used as a synonym for Christian Communion.
>
> תּוֹרָה **(Torah)**. Literally, "Teaching," but often translated as "the Law." Refers to the Five Books of Moses and, by extension, to the oral legal traditions that evolved into the Talmud and codes.
>
> הֲלָכָה **(halachah)**. The spectrum of Jewish law and legal discourse.
>
> מִצְוָה **(mitzvah)**. A commandment; moral and/or spiritual responsibility derived from Torah.
>
> עֲבֵרָה **(aveirah)**. Transgression; literally, "crossing over." Violation or failure to observe a mitzvah.
>
> חֵטְא **(cheit)**. Failure, sin, "missing the mark." Violation or failure to observe a mitzvah.

Moral and ethical. The terms "moral" and "ethical," which are roughly synonymous, have become vague in recent years. Both words come from roots meaning "custom." "Moral" is related to the word "mores" (conventions, manners, and customs of a group), while "ethical" seems to be distantly related to "ethnic" (of or relating to people). Both terms originally pertained to culture and customs, and with right and wrong behavior. Today both words apply to "right and wrong behavior," with "moral" sometimes associated with sexual conduct (or misconduct).

Virtue. From the Latin root *vir,* "man." In medieval English, "virtue" meant "valor" or "manly courage." The word "virtue" has a history that seems—at least to modern sensitivities—to be sexist. While the concept itself does not exclude women, the etymology and early usage of "virtue" do have a male bias. (The word *virile,* meaning "manly," derives from the same root.) Today it refers to good human character, as well as being used idiomatically to imply value, as in "by virtue of," and as a tag word for certain values (e.g., "the virtue of kindness," "the virtue of a good diet").

There is a positive parallel to "virtue" in the Yiddish word *mensch,* which literally means "man" but has the inferred meaning of "a good, moral person." The Yiddish word for "morality" is *menschlichkeit.*

Sacrament. In Latin, *sacramentum* was an oath, as in a military oath of allegiance, as well as a promissory note, a pledge, guaranty, or security on a loan or contract. The word derives from the Latin *sacer,* the same root as for "sacred." In Christianity, the word "sacrament" came to be associated with seven special acts or practices that were thought to bring the believer into union with Jesus and into the grace of God. Christian sacraments include baptism, confirmation, Eucharist (Communion), repentance, ordination, marriage, and anointing the sick.

תּוֹרָה *(Torah)*.   Even though *Torah* is frequently translated as "the Law," the word itself means "Teaching" and comes from the same root as *moreh* (teacher) and *horim* (parents). It comes from the verbal root *y-r-h,* which means "to aim." Many of the earliest usages of the verb *yarah* pertained to archery. In a very real sense, the purpose of Torah is to give Jews a target to shoot for.

מִצְוָה *(mitzvah)*.   The word *mitzvah* is often mistakenly translated as "good deed." From the Hebrew root צ-ו-ה (tz-v-h, "to command"), a mitzvah is something that is commanded or required of the Jewish people by God. *Mitzvah* is the term used for the various ethical and spiritual laws (according to Jewish tradition, there are 613 of them) found in the Torah. The word is sometimes understood as "a responsibility"; thus a bar mitzvah—and in modern times bat mitzvah—is "a responsible person," a person who has reached the age to be obligated under the law.

A mitzvah, like the Christian idea of a sacrament, is the very opposite of a sin. Mitzvot are often divided into categories:

- Positive mitzvot (*mitzvot aseih*—"you shall" mitzvot): "Write these words on the doorposts of your house and on your gates" (Deuteronomy 6:9) and "Honor your father and your mother" (Exodus 20:12).

- Negative mitzvot (*mitzvot lo taaseh*—"you shall not" mitzvot): "Do not murder" (Exodus 20:13) and "Do not turn to idols" (Leviticus 19:4).

- Moral mitzvot (*mitzvot bein adam l'chaveiro*—"mitzvot between people"): "When you build a new house, make a parapet around your roof so that you may not bring the guilt of bloodshed on your house if someone falls from the roof" (Deuteronomy 22:8) and "Do not deny justice to your poor people in their lawsuits" (Exodus 23:6).

- Spiritual mitzvot (*mitzvot bein adam laMakom*—"mitzvot between people and God"): "You shall be holy, for I, *Adonai* your God, am holy" (Leviticus 19:2) and "On the fourteenth day of the first month, there shall be a *pesach* offering to *Adonai*" (Numbers 28:16).

- Time-bound mitzvot (*mitzvot shehazman g'ramah*—"mitzvot that time causes"): "Remember the Sabbath day and keep it holy" (Exodus 20:8) and "At the age of eight days, every male among you shall be circumcised" (Genesis 17:12).

הֲלָכָה **(halachah).** From a Hebrew root meaning "walking" or "going," *halachah* can be understood as the "footpath" of proper conduct, or the comings and goings of a Jew. The analogy of "walking" is frequently associated with a person's relationship with God. The Bible tells us that Noah "walked with God" (Genesis 6:9) and that the Patriarchs "walked before God" (Genesis 24:40; 48:15). When the Books of Kings and Chronicles are describing the moral quality of the kings of Judah and Israel, the phrases used often refer to walking (e.g., "he walked in the ways of his father" and "he walked before God").

Halachah includes all mitzvot found in Torah, as well as legal discussions in Jewish law codes (such as the *Shulchan Aruch* and *Mishneh Torah*) and the ongoing discourse of responsa and various rabbinic councils. The word *halachah* also refers to the study of Jewish law and is sometimes used as a synonym for *mitzvah*.

עֲבֵרָה **(aveirah)** and חֵטְא **(cheit).** The words *aveirah* and *cheit,* both of which mean "sin," have interesting connections to the concept of Torah. *Cheit* literally means "missing the mark," and like the word *Torah,* it has roots in the vocabulary of archery. To commit a *cheit* is to fail to reach the target, to fall short or miss the aims of Torah. *Aveirah* means "crossing over" and is often translated "transgression." The concept of *aveirah* is serious, akin to "crossing the line" or "violating the boundary of right conduct." In practical terms, though, *cheit* and *aveirah* are used interchangeably.

Other Hebrew terms for "sin" include *pesha* (literally, "rebellion" or "to pass beyond") and *avon* (a wrongdoing). *Pesha* implies a willful disregard for Torah or rebellion against God. *Avon* (from the verbal root ע-ו-ה, "to be curved or crooked") is a somewhat harsher word for sin or wrongdoing.

Prescriptions, Prohibitions, and Precepts

Religious laws fit generally into three categories: prescriptions *(dos)*, prohibitions *(don'ts)*, and precepts (right attitudes and values).

Precepts

Precepts express positive ways of thinking or feeling without providing practical guidelines. An example of a precept from Western religions is the Golden Rule: "Love your neighbor as yourself" (Leviticus 19:18). Such a statement (it isn't precisely a law) suggests to its followers how they should behave, but doesn't in and of itself explain *how* one should love their neighbor. The first of the Ten Commandments (according to Jewish enumeration) is also a precept: "I am *Adonai* your God, who brought you out of Egypt, out of the land of slavery" (Exodus 20:1). Central to Buddhism is its Eightfold Path, a set of eight correct perspectives (see page 177).

Prescriptions

Prescriptions are acts that are prescribed or, literally, "written out" or "dictated." Just as a medical prescription might say "take two tablets before bed," a prescription is a set of positive directions or instructions. Jewish tradition distinguishes between prescriptions (positive laws) and prohibitions (negative laws) by labeling them as *mitzvot aseih* ("you shall" mitzvot) and *mitzvot lo taaseh* ("you shall not" mitzvot). Prescriptions include positive guidelines to ethical conduct, as well as ritual instructions.

Rituals. This type of prescription—or positive commandment—provides directions on how religious ceremonies are to be conducted. Examples include *puja* offerings of Hinduism, the Christian ceremony of Communion, and the Jewish act of lighting candles to mark the beginning of Shabbat and holy days.

Ethics. While rituals prescribe action performed between people and God, ethical prescriptions dictate conduct between people and other people. For example, the construction rule from Deuteronomy intended to prevent people from dying by falling off roofs: "When you build a new house, make a parapet around your roof so that you may not bring the guilt of bloodshed on your house if someone falls from the roof" (Deuteronomy 22:8).

Prohibitions

While prescriptions describe what actions are to be performed, prohibitions describe actions that are *not* to be performed. Examples of prohibitions include "You shall not murder" (Exodus 20:13), "You shall not steal" (ibid.), and "Don't boil a goat in its mother's milk" (Exodus 23:19).

Good and Evil in Judaism

A mitzvah is a command or responsibility believed by Jews to have been given to them by God. In order to understand how mitzvot fit into the Jewish worldview, it is necessary to take a look at the Jewish understanding of good and evil.

Western thought is divided regarding human nature and moral conduct. Are people innately good or innately bad? These two points of view are represented in the following table:

People Are Good	People Are Bad
If human beings were left on their own, then the best would come out. They would, by their nature, become caring, ethical beings. Evil comes from outside forces and institutions. If people were liberated from cultural constraints, they would rise to moral perfection. This is the view held in humanist philosophy as well as in the Unitarian Universalist Church.	If human beings were left on their own, then the worst would come out. People are not born good. They are essentially sinful. Through training, indoctrination, and civilization, the evil nature can be removed from a person. People require outside intervention (the Church, laws, teaching, God's grace) in order to rise to moral perfection. This is the view of classical Christianity as well as the behaviorist school of psychology of B. F. Skinner.

Judaism doesn't accept either of these options, finding both unrealistic and pragmatically ineffective. "Good" and "evil" do not describe "natures" or "forces" but instead describe behaviors. Jewish tradition teaches that every human being has two competing urges or inclinations: one toward self-interest, the other toward self-lessness. When these two urges are kept in balance, a person is able to conduct oneself in an ethical manner. When they are out of balance, a person becomes either selfish or ineffectual. When the urge for self-interest goes awry, a person begins to act in immoral, evil ways.

The Hebrew terms for these two urges are *yetzer hara* (evil inclination) and *yetzer hatov* (good inclination). The term "evil inclination" is somewhat misleading. In a midrash, Rabbi Shmuel bar Nachman said:

The words "Behold, it was good" [in the story of Creation] refer to the good inclination. The words "Behold, it was very good" refer to the evil inclination. But how can the evil inclination be termed "very good"? Because Scripture teaches that were it not for the evil inclination, a man would not be able to build a house, take a wife, beget children, or engage in commerce. All such activities come, as Solomon noted [quoting Ecclesiastes 4:4], "from a man's rivalry with his neighbor."

B'reishit Rabbah 9:7; *Kohelet Rabbah* 3:11

Thus, the Rabbis are suggesting that the *yetzer hara* is responsible for a person's drive for self-preservation. Without it, a person would lack the ability to care for oneself. But when the *yetzer hara* runs unchecked by the *yetzer hatov*, it leads a person to act in a greedy or malicious manner.

The *yetzer hara* has a stronger pull than the *yetzer hatov*, making it easy to slip off the target. To help us to stay on track, Jewish tradition teaches that God gave the Torah—literally, "teaching," "direction," or "aim"—to help us to become righteous, ethical people. Each mitzvah is like an arrow we pull from our quiver. When we miss the target, we commit a *cheit*—a sin, literally "missing the mark." And when we miss, our task is to draw another arrow from the quiver and try again.

Mitzvot in the Torah

What then is the goal or target of Torah? Perhaps the best distillation of the message of the entire Torah is found in the passage "Love your neighbor as yourself" (Leviticus 19:18). The Hebrew Sage, Hillel, when asked by a non-Jew to explain the meaning of Torah while balanced on one foot, paraphrased it this way:

What is hateful to you, do not do to your fellow man. This is the entire Torah, all of it. The rest is commentary. Go and study it.

Babylonian Talmud, *Shabbat* 31a

The prophet Micah summarized God's expectations of humanity this way:

"What does *Adonai* require of you? To act justly, to love mercy, and to walk humbly with your God."

Micah 6:8

While the precepts of love, justice, mercy, and humility are paramount to Judaism and the Torah, they make no guarantee that a person will behave in an ethical way. Jewish wisdom, recognizing the dynamics of human nature, provides mitzvot as guides to make the abstract precepts more concrete.

The most famous set of mitzvot found in the Torah are the Ten Commandments, or in Hebrew, *Aseret HaDibrot* (the Ten Utterances). At close examination, the first "commandment" is not a law at all, but more of a preamble, linking the giving of Torah to God and the Exodus from Egypt. The Ten Commandments as they appear in the Book of Exodus are as follows:

1. I am *Adonai* your God, who brought you out of Egypt, out of the land of slavery.

2. You shall have no other gods before Me. You shall not make for yourself an idol in the form of anything in heaven above or on the earth beneath or in the waters below. You shall not bow down to them or worship them; for I, *Adonai* your God, am a jealous God, punishing the children for the sin of the fathers to the third and fourth generation of those who hate Me, but showing love to a thousand generations of those who love Me and keep my commandments.

3. You shall not misuse the name of *Adonai* your God, for *Adonai* will not hold anyone guiltless who misuses His name.

4. Remember the Sabbath day by keeping it holy. Six days you shall labor and do all your work, but the seventh day is a Sabbath to *Adonai* your God. On it you shall not do any work, neither you, nor your son or daughter, nor your manservant or maidservant, nor your animals, nor the alien within your gates. For in six days *Adonai* made the heavens and the earth, the sea, and all that is in them, but He rested on the seventh day. Therefore *Adonai* blessed the Sabbath day and made it holy.

5. Honor your father and your mother, so that you may live long in the land *Adonai* your God is giving you.

6. You shall not murder.

7. You shall not commit adultery.

8. You shall not steal.

9. You shall not give false testimony against your neighbor.

10. You shall not covet your neighbor's house. You shall not covet your neighbor's wife, or his manservant or maidservant, his ox or donkey, or anything that belongs to your neighbor.

Exodus 20:1–14

A second, more lengthy set of laws is the so-called Holiness Code found in Leviticus 17–26. The focus of these laws is how a Jew can achieve holiness. The answer is a variety of ethical and spiritual prohibitions and prescriptions. Among them:

Be holy because I, *Adonai* your God, am holy.

Each of you must respect his mother and father, and you must observe My Sabbaths. I am *Adonai* your God.

Do not turn to idols or make gods of cast metal for yourselves. I am *Adonai* your God. . . .

When you reap the harvest of your land, do not reap to the very edges of your field or gather the gleanings of your harvest. Do not go over your vineyard a second time or pick up the grapes that have fallen. Leave them for the poor and the alien. I am *Adonai* your God. Do not steal. Do not lie. Do not deceive one another. Do not swear falsely by My name and so profane the name of your God. I am *Adonai*.

Do not defraud your neighbor or rob him. Do not hold back the wages of a hired man overnight. Do not curse the deaf or put a stumbling block in front of the blind, but fear your God. I am *Adonai*.

Do not pervert justice; do not show partiality to the poor or favoritism to the great, but judge your neighbor fairly. Do not go about spreading slander among your people. Do not do anything that endangers your neighbor's life. I am *Adonai*.

Do not hate your brother in your heart. Rebuke your neighbor frankly so you will not share in his guilt. Do not seek revenge or bear a grudge against one of your people, but love your neighbor as yourself. I am *Adonai*. . . .

Rise in the presence of the aged, show respect for the elderly, and revere your God. I am *Adonai*.

When an alien lives with you in your land, do not mistreat him. The alien living with you must be treated as one of your native-born. Love him as yourself, for you were aliens in Egypt. I am *Adonai* your God.

Do not use dishonest standards when measuring length, weight, or quantity. Use honest scales and honest weights, an honest ephah and an honest hin. I am *Adonai* your God, who brought you out of Egypt. Keep all My decrees and all My laws and follow them. I am *Adonai*.

Leviticus 19:2–4, 9–18, 32–37

You may have noted how most (if not all) of the Ten Commandments are repeated in the Holiness Code. Note also how being holy and loving your neighbor are tightly interconnected. The myth of the Exodus is again used as a basis for fair, ethical conduct (in this case, toward aliens). And love is not merely a feeling of emotional attachment; it is the practice of treating other people in a way we would want to be treated. While the Torah mandates the care and concern for the poor and weak, it specifically commands that one should not show bias or partiality toward them. Rather, fair and equal standards for all people are required.

Mitzvot in the Mishnah and Talmud

Even before Romans destroyed the Temple in 70 C.E., Jewish scholars were finding that many of the laws in the Torah were out of touch with the lifestyles of Jews living in that time. Many of the agricultural, commercial, and sacrificial laws in the Torah reflect a culture of Israelites living in their own kingdom. After the destruction of the Temple and the conquest of Jerusalem by Rome, Jews had no place to offer sacrifices, which was just one of the many difficulties facing them.

From the year 70 C.E. until 135 C.E., Rabbis such as Yochanan ben Zakkai, Eliezer ben Hyrcanos, Y'hoshua ben Chananyah, and Akiva ben Yosef met, discussed, and debated interpretations of Torah laws. Their students wrote down many of the debates and discussions, and these collections of transcribed lessons became the basis for the Mishnah, which was completed some time around 200 C.E. under the authority of Y'hudah HaNasi.

HaNasi divided the discussions into some sixty-odd chapters, called *masechtot,* or tractates. These tractates were divided into six major sections, called *s'darim,* or orders. The six orders of the Mishnah are as follows:

- *Z'raim* (seeds)—laws pertaining to agriculture, food, and produce set aside for the priests and the poor, as well as prayer
- *Mo-eid* (seasons)—primarily laws about Shabbat and holidays
- *Nashim* (women)—laws about betrothal, marriage, and divorce, as well as other forms of contracts, oaths, and vows
- *N'zikin* (torts)—discussions of legal procedures and the authority of the Rabbis; a variety of issues of civil and criminal law, including theft, murder, damages, and real estate
- *Kodashim* (sacred things)—laws about the Temple, the priesthood, and sacrificial procedures
- *Tohorot* (purity)—laws about ritual objects, and the purity of homes, people, foods, etc.

During the third through the sixth centuries C.E., scholars at academies in Tiberias (near the Sea of Galilee in northern Israel) and in Babylonia were engaged in writing commentaries and explanations of the Mishnah. Their works were called the Gemara ("completion"). The Mishnah combined with the Gemara came to be called the

Talmud ("study"). Since there were two different Gemaras, the one composed in Tiberias and the one composed in Babylonia, there are two different Talmuds: the Palestinian Talmud *(Talmud Y'rushalmi)* and the Babylonian Talmud *(Talmud Bavli)*. To this day, these two versions of the Talmud remain important encyclopedias of Jewish law and learning. Since the Babylonian Talmud is used much more widely than its Palestinian counterpart, the term *Talmud* usually refers to the *Talmud Bavli.*

Reform Judaism recognizes the Talmud as a historical development and not as law delivered by God at Sinai, and as such, talmudic law is not binding on Reform Jews. But Reform rabbis and scholars still treat the Talmud as inspired text and as an important source of Jewish wisdom and legal understanding. When Reform rabbis discuss and interpret halachah, they will often refer to talmudic sources.

In its 1999 Statement of Principles, the Central Conference of American Rabbis (CCAR) adopted the following statement regarding halachah:

> We are committed to the ongoing study of the whole array of מִצְוֹת *(mitzvot)* and to the fulfillment of those that address us as individuals and as a community. Some of these מִצְוֹת *(mitzvot),* sacred obligations, have long been observed by Reform Jews; others, both ancient and modern, demand renewed attention as the result of the unique context of our own times.

Judaism is often regarded as a "legalistic" religion. The term "Old Testament justice" refers to harsh, rigid, uncaring judgment. These generalizations are overly simplistic, and more often than not, they serve as subtle anti-Jewish slurs.

The famous *lex talionus* ("law of teeth" in Latin), "an eye for an eye, a tooth for a tooth," is frequently given as an example of Judaism's severe punishment. In point of fact, at the time this law first appeared in the Torah (Exodus 21:23–25; Leviticus 24:19–20), it represented a progressive reform in the way justice was meted out. When other ancient cultures sought revenge for minor injuries by massacring entire families, Judaism taught that punishment must not exceed the crime. There has, in fact, been no capital punishment performed in Judaism for well over two thousand years, an assertion that cannot be made by religions that claim to be more merciful.

Judaism is concerned with law. Mitzvot are taken seriously not as cruel restrictions of freedom, but as subtle guides to ethical and spiritual behavior. Torah and mitzvot are God's way of showing love, as evidenced by the *Ahavah Rabbah* and *Ahavat Olam* prayers. When considering the nature of Jewish legalism, it is a good idea to keep in mind Hillel's great teaching:

> What is hateful to you, do not do to your fellow man.

Hillel restates the "Golden Rule" of Leviticus 19, providing some practical direction on how one should go about loving one's neighbor.

> This is the entire Torah, all of it.

In other words, the message of the entire Torah can be summed up in the Golden Rule.

> The rest is commentary.

All 613 mitzvot, as well as all of the myths, stories, commentaries, and midrashim, serve as practical examples, lessons, and suggestions that illustrate the Golden Rule.

Hillel doesn't stop there. In his final line he takes the message to the next level. He points to each of us and says:

> Go and study it.

It is not enough to know the Golden Rule. One should learn the commentaries, gain understanding of all the subtleties of morality and spirituality, and make them a part of our lives by observing the mitzvot. The task of Jewish law and morality is not to purge the human being of sin. Rather, it is to make the world a better place.

Hindu Commandments

The central concept in Hindu morality is karma, a Sanskrit word that literally means "action" or "deed." The Law of Karma, a key principle of both Buddhism and Hinduism, is the idea that all action has consequences. Our actions affect who we are and what the future has in store for us.

Karma can be understood as a form of attachment—like an invisible appendage—that people acquire through behavior. Every action people perform results in karma becoming attached to their soul. Good behavior causes positive karma to be attached. Wicked behavior causes negative karma to become attached. The karma that people acquire through action is carried forward not only in their future life and behavior, but in their next life as well. A person who behaves poorly in this life may be born, in the next life, as a dog, an insect, or worse. One who behaves well in this life is likely to be reborn as a scholar or prince.

Another important element of Hindu ethics is the strong division of humans into various classes, or castes. Every Hindu is born into a specific caste and will remain in that caste until death. The Sanskrit word for these divisions is *varna* (color). Hindus are required to marry within their caste, and interactions between the castes have many limitations. The specific delineations of castes vary between different regions of India and ethnic traditions, with as many as 3,000 different castes and over 25,000 subcastes. But the general overall scheme of castes includes the following four *varnas:*

- **Brahmins** (also spelled Brahmanas and Brahmans): Traditionally the priestly and scholarly class, these were the protectors of sacred texts and sacrifices and the most pure of the castes. According to the Rig Veda (10:90:12), the Brahmins were born from the mouth of the primal man, Purusha. (In other versions of this myth, Brahmins came from the head or brain of Purusha.) They are associated with the color white. The term is related to the creator god Brahma as well as Brahman, the Hindu concept of ultimate reality or world soul.

Brahmins, Butkara, Pakistan, 1st–7th century C.E.

- **Kshatriyas:** The warrior class, later associated with the role of being protectors of cows. According to myth, the people of this caste were born from the arms of Purusha. The Kshatriyas are associated with the color red.
- **Vaisyas:** Merchants, traders, and farmers, according to myth, are derived from the belly of Purusha and are associated with the color yellow.
- **Sudra:** The people who emerged from the feet of Purusha, according to myth, became the artisans, menial laborers, and servants. This is the lowest and least pure of the four *varnas* and is associated with the color black.

A fifth group, known as the untouchables, are considered lower than any of the other castes. Members of this group are generally prohibited from entering temples and shrines or from having interactions with the higher castes.

Hindus of different castes observe different sets of rituals. In addition, there is a huge amount of regional variety of observances. So not only will a Punjabi Brahmin's observances be different from those of a Punjabi Sudra, but his observances will differ from those of a Kashmiri Brahmin or a Tamil Brahmin.

Sacrifice, which will be explored in greater detail in the next chapter, is a key element of Hindu ritual. Hindus have a multitude of *puja* (offering) ceremonies that are observed at various times and for various events. These typically involve offering flowers, incense, and food items to a god, accompanied by chanting certain hymns.

Hindu scriptures include several law texts, the most important of which is a collection called the Laws of Manu, named for the mythical first lawgiver. This law code and moral guide contains precepts as well as specific rules. In the passage below, addressed to Manu, the importance of proper action is announced, and examples of sinful thought, speech, and physical behavior are given:

> O sinless One, the whole sacred law, [applicable] to the four castes, has been declared by thee; communicate to us [now], according to the truth, the ultimate retribution for [their] deeds.
>
> Action, which springs from the mind, from speech, and from the body, produces either good or evil results; by action are caused the [various] conditions of men, the highest, the middling, and the lowest.
>
> Coveting the property of others, thinking in one's heart of what is undesirable, and adherence to false [doctrines], are the three kinds of [sinful] mental action.
>
> Abusing [others, speaking] untruth, detracting from the merits of all men, and talking idly, shall be the four kinds of [evil] verbal action.
>
> Taking what has not been given, injuring [creatures] without the sanction of the law, and holding criminal intercourse with another man's wife, are declared to be the three kinds of [wicked] bodily action.
>
> Laws of Manu 12:1, 3, 5–7

Note that in this passage above, a distinction is made between thought, speech, and physical behavior. Yet all are considered forms of action and fall under the Laws of Manu.

Buddhist Commandments

To a Buddhist, legal and moral issues are far less important than following the path to enlightenment. Meditation and the casting off of desire take precedence over rules of right and wrong behavior. However, one cannot become enlightened if one is acting in a base or hurtful way. Buddhist sacred texts include several collections of rules—such as the Patimokkha (monks' code of conduct) and the Sigalovada Sutta (laypersons' code of discipline)—outlining behaviors to be avoided.

The highest precept in Buddhist morality is ahimsa (nonviolence), a concept borrowed from Hinduism. Like the Golden Rule in Western ethics, the precept of ahimsa serves as an umbrella value for all Buddhist morals, and nearly every Buddhist rule can be distilled down to this idea of nonviolence.

The message revealed in the Buddha's Four Noble Truths is that the way to end suffering is to end desire, and the key to casting off desire is following the Eightfold Path. These are a set of eight perspectives or ways of thinking, acting, and meditating:

**The Noble Eightfold Path
to the Cessation of Desire and the End of Suffering**

1. Right perspective	Wisdom
2. Right intention	
3. Right speech	
4. Right action	Morality
5. Right livelihood	
6. Right effort	
7. Right mindfulness	Meditation
8. Right concentration	

These steps are part of an ongoing, lifelong practice that are intended to guide the Buddhist away from desire and suffering and toward enlightenment. Note how the steps of the Eightfold Path are divided into three categories: wisdom, morality, and meditation. Western ethics tend to focus on the three "morality" steps of the path, but to a Buddhist, all eight steps are ongoing, interrelated steps, sometimes understood as a spiral staircase, on which each step brings one higher, and every cycle of the eight steps brings one to the same spot, but on a higher plane.

Buddhist teachings contain many writings attributed to the Buddha. The Dhammapada is such a document, a collection of moral proverbs believed to have been written by the Buddha. The following passage assures that proper conduct in this life will assure happiness in this world and in one's next life:

Do not follow an evil way of life.

Do not live based on careless attitudes.

Do not follow false views.

Do not be attached to the world.

Wake up and pay attention.

Follow the *dhamma* (good teaching).
Whoever follows the path of *dhamma* lives happily in this world and in the next.
Lead a moral life, and not a life of wrongdoing.
Whoever follows the path of *dhamma* lives happily in this world and in the next.

Dhammapada 167–169

This passage, also from the Dhammapada, summarizes Buddhist ethics in a way that is surprisingly similar to the summary of the prophet Micah in the Bible (see passage earlier in this chapter):

To abstain from evil,
To practice good deeds,
And to purify one's mind,
This is the teaching of the Buddhas.

Dhammapada 183

Every Buddhist is expected to follow the Five Precepts:

1. To abstain from taking life.
2. To abstain from taking what is not given.
3. To abstain from sexual misconduct.
4. To abstain from false speech.
5. To abstain from intoxicants causing heedlessness.

In addition, monks and others striving for a higher level of morality follow the Eight Precepts:

1. To abstain from taking life.
2. To abstain from taking what is not given.
3. To abstain from unchastity.
4. To abstain from false speech.
5. To abstain from intoxicants causing heedlessness.
6. To abstain from untimely eating.
7. To abstain from dancing, singing, music, and unseemly shows, from wearing garlands, smartening with scents, and beautifying with perfumes.
8. To abstain from the use of high and large luxurious couches.

Confucian Obligations

The ethics of K'ung-Fu-tzu (Latin spelling, Confucius; 551–479 B.C.E.) and his followers emphasize etiquette, respect, and protocol—coupled with kindness and grace—to maintain universal order. The most important writings to come out of the Confucian tradition are the collection of teachings known as Lunyu, known in English as the Analects.

Like the biblical Book of Proverbs, the Analects of Confucius is a collection of moral teachings and aphorisms. Both books teach the importance of respect, modesty, and honoring one's parents and teachers. While the Book of Proverbs focuses on the importance of being a diligent student, the Analects focus on being a good leader.

Some of these values are expressed in the following passage from the opening chapter of the Analects:

> The philosopher Tsang said, "I daily examine myself on three points: whether in transacting business for others, I may have been not faithful; whether in intercourse with friends, I may have been not sincere; whether I may have not mastered and practiced the instructions of my teacher."
>
> The Master said, "To rule a country of a thousand chariots, there must be reverent attention to business, and sincerity; economy in expenditure, and love for men; and the employment of the people at the proper seasons."
>
> The Master said, "A youth, when at home, should be filial, and, abroad, respectful to his elders. He should be earnest and truthful. He should overflow in love to all, and cultivate the friendship of the good. When he has time and opportunity, after the performance of these things, he should employ them in polite studies."
>
> Analects 1:4–6

Chinese philosophy provides several important concepts that are key to Confucian teachings:

Rin—morality
Li—rituals, ceremonies, procedures
Yi—duty, proper behavior
Chi—wisdom

Confucian rituals include a variety of blessings, offerings, and sometimes music used to pay respect to parents, teachers, and leaders. Confucianism, more than any other philosophy, has made a religion out of filial piety (acts of devotion toward parents and ancestors). In the following passage from the Analects, Master K'ung explains to a student how one should approach ritual observances:

> Lin Fang asked what was the first thing to be attended to in ceremonies.
>
> The Master said, "A great question indeed! In festive ceremonies, it is better to be sparing than extravagant. In the ceremonies of mourning, it is better that there be deep sorrow than minute attention to observances."
>
> Analects 3:4

Christian Obligations

We have seen, in Hindu and Buddhist religions, that there is often little differentiation between what a person does and what a person thinks. Belief and behavior are as inseparable as the warp and weave of a sheet of fabric. In Christianity, by contrast, faith is far more important than conduct. It is the consensus of classic Christian theologians that (a) faith in Christ is the only way to redeem us from sin, and (b) good behavior will be a natural consequence of faith in Christ.

The British writer and theologian C. S. Lewis explains this dichotomy between faith and works and then dismisses it:

> Christians have often disputed as to whether what leads the Christian home is good actions, or Faith in Christ. I have no right really to speak on such a difficult question, but it does seem to me like asking which blade in a pair of scissors is most necessary.
>
> C. S. Lewis, *Mere Christianity* (HarperCollins, 2001), p. 115

The earliest Christians were Jewish followers of Jesus. Like other Jews, they saw that proper behavior, as dictated in the Torah through mitzvot, was essential to being a good person and a follower of God. In the following Christian Bible passage, attributed to James, the brother of Jesus, it is argued that it is a person's actions, not merely faith, that make a person righteous before God:

> Speak and act as those who are going to be judged by the law that gives freedom, because judgment without mercy will be shown to anyone who has not been merciful. Mercy triumphs over judgment! What good is it, my brothers, if a man claims to have faith but has no deeds? Can such faith save him? Suppose a brother or sister is without clothes and daily food. If one of you says to him, "Go, I wish you well; keep warm and well fed," but does nothing about his physical needs, what good is it?
>
> James 2:12–16

The passage above is making the same arguments that Jewish thinkers would make. James later says, "I will show you my faith by my works" (James 2:18), expressing the Jewish sentiment that Jews show their devotion to God by following mitzvot and good deeds. He makes his point even stronger several verses later when he says, "Faith without works is dead" (James 2:26). James gives Abraham and Rahab as examples of how faith and works act together and how both heroes showed their belief in God through their actions, and not merely by giving lip service to God.

James was not typical of what came to be predominant thought in Christianity. Most classical Christian writers believed that faith took precedent over deeds. The leading voice in shaping the Christian religion was the apostle Paul, a former Jew through whose efforts Christianity transformed itself from being a Jewish fringe sect to being a major world religion. In stark contrast to James, Paul wanted to appeal to Romans and other non-Jews by asserting that observance of Torah was not necessary to being Christian. Paul argued that despite the observance of mitzvot, Jews, like all human beings, are sinful in their nature. The only way to be redeemed from sin is through faith in Christ:

> No one can be declared righteous in His sight by observing the law; rather, through the law we become conscious of sin. But now God has shown us a new righteousness, apart from law, to which the Law and the Prophets promise.
>
> This righteousness from God comes through faith in Jesus Christ to all who believe. There is no difference, for everyone has sinned and falls short of the glory of God, and everyone is justified freely by His grace through the redemption that came by Jesus Christ.
>
> Romans 3:20–24

Paul further separated himself and his fellow Christians from their Jewish origins by stressing that his religion was not restricted to the Jews and that observance of the law (i.e., Torah) was no longer required:

> We maintain that a man is justified by faith apart from observing the law. Is God the God of Jews only? Is He not the God of gentiles too? Yes, of gentiles too, since there is only one God, who will justify the circumcised by faith and the uncircumcised through that same faith. Do we, then, nullify the law by this faith? Not at all! Rather, we fulfill the law.
>
> Romans 3:28–31

Christians at the time of Paul believed that the world would soon come to an end, to be replaced by God's kingdom. Rules, possessions, and even family held little meaning for them, knowing that they would soon witness the messianic age. But years passed without the return of Christ, and short-term ethics were supplanted by institutionalized law codes. The organized Christian community began holding meetings, beginning with the council of Nicea in 325 C.E., in which Church law—which has come to be known as canon law—was legislated.

The Seven Deadly Sins by Hieronymus Bosch, 15th century.

Among the important ethical doctrines of the Christian Church are the seven cardinal sins and the seven sacraments. The seven sins—also called the seven deadly sins—are considered significant because committing any of them serves as a trap to commit more. A frequent subject of Christian art and literature, the seven cardinal sins are as follows:

1. Pride—vanity, lack of humility, excessive faith in one's own abilities
2. Envy—the desire for what others possess
3. Lust—illicit or inordinate sexual desire
4. Greed—insatiable desire for material possessions
5. Gluttony—the desire to eat or drink more than one needs
6. Anger—wrath, hatred rather than love
7. Sloth—laziness, avoidance of work

The seven sacraments are holy acts, similar to the Jewish mitzvot, that a Christian may perform. The precise origin of the seven sacraments is vague and uncertain. But the list as we have it today was widely accepted as early as the Council of Trent (1545–1563), during which Roman Catholic leaders defined each of the seven sacraments. The seven sacraments are as follows:

1. Baptism	Based on the Jewish ritual of *t'vilah,* or ritual immersion in a *mikveh* (a ritual of purification and renewal still practiced by Jews today). In the years just prior to the rise of Christianity, a Jew named John the Baptist (possibly a cousin to Jesus) began preaching the importance of ritual immersion as a means to prepare for the coming of the messianic age. As Christianity evolved, baptism became a substitute for circumcision to initiate infants and converts into the Church.
2. Confirmation	The earliest ceremony of confirmation is recorded in the Christian Bible (Acts 8:14–17) when the apostles Peter and John caused the spirit of God to come to baptized Christians by laying their hands on them. The "laying on of hands" and sometimes anointing with oil became the sacrament of confirmation, occasionally performed on babies or young children sometime after baptism or, more often, as a ceremony to mark a child's accomplishments in religious study and their ability to confirm their faith.
3. Eucharist	From the Greek word meaning "thanksgiving," Eucharist is the act of Holy Communion, in which the Christian symbolically shares a meal with Christ, re-creating the Last Supper (possibly a Passover seder) by eating a wafer or bread (symbolizing Christ's body) and drinking wine (symbolizing Christ's blood).
4. Repentance	The act of absolving sins through penance and confession. While generally not practiced as a formal rite among Protestant Christians, it remains an important ceremony for Roman Catholics and Eastern Orthodox Christians in the form of the confessional.
5. Ordination	The transfer of religious power to bishops, priests, and deacons.
6. Marriage	The ceremony of marriage presided and witnessed by a priest.
7. Anointing the sick	Conveying blessing and healing to a person suffering illness. This also includes administering "last rites" by a priest or minister to a person on a deathbed.

Pillars of Islam

The Quran, according to Muslims, is God's clearest and most complete message to humankind. Everything a Muslim needs to know can be derived from the words of the Quran, and thus the Quran is the basis and guide to Islamic law, conduct, and morality.

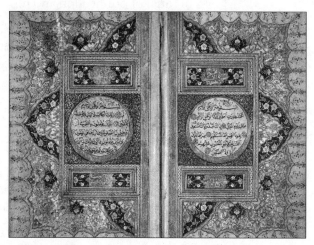

Page from the Quran, Turkey.

The two words for Islamic law are *Sharia* (from the Arabic word meaning "prescribed" or "ordained") and *Fiqh* (meaning "knowledge"). *Sharia,* like Jewish halachah, is a broad field of jurisprudence covering all aspects of life: personal, political, commercial, and religious. Like halachah, there are special rules and procedures for interpreting and explaining the laws of *Sharia,* a job performed by a trained scholar called a mufti.

Although the Quran is the primary source for the Muslim way of life, many conditions and situations are not directly addressed in its pages. To determine the rules of *Sharia,* scholars look to the following sources in order:

1. **Quran,** the first and most important source of Islamic law
2. **Hadith,** a body of writings attributed to Muhammad and his companions
3. *Ijma,* the consensus of Islamic scholars and leaders
4. *Istibsan* (extrapolation), *ijtibad* (interpretations), and *qiyas* (analogy)

Like the sacraments of Christianity and the mitzvot of Judaism, Islam has a set of five central prescriptions, referred to as the Five Pillars *(Arkan Al-islam)*. These are the five duties that every Muslim is required to fulfill:

1. *Shahada* The declaration of faith that there is no God but Allah, similar to the Jewish prayer *Sh'ma*. Every Muslim is required to proclaim: "There is no god but Allah, and Muhammad is His Prophet." This message is central to Islamic belief and way of life. Conversion to Islam, in fact, is the simple act of proclaiming the *Shahada*.

2. *Zakat* Paying alms to the poor. Muslims are required to pay a tax, based on a percentage (2$\frac{1}{2}$%) of personal income, to provide for the poor and for other religious and community needs. *Zakat* is a sort of religious Social Security without retirement entitlements. Islam also has a separate precept called *sadaqa* (related to the Hebrew *tzedakah*), roughly translated as "charity." *Sadaqa* can involve giving financial or material donations, as well as intangible gestures of kindness. The amount of *sadaqa* given is up to the individual Muslim, whereas the amount of required *zakat* is a set percentage and is always in monetary form.

3. *Siyam* During the holy month of Ramadan, Muslims fast during daylight hours in observance of the third pillar of Islam: *siyam*—fasting. Ramadan is a time of introspection, repentance, and striving for a closer relationship with God. Ramadan is much like Christian Lent (the forty-day period beginning 6$\frac{1}{2}$ weeks prior to Easter) and the Jewish Ten Days of Repentance and Yom Kippur. The word *siyam* is related to the Hebrew word *tzom* (fast).

4. Hajj All Muslims who are financially and physically able are required to make pilgrimage to Mecca at least once during their life and to march seven times around the Kaaba (shrine at the Great Mosque in Mecca).

5. *Salat* Five times per day, at specific appointed times, Muslims are required to pause from their daily routine, face toward Mecca, and perform a prescribed ritual of prayer. *Salat* involves reciting a brief series of prayers, pronouncements, and readings accompanied by certain gestures and postures. It may be performed individually, although public prayer is preferred.

Another important aspect of Islamic law is *halal,* the dietary laws prescribed in *Sharia.* The word *halal* (similar to the Hebrew *kasheir,* or "kosher," meaning "fit") means "permitted" or "lawful." The laws of *halal* bear many similarities to kashrut:

- All pork products and foods derived from pork are forbidden.
- Carnivorous animals and birds of prey are forbidden.
- Animals are required to be slaughtered in a specified manner.
- Blood and blood by-products are forbidden.

In addition to the above rules, which Islam shares with Judaism, the following rules also apply:

- The name of Allah is to be pronounced on the animal as it is being slaughtered.
- Alcoholic beverages (wine, beer, and spirits) are prohibited, as are flavoring extracts containing alcohol.

Responsibility and Commitment

There is great variety in the ways different religions view ritual and ethical behavior. While prescriptions and prohibitions exist in all religions, morality is usually expressed in nonspecific precepts and values. The Hindu doctrine of karma—that behavior has consequences—is reflected in most religions. The Christian concept of sacrament provides us with a good understanding of rituals. A sacrament is an act that brings the worshiper closer to the sacred. For Muslims, the Five Pillars are the beginning of observance, but Islamic law extends into all aspects of life as expressed in *Sharia*. In Jewish tradition, there is little distinction made between moral and ritual laws. Both fall under the category of *mitzvot*. And both are responsibilities under Torah.

Chapter Eleven

קָרְבָּן

Korban

Sacrifice, Offerings

> Make an altar of earth for Me and sacrifice on it your
> burnt offerings and fellowship offerings, your sheep and
> goats and your cattle. Wherever I cause My name to be
> honored, I will come to you and bless you.
>
> Exodus 20:21

When people speak about sacrifice, they are usually using the word in one of two ways:

1. Sacrifice is the selfless giving up of something important, or
2. Sacrifice is a primitive and barbaric ritual in which people or animals are brutally killed.

There is an element of truth to both of these definitions, but as we have seen with so many other religious concepts, the true meaning is something much more, and something that modern students of religion often miss.

This chapter will look at examples of sacrifice in the history of world religions. It will focus on the Israelite sacrificial rituals that ceased when Jerusalem fell to Rome in 70 C.E. and identify relics of past rituals that persist in Jewish tradition today.

Word Histories

Sacrifice. The word "sacrifice" is composed of two Latin roots: *sacer* (sacred, holy, special, set apart) and *facere* ("to make," which is also the basis for the words "manufacture," "factory," "artifice," and "office"). To make a sacrifice is to take some object, usually food, and set it aside for a special purpose, namely to give it to a god.

The English word "sacrifice" has come to mean giving something up for a higher good, or even giving something up for *less* than its actual value. In baseball, for instance, a "sacrifice" is when a batter hits a ball such that he will likely be tagged out in order to get one of his teammates home.

Holocaust. The Hebrew word עוֹלָה *(olah)* has an interesting history. From a root meaning "to go up" or "ascent," an *olah* was a burnt offering in which all or most of the animal was burnt, so that

> ## Key Terms
>
> **Sacrifice**. Literally, "to make holy." The act of offering a gift to a deity.
>
> **Offering**. Synonym for sacrifice. Often refers to the object being offered to the god.
>
> **Altar**. A raised platform, mound, or table used for making an offering.
>
> קָרְבָּן *(korban)*. Offering, sacrifice. From the root ק-ר-ב *(k-r-b)*, meaning "to bring close, to approach, to come near."
>
> זֶבַח *(zevach)*. Sacrifice. From the root meaning "to kill." To slaughter an animal for offering and partaking.
>
> מִזְבֵּחַ *(mizbei-ach)*. Altar. From the same root as *zevach*. A place for offering a sacrifice, usually a table or platform of unhewn stone.
>
> מִנְחָה *(minchah)*. Meal offering. Literally, "gift, apportion, present." An offering of flour (mixed with oil) or baked bread.
>
> עוֹלָה *(olah)*. Whole burnt offering. From the root meaning "to go up, to ascend." A special *zevach* in which the entire animal is burnt.

nothing was left over for the people to eat. In biblical times, the *olah* was voluntarily performed by a person as an acknowledgment that he or she failed to observe a particular mitzvah. By burning the animal entirely, the person demonstrated total submission to God.

When Jewish Sages wrote the Septuagint (a translation of the Bible into Greek around 250 B.C.E.), they used the word ολοκαυτωμα *(olokautoma),* derived from *olo,* "whole" (a convenient homophone—soundalike—to the Hebrew *olah*) and *kaustos,* "burn." In English, the *olah* came to be referred to as a whole offering, or by the Latin form of ολοκαυτωμα, holocaust.

The word "holocaust," then, came to mean total destruction by fire. When the Nazis systematically killed six million Jews and millions of others during the Second World War, the word "holocaust" was occasionally used to describe the genocide. By the late 1950s, the phrase "the Holocaust" became the established name for the Nazi destruction of European Jewry. It is worth mentioning that in modern Hebrew, a different word is used to describe the Nazi Holocaust. Rather than using עוֹלָה *(Olah)*, inferring that six million Jews died as a sacrifice, the word שׁוֹאָה *(Shoah)*, meaning "disaster," is used.

Overcoming Modern Biases and Understanding Sacrifice

It is very easy to tag animal sacrifices as cruel rituals of primitive, barbaric people. To a certain extent, this is a fair evaluation. However, before making such a leap and asserting moral superiority over primitive civilization, we have to carefully take into account the historical and sociological meaning of sacrifice, separating the melodramatic hype from historical reality. People kill animals for food. In modern civilization, most of us prefer not to witness the killing. Slaughter occurs far from our awareness in meatpacking factories. Yet, with the exception of vegetarians—the only people with a legitimate reason to criticize animal sacrifice—we reap the rewards of killing whether we witness it or not. When we go to the fast-food drive-through window or take a pound of neatly plastic-wrapped meat to the checkout stand, we rarely consider where that food actually came from.

Our ancient ancestors, by contrast, were acutely aware of the source of their meat. They took killing much more seriously than we do today. Sacrifice, for them, was a means of paying respect for the life that was taken for the sake of their own nourishment.

A common misconception about sacrifice is that when an animal was being offered, it was completely destroyed for the exclusive benefit of the god. As explained previously, this was only the case with the *olah* sacrifice. An animal sacrifice was a communal event in which humans shared a feast with a god, spirit, or ancestor. This is made very clear in the Bible: with the exception of the *olah* offering, God received the blood, the fat, and the aromatic smoke—all the animal by-products that people normally wouldn't eat anyway—while the priests, attendants, and the family bringing the offering shared the meat:

> From what he offers he is to make this offering to *Adonai* by fire: all the fat that covers the inner parts or is connected to them, both kidneys with the fat on them near the loins, and the covering of the liver, which he will remove with the kidneys. The priest shall burn them on the altar as food, an offering made by fire, a pleasing

aroma. All the fat is *Adonai*'s. This is a lasting ordinance for the generations to come, wherever you live: you must not eat any fat or any blood.

Leviticus 3:14–17

Lest there be any doubt about the use of the meat, the text of Leviticus also instructs that the person bringing a thanksgiving offering

> . . . is to bring one of each kind as an offering, a contribution to *Adonai*; it belongs to the priest who sprinkles the blood of the fellowship offerings. The meat of his fellowship offering of thanksgiving must be eaten on the day it is offered; he must leave none of it till morning. If, however, his offering is the result of a vow or is a freewill offering, the sacrifice shall be eaten on the day he offers it, but anything left over may be eaten on the next day.

Leviticus 7:14–16

In addition, it is often overlooked that Israelite sacrifices didn't always involve animal products. Wheat, bread, fruits, olive oil, and incense were integral parts of Temple ritual. Animal sacrifice was, by and large, a conscientious and spiritual way to slaughter meat for food. Sacrificial ceremonies were feasts, much like modern barbecues. The major difference between an ancient sacrifice and a modern picnic is that God is rarely invited to the latter.

History of Sacrifice

Archeologists have found Paleolithic burial sites and cave paintings that suggest that communities were performing sacrifices at least as early as forty thousand years ago, and possibly much earlier. Because these cultures had no written records, and because the artifacts are scanty, we cannot say for certain how elaborate and involved these sacrificial ceremonies were or to whom (or what) they were being offered. We don't know whether these Stone Age people believed in a god, in nature spirits, or in the power of animals and ancestors. In any event, they slaughtered animals in a ritualized manner, imbuing the experience of killing with special meaning.

According to Joseph Campbell, "Man lives by killing, and there is a sense of guilt connected with that." He continues, "The basic hunting myth is a kind of covenant between the animal world and the human world. The animal gives its life willingly, with the understanding that its life transcends its physical reality" (*Power of Myth*, p. 72). In *Transformations of Myth through Time* (Harper and Row, 1990), Campbell further explains that, "the animal comes with the understanding that it will be killed with gratitude, that a ceremonial will be conducted to return its life to the mother source for rebirth, so that it will come again next year" (p. 10).

Muslim butchers never slaughter an animal without calling out the name of Allah. This is one of the requirements for meat to be *halal* (permitted). Thus, every piece of meat prepared according to Muslim law is an offering to God.

Why Sacrifice?

People's motives for offering sacrifices are many, and the reasons often overlap. Sacrifices are given as gifts, as payments, as penalties, and as acts of communion.

In its simplest form, a sacrifice is a gift to a god or spirit. The sacrifice is presented with the assumption that the god or spirit needs or desires what is offered. Such gifts are given in order to make a request, ask for fertility, give thanks, or demonstrate devotion. As primitive as it may seem, sacrifice was often understood in the ancient world as a magical quid pro quo—"I'll scratch your back if you scratch mine"—with the gods.

Sacrifice is also an act of communion, celebrating a meal with the larger community as well as with the deity. In some cultures, the only time a person eats meat is when sharing the meal with a god.

Sacrifice could serve as a form of expiation or atonement for a sin. The ancient Israelites atoned for inadvertent sins solely through sacrifice. Intentional violations required other forms of punishment or recompense, often accompanied by sacrifice.

Filial piety, the worship of ancestors, is particularly common in Africa and Central Asia. In such cultures, ancestors are the main recipients of sacrifices, given at tombs, in household shrines, and during funeral rites. Flowers, incense, and gifts of food are often laid on ancestral altars.

Methods of Sacrifice

The most familiar form of sacrifice is burning an offering on an altar. Perhaps out of a Promethean appreciation of flame, ritual fire is often used as a sacrifice—even in the absence of food offerings. This can be seen in the Hindu (Vedic) offerings to Agni, in the Zoroastrian lighting of the sacred fire, and even in the Jewish ritual of lighting candles at the onset of Shabbat and holidays. Although nothing is consumed—except fuel or candle wax—these acts indicate a communion with God and are an act of making sacredness.

Just as sacrifice by fire sends the offering upward to the heavens, so do many sacrificial rites send an offering downward to the earth. Ancient Paleolithic burials that involved interring the dead in the ground were understood as returning the dead to its source. This idea is expressed in the Bible when God tells Adam: "You shall return to the ground from which you were taken, for you are dust, and to dust you shall return" (Genesis 3:19).

Burial as sacrifice also may include the belief that burying somehow nourishes the earth or earth gods. The Native American custom of burying fish near crops with the "magical" effect of producing better crops, has a scientific basis: the body of the fish fertilizes the soil. In some cultures, such as ancient Greece and Central America, sacrificial victims—animal and human—were buried alive. This is also true with reindeer sacrifices, common in ancient Northern Europe and Asia, in which a live reindeer was drowned in a lake or buried alive.

Bloodletting is another common form of sacrifice. In this ritual, the purpose is to provide the god or spirit with the life-giving force of blood. This is often done without killing the victim, particularly in cases of human bloodletting, where people willingly offer their blood by piercing or cutting their limbs, ribs, face, or genitals in order to spill blood on an altar. Animal sacrifices frequently involve bloodletting.

When making a sacrifice, the offering is not always destroyed. In Hindu ritual, fruit, flowers, baked goods, and incense are displayed on an altar. In the Israelite Temple in Jerusalem, twelve loaves of bread were set out on a golden table each week. In Hebrew the bread is called לֶחֶם הַפָּנִים, *lechem hapanim* (face bread), and in English it is usually translated as "shewbread"—bread for show. Each Shabbat, according to Leviticus 24:8–9, this bread was eaten by the priests and replaced with fresh loaves.

When, Where, Who, and What?

The frequency, the location, and the participants in sacrifices varied from culture to culture. Many religions, including ancient Judaism, held sacrifices on a daily basis, with special additional services held for holidays and special events.

In some nations, sacrifice was the province of kings, as in Mayan, Aztec, and Mesopotamian religions. In others, it was the domain of a priestly class. Many Greek and Roman religious movements were secret societies that held sacrificial ceremonies in which only the initiated could participate. In India and ancient Israel, most citizens could and did participate in sacrifices, but the extent of their participation depended on their caste or tribe.

Korban: Sacrifice, Offerings

Sacrifices were generally held on altars or shrines. These shrines may have been located at tomb sites, at unique geological settings (mountains, rocks, hills, caves), or in private family homes. Often huge monuments were erected, such as the pyramids of Mesoamerica and the temples of Greece, Rome, and the ancient Near East. Offerings included nearly every type of animal, typically birds and field-grazing animals. Although less dramatic than blood sacrifices, food offerings (grain, fruits, oil, and baked goods), as well as wine, flowers, and incense offerings, were probably sacrificed in greater proportions than were animal offerings.

Although rare, there have been cultures that sacrificed people. The widest use of human sacrifice occurred in Central and South America where, by some estimates, twenty thousand people were sacrificed to the Aztec sun god annually. In China, Egypt, and Sumeria, deceased kings were sometimes buried with entire retinues of live servants and attendants. Various ceremonies are recorded in Africa, Europe, and the Americas in which slaves, prisoners of war, and children were slaughtered for the benefit of gods.

Sacrifice in Ancient Mesopotamia

The care and feeding of gods was an essential economic and political element in ancient Sumerian, Akkadian, and Babylonian society. The gods, as the people of Mesopotamia believed, enjoyed eating, drinking, and celebrating. Tablet 3 of *Enuma Elish,* the Babylonian Creation epic, records the gods' preparations for war against their mother, Tiamat:

> Let them speak, let them sit down to banquet together, they shall eat the feast and drink the new-drawn liquor and then they shall all confirm in his destiny the avenger, Marduk!

> *Enuma Elish,* tablet 3 (trans. N. K. Sandars)
> *Poems of Heaven and Hell from Mesopotamia* (Penguin Books, 1971)

After the gods were victorious, a ziggurat (pyramid-style temple) named Esagila was erected, and the gods again celebrated:

> When all the gods sat down together there was wine and feasting and laughter; and after the banquet in beautiful Esagila they performed the liturgy from which the universe receives its structure, the occult is made plain, and through the universe gods are assigned their places.

> Ibid., tablet 6

The *Epic of Gilgamesh* records how, after Enkidu slays the Bull of Heaven, he and Gilgamesh "tore out his heart and placed it before Shamash [the sun god]" and prostrated themselves before Shamash (*Gilgamesh,* tablet 6:153–155).

The *Gilgamesh Epic* also contains the story of Utnapishtim, the Babylonian Noah, who described to the king of Uruk how he thanked the gods for allowing him to survive the flood:

> I sent forth [the animals] to the four winds and offered a sacrifice.
> I poured out a libation on the peak of the mountain.
> Seven and seven kettles I set up.
> Under them I heaped up sweet cane, cedar, and myrtle.
> The gods smelled the savor,
> The gods smelled the sweet savor.
> The gods gathered like flies over the sacrificer.
> As soon as the great goddess [Ishtar] arrived,
> She lifted up the great jewels [a lapis lazuli necklace], which Anu had made according to her wish, [and said]:
> "You gods gathered here, as surely as I will never forget this lapis lazuli about my neck,
> I shall remember these days forever.
> Let the gods come near the offering."

Gilgamesh, tablet 2: 155–166

Mesopotamian sacrifices, held daily, included beer, wine, milk, bread, dates, and meat. Offerings were generally not burnt among the Akkadians and Babylonians. The meat was cooked elsewhere and brought to an altar that served more as a serving table than a brazier. In Mesopotamian practices the person or family bringing the offering did not share in any of the food, which was eaten exclusively by the king, priests, and staff. In addition to the daily sacrifices, special offerings were made on holidays and when wealthy members of society wanted to make a special request of the gods. Whole offerings (like the Israelite *olah*) were not practiced.

There is evidence that Mesopotamian cultures held human sacrifices, not the least of which is the Bible's condemnation of the Canaanites and Assyrians for sacrificing their children to Molech (see Leviticus 18:21). Between 1922 and 1934, British archeologist Leonard Woolley led an excavation at Tel el-Mukayyar (the site of ancient Ur) in southern Iraq, where he found a series of sixteen royal tombs dated around 2600 B.C.E. In one tomb, Woolley found evidence that a large number of royal ministers, soldiers, servants, and women were served a strong narcotic drink and were buried alive along with their dead king.

Sacrifice in Ancient America

Aztec (Mexico) rituals included animal sacrifice and human bloodletting. Particularly graphic records were made of priests removing still-pumping hearts from living human victims and burning them for the sun god Huitzilopochtli. Human offerings to the agricultural fertility god Xipe Totec were tied to a post and shot full of arrows, the flowing blood representing spring rain. An annual harvest

Human sacrifice, Aztec manuscript.

sacrifice was made to the earth mother goddess, Teteoinnan, during which a female victim was flayed and her skin used as a costume worn by a priest.

The Incas, who lived in the Andes region (Chile, Peru, etc.) regularly offered grain on an open fire. Monthly offerings of animals (llamas) and articles of clothing were burnt in sacrifice. The Incas were also known to perform human sacrifice. Pat Tierney, in *The Highest Altar: Unveiling the Mystery of Human Sacrifice* (Penguin Books, 1989), on page 28, describes the various types of human sacrifice that the Andean people performed:

> The Incas used many methods of sacrifice, including strangling, garroting [sacrifice by strangling with an iron collar], breaking the cervical vertebrae with a stone, tearing out the heart, and burying alive. But freezing to death at high altitude was probably the least painful.

Numerous well-publicized archeological discoveries of mummified remains confirmed that Incas regularly sacrificed children, called *capochas,* by drugging them, strangling them, or giving them a severe blow on the head before burying them.

Jewish Sacrifice

Unique characteristics of Israelite sacrifice are that sacrifice was a gesture of appreciation to God and rarely—if ever—did it serve as divine bribery or "payment for services rendered." The use of sacrifice as a means of absolving sins seems to have developed fairly late. The Israelites were performing communion offerings *(zevach sh'lamim)* and whole burnt offerings *(olah)* from the time of their settlement in Canaan (ca. 1200–1100 B.C.E.). But there is evidence that sin *(chatat)* and guilt *(asham)* offerings were not practiced by the Israelites prior to the return from the Babylonian exile (538 B.C.E.).

As the following text indicates, the effectiveness of sacrifice for absolving guilt or removing sin was very limited:

> When a man or woman wrongs another in any way and so is unfaithful to *Adonai,* that person is guilty and must confess the sin he has committed. He must make full restitution for his wrong, add one fifth to it, and give it all to the person he has wronged. But if that person has no close relative to whom restitution can be made for the wrong, the restitution belongs to *Adonai* and must be given to the priest, along with the ram with which atonement is made for him.
>
> Numbers 5:6–8

As the text suggests, restitution for offenses must be paid to the injured party, and sacrifice is only used in a case of last resort. This seems to be at odds with the Christian interpretation of sacrifice as stated by Paul, which asserts that sacrifice is the necessary element for atonement. This approach to sacrifice is one of the most important differences between Judaism and Christianity.

Sacrificial traditions go back to the prehistory of the Israelite nation. One of the best-known stories of the Patriarchs is the story of the *Akeidah,* the Binding of Isaac, in which God tests Abraham by asking him to sacrifice his favorite son. This story has been variously interpreted to show Abraham's faithfulness to God, to his heartlessness as a father. Yet, on the simplest level, the story serves as a polemic against human sacrifice and as a historical landmark indicating the transition between a theology that tolerates human sacrifice and one that does not. The following text, while condemning worship of the Assyrian god Molech, is a clear prohibition against human blood offerings:

Any Israelite or any alien living in Israel who gives any of his children to Molech must be put to death. The people of the community are to stone him. I will set My face against that man and I will cut him off from his people; for by giving his children to Molech, he has defiled My sanctuary and profaned My holy name.

Leviticus 20:2–3

Likewise, Judaism prohibits ritual bloodletting, scarification, and self-flagellation, all of which were—and still are—practiced in some cultures as signs of devotion or mourning:

Do not cut your bodies for the dead or put tattoo marks on yourselves. I am *Adonai*.

Leviticus 19:28

For the earliest Israelites, sacrifice was informal and noninstitutional. The stories of the Patriarchs suggest that men like Abraham and Jacob would stop where they were whenever faced with a spiritual turning point and set up an altar. The sacrifices involved fire and generally animal offerings. Nonetheless, detailed procedures for the sacrifices remained nonspeci-

Jewish sacrifice, as imagined by Alessandro Franchi, 19th century.

fic until the stories of the Tabernacle in Sinai and continued to evolve until the Second Temple period.

During the time of the Temple, there were two regular sacrificial services held each day. These were the *shacharit* (morning) sacrifice and the *minchah* (gift) sacrifice. On Shabbat, Festivals, and other holy days, a third service, the *musaf* (additional) sacrifice was offered.

In addition to the regularly sacrifices, any person could bring an offering to commemorate, celebrate, or make restitution. As a rule, however, the Jerusalem Temple was the only acceptable place to bring offerings for the people of Judah during the First Temple period and for all Jews in the Second Temple period.

Among the types of sacrifices offered in Israelite sanctuaries were the following:

197

Zevach sh'lamim	Communion offerings, or literally "well-being slaughtering." These were animal offerings that served as welcoming ceremonies, to give thanks to God for well-being and bounty, and to celebrate communal eating with God and with the community.
Olah	Holocaust or whole burnt offerings (literally "rising"). These were animal sacrifices in which the offering was entirely burned, so that the priests or people who brought the offering didn't receive any of the meat.
Minchah	Literally "gift," these sacrifices largely consisted of cereal offerings, that is, fresh grains, bread, or flour mixed with oil and incense.
Chatat and *asham*	The sin offering and guilt offering were sacrifices of expiation and reparation performed by people who had committed offenses. The exact distinction between these two sacrifices is uncertain, but they seemed to cover inadvertent sins and sins of omission or negligence, and not intentional violations such as theft, murder, idolatry, and adultery. It is uncertain whether these sacrifices were performed prior to the Babylonian exile, but they certainly became prevalent in the Second Temple period.
Lechem hapanim	The "shewbread" were twelve loaves of bread set out on a table as an unburnt offering, displayed weekly.
Incense	Mixtures of aromatic powders were used together with all the other sacrifices, as well as being used on their own, placed on burning coals.

Israelite sacrifices served as opportunities for the people to give gifts to God, to improve their relations with God, and to share with their families and community in a devotional meal. In the Israelite civilization, it is likely that meat and poultry were rarely—if ever—eaten outside of sacrifices.

With the exception of the *olah* (whole burnt offering), most Israelite sacrifices can be understood as prayer meals. They were feasts for which the primary purpose was devotion to God. So it is understandable, when the sacrifices ceased after the destruction of the Second Temple, that the sacrificial traditions evolved into the prayer liturgies that are still in use today.

The Prophet's Challenge

Sacrifices were not universally popular among the Israelites. In particular, many of the prophets would rail against what they saw as hypocritical use of rituals while ignoring the ethical tenets of Torah. The prophet/judge Samuel is recorded asking:

> "Does *Adonai* delight in burnt offerings and sacrifices as much as in obeying the voice of *Adonai*? To obey is better than sacrifice, and to heed is better than the fat of rams."
>
> I Samuel 15:22

The prophet Hosea wrote about the sanctuaries of the Northern Kingdom of Israel:

> Though Ephraim built many altars for sin offerings, these have become altars for sinning. I wrote for them the many things of My law, but they regarded them as something alien. They offer sacrifices given to Me and they eat the meat, but *Adonai* is not pleased with them.
>
> Hosea 8:11–13

Lastly, Isaiah, perhaps the best known and one of the most outspoken of the prophets spoke these strong words of God:

> "The multitude of your sacrifices—what are they to Me?" says *Adonai*. "I have more than enough of burnt offerings, of rams and the fat of fattened animals; I have no pleasure in the blood of bulls and lambs and goats. When you come to appear before Me, who has asked this of you, this trampling of My courts? Stop bringing meaningless offerings! Your incense is detestable to me."
>
> Isaiah 1:11–13

Rather, according to Isaiah, what God desired was:

> "Stop doing wrong, learn to do right! Seek justice, encourage the oppressed. Defend the cause of the fatherless, plead the case of the widow."
>
> Isaiah 1:16–17

Ultimately the offerings did stop. When the Romans destroyed the Second Temple in 70 C.E., Jews no longer had a place consecrated for sacrifice. Worship continued, but without the blood offerings, and the study of Torah became the principal act of Jewish life.

Vestiges of Sacrifice

Although the Roman conquest of Judea brought an end to the rituals of burnt offerings, Jewish sacrifice didn't disappear altogether after the destruction of the Second Temple. Certain remnants of the old sacrificial rites still persist in subtle ways, even in modern Judaism:

Prayer.   The set times of Hebrew liturgy are based on the sacrificial services that were held in the Jerusalem Temple. The daily morning *(Shacharit)* and afternoon *(Minchah)* services are named for and patterned after the sacrificial services that bore the same names. The additional *(Musaf)* service held on Shabbat and holidays is also a vestige of the Israelite sacrificial calendar. Traditional *Shacharit* liturgy begins with several pages of readings outlining and recalling the rites of sacrifice in the Temple.

Festivals and Holy Days.   The Three Pilgrimage Festivals (Sukkot, Pesach, Shavuot) and the High Holy Days (Rosh HaShanah and Yom Kippur) were tightly bound with the sacrificial services. While all of these holy days predated the Temple and in the case of the Pilgrimage Festivals had strong agricultural origins, ritual offerings had always been integral to their celebration.

Kashrut.   The dietary laws found in the Torah (Leviticus 11 and Deuteronomy 14) provide the outline not only for what foods may be eaten, but also what foods are considered "clean" or "fit" for God and humans. Only kosher foods were acceptable as offerings. The process of kosher slaughtering *(sh'chitah)* of animals for food follows a strict and solemn procedure that bears a resemblance to the preparation of meat in the days of the Temple.

Challah.   The word *challah* appears ten times in the Torah, always pertaining to sacrifices, and always referring to a loaf or cake of bread. *Challah* could be leavened (i.e., made with yeast; see Leviticus 7:13) or unleavened (i.e., matzah; see Leviticus 2:4), but was distinguished from crackers, wafers, or biscuits by its size. The original *challah* loaves were probably pierced or perforated, as matzah is designed with rows of pinholes. The *challah* was a sacrificial loaf, offered as the priests' portion, as seen in the following example:

> Along with his fellowship offering of thanksgiving *(zevach todat sh'lomav)* he is to present an offering with *challot* of raised bread *(challot lechem chameitz)*.
>
> Leviticus 7:13

The shewbread, the twelve loaves displayed in the Temple, are usually referred to as *lechem hapanim* or *lechem hamaarechet*. In Leviticus 24 the shewbread is referred to as *challot:*

Take fine flour and bake twelve *challot,* using two-tenths of an ephah for each *challah.*

Leviticus 24:5

An ephah equals approximately one bushel, or eight gallons dry measure. At that rate, it would take about fifty modern cups of flour for each *challah.* What distinguished *challah,* other than its size, was the small ball of dough that was separated from the loaf before baking and allowed to burn whole. To this day, when challah is baked according to halachah, an olive-sized ball of dough is baked alongside the loaf and allowed to burn. When you read the words on the side of a matzah box, you'll find the message "CHALLAH IS TAKEN," meaning that the matzah was baked according to this custom.

Sacrifice in World Religions

Hinduism

Sacrifice is the most pervasive element in ancient Vedic Hinduism. The Sanskrit word for sacrifice is *yajna,* from a root, *yaj,* meaning both "to worship" and "to sacrifice." Agni—god of fire and messenger to pantheon—is the conduit through which Vedic Hindus reach the other gods. The name for fire offering is *agnicayana,* which commemorates and reenacts the cycle of the birth-death-rebirth of the universe.

Goats and horses, barley cakes, butter, and soma (a psychotropic liquor) were common offerings on the altar of Agni. Sacrifices were held on new moons, half moons, and quarterly on the seasons, in addition to daily offerings and special offerings, and were always accompanied by chanting mantras or verses from the Vedas.

The original sacrifice, according to Vedic thought, was the mythical slaughtering of Purusha, the primal man whose body formed the four castes (see chapter 10). Human sacrifice, considered the highest form of sacrifice in Vedic times, was a reenactment of that sacrifice that began humanity.

Over the past several thousand years, blood sacrifices have largely given over to offerings of flowers, fruit, baked goods, and butter. The primary modern form of sacrifice is the *puja,* or worship. Performed at temples as well as in household shrines, the worshiper addresses a picture or statue of the god, invites the god to the ceremony, and offers sweetened water, perfume, flowers, incense, and platters of food to the god. Ornate oil lamps, bells, and serving implements are reserved for these ceremonies. Prayers and chants accompany every gesture and step in the offering ceremony. Additional offerings include cloth, string rice, coconut, and sandalwood paste.

A Hindu offers food to a god prior to having a meal in a tradition that somewhat parallels the "saying Grace" in Christianity or *HaMotzi* in Jewish tradition. The meaning behind the Hindu offering is unique. Once the food is given to the god, it becomes *prasad,* the god's possession. The meal then is considered to belong to the deity. When the human accepts it back, it is accepted with a special reverence, since the hand of the god has touched it. Note how this ceremony reflects the notion of communion that we have seen both in ancient sacrifices and in the Christian Eucharist.

Christianity

Christianity is not usually thought of as a religion that performs sacrifices. Yet much of Christian belief and ritual observance is based on pre-Christian sacrifice.

As has been suggested, Israelite sin offerings had a limited power to absolve a person of sin. If a sin was performed intentionally, no amount of sacrifice, according to the Torah, could pardon that person unless prior to the sacrifice, the sinner confessed, apologized, made material amends, and changed his behavior patterns. Sacrifice, for the Israelites, was much more a form of communal worship than it was a means of pardoning sins.

This attitude toward sacrifice was more or less shared by early Christians. The Gospel writers had a mixture of respect for the Leviticus rites of sacrifice and a disdain for the hypocrisy they often saw in the running of the Temple. In one of Paul's letters, he criticized the Temple sacrificial system as being inadequate:

> Day after day every priest stands and performs his religious duties; again and again he offers the same sacrifices, which can never take away sins.
>
> Hebrews 10:11

Paul introduced new meaning to the idea of sacrifice. As an alternative, God offered Christ as the perfect and final sacrifice:

> We have been made holy through the sacrifice of the body of Jesus Christ once and for all.
>
> Hebrews 10:10

According to Paul's interpretation, humanity was cursed because of their original sin, and sacrifice was necessary in order to remove the sin. Jesus was the ultimate sacrifice. As Jesus died on the cross, he represented the ram caught in the thicket, the Passover lamb, the final fragrant offering needed to expiate the sins of all believers.

According to the Christian Bible, God "loved us and sent His Son as an atoning sacrifice for our sins" (I John 4:10) and "God presented him as a sacrifice of atonement, through faith in his blood" (Romans 3:25).

In the first through third centuries C.E., when Church fathers were institutionalizing the ritual of Communion based on accounts of the Last Supper and Jesus' own instructions, they intentionally presented it as a sacrifice. Quite early, the table on which the Communion Offering was prepared was called *altare* (the Latin form of "altar," which literally means "high place," but implies a platform for ritual slaughter).

The Communion ritual, in which Christians eat bread and wine, consists of transubstantiation. The doctrine of transubstantiation means that the bread actually becomes Jesus' body and the wine actually becomes Jesus' blood. Catholic popes as well as Martin Luther promoted the sacrament of Eucharist as a very real—albeit mythologized—consumption of the flesh and blood of Christ. The name for the Communion wafer, "Host," comes from the Latin *hostia*, "sacrifice." Not all Christian denominations currently hold fast to the idea of transubstantiation, but interpret the Eucharist as a representation of Jesus. Yet, since Jesus was the final sacrifice according to Christianity, Communion is an example of "sacrifice" practiced still.

Sacrifice is prayer with food; an active form of worship in which food and eating are the vehicle for communicating with God. Some relics of the ancient rituals have remained in Judaism and other world religions. After the fall of the Second Temple, the Israelite sacrifices evolved into the prayer liturgy that is still in use today.

Chapter Twelve

תְּפִלָּה

T'filah

Prayer, Meditation, and Devotion

May the words of my mouth and the meditation of my
heart be pleasing in Your sight, O *Adonai,* my Rock and
my Redeemer.

Psalm 19:15

The last chapter explored how sacrifice—the offering of food and other gifts to a
god—was an active form of worship, in which participants communed with the deity
as they sought to give praise, offer thanks, or beg for intercession. This chapter will
look at prayers—verbal communications between human and divine—as well as the
process of praying in Judaism and various world religions.

"Prayer," wrote William James in *The Varieties of Religious Experience,* "is the very
soul and essence of religion. . . . Prayer is religion in act; that is, prayer is real religion."
Prayer is one of the central acts of religious life. Prayer can mean the words on the
pages of a prayer book, just as well as it can mean the white spaces between the
words and letters. Prayer is a structure and a framework for religious expression.

Word Histories

Prayer.   Prayer is actually a very paradoxical word, in that it has two very different,
and opposite, meanings. To pray means both to give selflessly and to beg for favors. It
is both a sacrifice and a request. The Latin root *precari* (to ask or beg) is the source of
the Old French *preier* and the Middle English *praien.* Both of these words imply asking
for something, whether from a person or a god. The Elizabethan word *prithee*

(contraction for "I pray thee") meant "please." Occasionally the word "pray" is still used as a word of request, as in "pray tell."

תְּפִלָה **(t'filah)**. The Hebrew word for "prayer," *t'filah* (plural, *t'filot*), has a rather different origin and history. The root פ-ל-ל *(p-l-l)* means "to intervene, arbitrate, or judge." *T'filah,* from the reflexive *(hitpaleil)* form of the verb, means "to judge oneself." *L'hitpaleil* means "to pray." *T'filah* is also the basis for *t'fillin,* the leather prayer boxes traditionally worn by men during weekday morning prayers. (The Greek name for *t'fillin—phylacteries*—comes from a root meaning "guard or watch" and probably refers to the purpose of the *t'fillin,* to remind the wearer to keep God's mitzvot.) In Arabic, this root, *p-l-l,* means "to cut" and is used to refer to the notch edge of a knife or sword. A possible connection between the Hebrew meaning and the Arabic meaning may be

---

Key Terms

Pray. The act of addressing praise, thanks, or requests to a deity; worshipful meditation. Originally, "to beg or beseech."

Prayer. A composition of words used to address a deity.

Worship. Reverent love and devotion, sometimes expressed through prayer. From the Anglo-Saxon *weorethscipe* (worth + ship), the quality or state of being worthy.

תְּפִלָה **(t'filah).** Prayer, from the root פ-ל-ל *(p-l-l),* "to judge." In the reflexive *hitpaleil* form, it means "to judge oneself." Also used as a name for the *Amidah* service.

סִדּוּר **(siddur).** Prayer book, from ס-ד-ר *(s-d-r),* "order." The *siddur* is the written order of daily prayers in book form.

שְׁמַע **(Sh'ma).** "Listen," the name of the prayer-proclamation "Hear O Israel, *Adonai* is our God, *Adonai* is One," as well as the group of prayers that surround it in the daily service.

עֲמִידָה **(Amidah).** The "standing" prayers, also known as T'filah (Prayer) and Sh'moneh Esreih (Eighteen), the group of blessings (18 + 1 on weekdays, 7 on Shabbat) that are read while standing in every daily service.

---

found in the ancient Middle Eastern custom of cutting one's body (bloodletting, as briefly discussed in the previous chapter) as a sign of devotion.

The Yiddish word for "prayer," *daven,* has a less certain origin, but may be related to the Latin *divine,* possibly indicating an attempt to intercede with the Divinity or to predict or foretell.

What Is Prayer?

Prayer is a verbal communication—a message in words—delivered by a human to a god or God. Sometimes these words are spoken from the first-person singular (I, me, my) and sometimes from the first-person plural (we, us, our). Sometimes prayer is addressed to God in the second person (You, Your) and at other times in the abstract third person (addressing "the One who . . . ," "Creator," "Ruler," or "Savior").

Prayer is always poetic, in that it employs metaphors and symbolism and often is composed in verse. Some prayers involve unique structures, such as sonnet-like patters, acrostics, and incantations. Prayers are often musical, whether read, chanted, or sung. People say prayers alone and in groups, at set times and on special occasions. Prayers are also said spontaneously.

The act of praying, whether read or chanted, sometimes requires special objects (rosary beads, Eucharist, Tibetan prayer wheels, bells, drums, incense), special garments (robes, frocks, habits, Muslim *jubba* and *ihram,* the Hindu *angarkha* and *upavita,* the Buddhist *civara,* the Jewish *tallit* and *t'fillin*), and special gestures and motions (kneeling, bowing, genuflecting, facing east,

Rosary, 16th century.

closing eyes, making the sign of the cross). A prayer can be a single word or phrase, repeated over and over as a mantra, or a long reading or composition.

Types and Functions of Prayer

The two primary functions of prayer are adoration and petition. Adoration prayers praise and glorify God. Petitionary prayers ask God for something. Nearly every prayer fits into these two general categories. We will explore these, as well as the several overlapping subcategories of prayers.

Adoration

Adorations are laudatory prayers—prayers whose entire function is to express loving admiration of a god. These prayers often have a mystical, sacred quality of taking a person beyond the self. Adorations stress the majesty, wondrousness, and awesome power of God. Sometimes they contain repetitions of special names or words, like "Hallelujah" (praise *Yah*) in Hebrew and Christian prayer, and the Hindu mantra "Hare Krishna." The *Kaddish* is another example of a prayer of adoration.

Islamic prayer consists almost entirely of laudatory prayers, such as the words of the call of the muezzin announcing the beginning of the worship service:

Allah is Greatest! Allah is Greatest!

Allah is Greatest! Allah is Greatest!

I bear witness that there is nothing worthy of worship but Allah.

I bear witness that there is nothing worthy of worship but Allah.

I bear witness that Muhammad is the Messenger of Allah.

I bear witness that Muhammad is the Messenger of Allah.

Hasten to Prayer! Hasten to Prayer!

Hasten to real success! Hasten to real success!

Allah is Greatest! Allah is Greatest!

There is nothing worthy of worship but Allah.

Al-Adhan (The Call to Prayers)

The following Hindu prayer, from the Rig Veda, offers words of adoration to Indra, the Indian god of war:

I bring my song of praise as dainty dishes, my thought to him resistless,
    praise-deserving, prayers offered most especially to Indra.
Praise, like oblation, I present, and utter aloud my song, my fair hymn to the Victor.
For Indra, who is Lord of old, the singers have decked their lauds with heart and
    mind and spirit.
To him then with my lips give adoration, winning heaven's light, most excellent,
    I offer,
To magnify with songs of invocation and with fair hymns the Lord, most bounteous
    Giver.
Even for him I frame a laud, as fashions the wright a chariot for the man who
    needs it—
Praises to him who gladly hears our praises, a hymn well-formed, all-moving,
    to wise Indra.

Rig Veda 1:61:1–4

Note how the following two prayers, one from the Hindu Mundaka Upanishad, the other from the Hebrew Psalms, both show adoration of God (Brahma in the Hindu prayer) using the image of the stars and heavenly bodies to highlight God's grandeur:

The sun does not shine there, nor the moon and the stars, nor these lightnings, not to speak of this fire. When He shines, everything shines after Him; by His light everything is lighted.

That immortal Brahma alone is before, that Brahma is behind, that Brahma is to the right and left. Brahma alone pervades everything above and below; this universe is that Supreme Brahma alone.

Mundaka Upanishad 2:10–11

Praise *Adonai*. Praise *Adonai* from the heavens, praise Him in the heights above.

Praise Him, all His angels, praise Him, all His heavenly hosts.

Praise Him, sun and moon, praise Him, all you shining stars.

Praise Him, you highest heavens and you waters above the skies.

Let them praise the name of *Adonai*, for He commanded and they were created.

He set them in place forever and ever; He gave a decree that will never pass away.

Psalm 148:1–6

The psalm, which is read each morning as part of the *P'sukei D'zimrah* (Songs of Praise) in the Jewish *Shacharit* service, continues with more samples of God's grandeur in nature:

Praise *Adonai* from the earth, you great sea creatures and all ocean depths,

Lightning and hail, snow and clouds, stormy winds that do His bidding,

You mountains and all hills, fruit trees and all cedars,

Wild animals and all cattle, small creatures and flying birds,

Kings of the earth and all nations, you princes and all rulers on earth,

Young men and maidens, old men and children.

Let them praise the name of *Adonai*, for His name alone is exalted; His splendor is above the earth and the heavens.

He has raised up for His people a horn, the praise of all His saints, of Israel, the people close to His heart. Praise God.

Psalm 148:7–14

Petition

Petition is the most common form of prayer and is, in fact, the very definition of the English word "prayer"—"to ask or beg" for something. Sometimes these requests are for tangible, material, and personal items, as in the following Upanishad prayer:

The dazzling bill among Vedic hymns,
Sprung from the immortal
Sprung from the Vedic hymns—that is Indra!
May he deliver me with wisdom!
In my memory, O God, may the immortal be fixed!
May my body be competent;
May my tongue say the sweetest things;
May I hear the wealth of sacred lore!
You are Brahma's chest, covered in wisdom.
Guard what I have heard.
Bring me, without delay, fortune accompanied by clothes and cattle, food and drink.
Bring prosperity, bring her to me, rich with sheep and cows.
May students come to me!
May I become famous among men!
May I become richer than the rich!
O Dispenser of Wealth, may I enter you!

Taittiriya Upanishad 1:4

Often, petitionary prayers ask for something for the benefit of a third party, as in the following intercessional prayer, a customary (Sunna) response to the Islamic Call to Prayers said on behalf of Muhammad:

> O Allah, Lord of this most perfect call, and of the prayer which is about to be established, grant to Muhammad the favor of nearness to You and excellence.

A response to the Call to Prayers

Similarly, the following prayer, said by members of the Pure Land sect of Buddhism, is a petition on behalf of "all beings":

May all beings have happiness and its causes,
May they never have suffering nor its causes;
May they constantly dwell in joy transcending sorrow;
May they dwell in equal love for both near and far.

Four Immeasurables

The following Blackfoot Indian prayer, composed by Chief Yellow Lark, asks the Great Spirit for positive personal attributes like strength and wisdom:

Oh, Great Spirit, whose voice I hear in the winds and whose breath gives life to all the world, hear me. I come before you, one of your many children. I am weak and small. I need your strength and wisdom. Let me walk in beauty and make my eyes ever behold the red and purple sunset; my ears sharp so I may hear your voice. Make me wise, so I may learn the things you have taught my people, the lessons you have hidden under every rock and leaf. I seek strength, not to be superior to my brothers, but to be able to fight my greatest enemy—myself. Make me ever ready to come to you with clean hands and straight eyes, so whenever life fades, like the fading sunset, my spirit will come to you without shame.

The *Mi Shebeirach* prayer that is said following a Torah reading is an example of a Hebrew petitionary prayer. The traditional *Mi Shebeirach* said for the recovery of a sick woman is as follows:

May the One who blessed our ancestors—Abraham, Issac, and Jacob, Moses, Aaron, David, and Solomon—bless this sick woman, because the entire congregation prays on her account. In reward for this, may the Holy One, Blessed be, be filled with compassion for her and restore her health, to heal her, to strengthen her, and to revivify her. And may God send her speedily a complete recovery from heaven for all her organs and all her blood vessels, among the other sick people of Israel, a recovery of the body and a recovery of the spirit, swiftly and soon. And we say: Amen.

Thanksgiving

Prayers of thanksgiving express gratitude to a deity for help provided or for bounty received. Thanksgiving prayers are typically a response to surviving difficult situations (e.g., warfare, illness, droughts). Food is a common subject of thanksgiving prayers. The following Iroquois prayer offers thanks to the earth spirits for all things that they provide:

We return thanks to our mother, the earth, which sustains us.
We return thanks to the rivers and streams, which supply us with water.
We return thanks to all herbs, which furnish medicines for the cure of our diseases.
We return thanks to the moon and stars, which have given to us their light when the
    sun was gone.
We return thanks to the sun, that has looked upon the earth with a beneficent eye.
Lastly, we return thanks to the Great Spirit, in whom is embodied all goodness, and
    who directs all things for the good of her children.

The word "Grace" has taken on the popular meaning of "prayer of thanks over food." Nearly every world religion has prayers that are said prior to or after eating. The following is taken from *Birkat HaMazon*, the Jewish "Grace after Meals":

> Blessed are You, *Adonai* our God, Ruler of the universe, who nourishes the entire world by Your goodness, with grace, with love, and with compassion. You give food to all flesh, for Your kindness is eternal. Through Your great goodness we have never lacked and may we never lack sustenance, for all time. For the sake of Your great name, for You are God who nourishes and sustains all and does good to all, who prepares food for all Your creation that You have created. Blessed are You, *Adonai,* who nourishes all.

Thanks can be offered for a variety of matters. In thanking a god for some gift or quality, the worshiper makes that gift sacred. Judaism raises even the most mundane of actions to a state of sacredness through blessing. The following prayer, for instance, offers thanks to God for making human bodies function properly. It is said after using the toilet:

> Blessed are You, *Adonai* our God, Ruler of the universe, who formed humankind in wisdom, creating many openings and passageways. It is clear and known, by the Throne of Your Glory, that if one of these were opened [when it is supposed to be closed] or closed [when it is supposed to be opened], it would be impossible to survive and stand before You. Blessed are You, *Adonai,* Healer of all flesh and Doer of wondrous deeds.

The Muslim prayer said when a person rises from bed is another example of a thanksgiving prayer:

> Many thanks to Allah who gave us life after having given us death and our final return on the Day of Judgment is to Him.

Meditation/Reflection

One of the functions of prayer is to put the worshiper in a higher state of consciousness. Prayers help people to probe into deep, personal issues, asking life's more difficult questions. Prayers can also heighten focus, taking the worshiper to ecstatic feelings and exhilarating visions.

Ideally, all prayer involves focused attention and proper intention. Islamic prayer and Native American prayer have built-in mechanisms for transforming the saying of words into a sacred experience. Hinduism and Buddhism are especially known for meditative techniques that integrate sacred imagery with the inner self. The Mundaka Upanishad, for instance, instructs the worshiper on how to find truth between the flickering flames of a sacrificial fire and between the breaths of uttered prayers. The following passage asks the worshiper to use the sacred sound of "om" to find the bridge between the individual soul (atman) and the world soul (Brahman):

> The Luminous Brahman dwells in the cave of the heart and is known to move there.
> It is the great support of all.
> In it is centered everything that moves, breathes, and blinks;
> That which is adorable, supreme, and beyond the understanding of creatures;
> That which is radiant, subtler than the subtle;
> That by which all the worlds and their inhabitants are supported.
> That is the indestructible Brahman;
> It is breath, speech, and the mind;
> It is Truth and it is the Immortal. Strike it, my good friend!
> Take the Upanishad as the bow, the great weapon, and place upon it the arrow sharpened by meditation. Then, having drawn it back with a mind directed to the thought of Brahman, strike that imperishable target, my good friend.
> Om is the bow; the atman [soul] is the arrow;
> Brahman is said to be the target. It is to be struck by an undistracted mind.
> Then the atman becomes one with Brahman, as the arrow with the target.
> Within Brahman, heaven, earth, space, and mind are woven.
> Put away other talk. This is the bridge to Immortality.
> Within the heart, the arteries meet like the spokes fastened in the wheel of a chariot.
> Meditate on atman as Om. Good luck as you cross beyond the darkness!
>
> Mundaka Upanishad 2:2:1–6

Confession

Apologies and confessions have a powerful effect on the worshiper. They bare the soul and bring about a humbling creature feeling. Humility of this sort leads to a sense of renewal and empowerment. In Roman Catholicism and Orthodox Christianity, confession is a sacrament. Throughout the Christian world, the Lenten season that precedes Easter is a time of repentance and solemnity. Likewise, the month of Ramadan, the holy day of Yom Kippur, and the Ten Days of Repentance are times for Muslims and Jews to probe introspectively and to measure their personal failings.

The Book of Psalms records a confession that is attributed to King David. After David's adulterous relationship with Bathsheba and the ruthless betrayal of her husband, the prophet Nathan confronts David and helps the king realize his errors:

> Have mercy on me, O God, according to Your unfailing love;
> According to Your great compassion blot out my transgressions.
> Wash away all my iniquity and cleanse me from my sin.
> For I know my transgressions, and my sin is always before me.
> Against You, You only, have I sinned and done what is evil in Your sight,
> So that You are proved right when You speak and justified when You judge.
> Surely I was sinful at birth, sinful from the time my mother conceived me.
> Surely You desire truth in the inner parts;
> You teach me wisdom in the inmost place.
> Cleanse me with hyssop, and I will be clean; wash me, and I will be whiter
>   than snow.
> Let me hear joy and gladness; let the bones You have crushed rejoice.
>
> Psalm 51

Confessional prayers are usually general—unspecific about the exact nature of the sins, and broadly applicable to whomever says the prayers, such as the following, from the Rig Veda:

> Aditi, Mitra, Varuna, forgive us however we have erred and sinned against you.
> May I obtain the broad light free from peril: O Indra, let not during darkness
>   seize us.
>
> Rig Veda 2:27:14

The following Zoroastrian confession, like many such prayers throughout world religions, adds an admission for sins committed unknowingly:

> If I have offended you, O Wise Lord, whether by thought or word or deed,
>   whether intentionally or inadvertently, I earnestly seek to make amends
>   by offering you praise.
> If I have reduced the honor in which you are held,
> I proclaim your glory with even greater fervor.
> May your will rule in the hearts of all your creatures.
> May every animal and plant, as well as every man and woman, live according to
>   your laws, for the seed of righteousness lives in every living thing.
>
> Zoroaster (sixth century B.C.E., Persia)

Jewish Prayer

May my prayer be set before You like incense;
May the lifting up of my hands be like the evening sacrifice.
Set a guard over my mouth, O *Adonai,*
Keep watch over the door of my lips.

Psalm 141:2–3

Jewish prayer serves to bind the individual, the community, and the Creator in a tight and warm circle. Words are important in Judaism, and the Jewish prayer service—seemingly dauntingly complex at first glance—is a naturally formed pattern of words. Jewish prayer has its prototypes in the Bible, with the Patriarchs, Hannah, and King David providing examples of how we pray.

Biblical Models for Jewish Prayer

Abraham serves as a Jew's first model of prayer. Abraham first appears—as "Abram son of Terah"—at the end of the eleventh chapter of Genesis. Four verses later, God instructs Abram to leave Ur and travel to a new land. Along the way with his wife Sarai and nephew Lot, Abram pauses near Bethel and "called on the name of *Adonai*" (Genesis 12:8). This prayer marked the beginning of what became a long tradition of dialogue between Jews and God.

The first recorded communal prayer service is found in Genesis 14, when, after a successful rebellion against King Chedorlaomer, the leaders of several small clans gather in thanksgiving:

Jewish prayer book from Venice, 1772.

Then Melchizedek king of Salem brought out bread and wine. He was priest of God Most High, and he blessed Abram, saying, "Blessed be Abram by God Most High, Creator of heaven and earth. And blessed be God Most High, who delivered your enemies into your hand."

Genesis 14:18–20

Isaac twice blesses his son Jacob. In the first instance, Jacob is disguised as his brother Esau to deceive his father. Nevertheless, a perceptive reader may conclude that Isaac is not deceived by the disguise. Isaac blesses Jacob with the following blessing:

> "May God give you of heaven's dew and of earth's richness—an abundance of grain and new wine. May nations serve you and peoples bow down to you. Be lord over your brothers, and may the sons of your mother bow down to you. May those who curse you be cursed and those who bless you be blessed."
>
> Genesis 27:28–29

In the second blessing, Isaac is sending Jacob off to live with Isaac's brother-in-law Laban:

> "May God Almighty bless you and make you fruitful and increase your numbers until you become a community of peoples. May He give you and your descendants the blessing given to Abraham, so that you may take possession of the land where you now live as an alien, the land God gave to Abraham."
>
> Genesis 28:3–4

The story of Hannah adds some important elements to Jewish prayer. During a pilgrimage to the sanctuary at Shiloh, her husband's other wife—who has been blessed with children—torments the childless Hannah. She takes solace in the sanctuary, where she prays that she may have a child:

> In bitterness of soul Hannah wept much and prayed to *Adonai*. And she made a vow, saying, "O *Adonai* Almighty, if You will only look upon Your servant's misery and remember me, and not forget Your servant but give her a son, then I will give him to *Adonai* for all the days of his life, and no razor will ever be used on his head."
>
> As she kept on praying to *Adonai*, Eli observed her mouth. Hannah was praying in her heart, and her lips were moving but her voice was not heard.
>
> I Samuel 1:10–13

The story of Hannah and her prayer has a practical implication for Jewish worshipers. The text tells us "Hannah was praying in her heart, and her lips were moving but her voice was not heard." Thus, it is customary, when praying, to say the words silently to oneself, moving one's lips as though speaking.

The final model of prayer is King David. In addition to the many accounts of his praying (II Samuel 7:18–29; 15:31; 24:17; 24:25), approximately half of the hymns in the Book of Psalms are ascribed to David. The following account, from the Book of Chronicles, shows David leading the Israelites in worship and assigning special roles to the Levites, including responsibility for music in the sanctuary. This account is set inside a temporary sanctuary, as the Temple was not built until after David's death.

They brought the Ark of God and set it inside the tent that David had pitched for it, and they presented burnt offerings and fellowship offerings before God. After David had finished sacrificing the burnt offerings and fellowship offerings, he blessed the people in the name of *Adonai*. Then he gave a loaf of bread, a cake of dates, and a cake of raisins to each Israelite man and woman.

He appointed some of the Levites to minister before the Ark of *Adonai*, to make petition, to give thanks, and to praise *Adonai*, the God of Israel: Asaph was the chief, Zechariah second, then Jeiel, Shemiramoth, Jehiel, Mattithiah, Eliab, Benaiah, Obed-edom, and Jeiel. They were to play the lyres and harps, Asaph was to sound the cymbals, and Benaiah and Jahaziel the priests were to blow the trumpets regularly before the Ark of the Covenant of God.

That day David first committed to Asaph and his associates this psalm of thanks to *Adonai*:

Give thanks to *Adonai,* call out God's name;
Make known among the nations what God has done.
Sing to God, sing praise to God; tell of all God's wonderful acts.
Glory in God's holy name; let the hearts of those who seek *Adonai* rejoice.
Look to *Adonai* and God's strength; seek God's face always.
Remember the wonders God has done, God's miracles,
And the judgments God pronounced,
O descendants of Israel, God's servant,
O sons of Jacob, God's chosen ones.
Adonai is our God; God's judgments are in all the earth.
God remembers the covenant forever,
The word God commanded, for a thousand generations,
The covenant God made with Abraham, the oath God swore to Isaac.
God confirmed it to Jacob as a decree, to Israel as an everlasting covenant:
"To you I will give the land of Canaan as the portion you will inherit."

I Chronicles 16:1–18

The latter part of that passage—the prayer that King David instructed the Levites to recite—is the opening paragraph to the *P'sukei D'zimrah* (Songs of Praise), a section of Psalms and other hymns of praise that precede the *Bar'chu*.

Types and Sources of Hebrew Prayer

Jewish liturgy is comprised of various types of prayers and readings. The central form of prayer is the *b'rachah* ("blessing"; plural, *b'rachot*). A *b'rachah* is a very specific and easy to recognize kind of prayer. What distinguishes a *b'rachah* is the following formula:

Baruch atah Adonai	בָּרוּךְ אַתָּה יי	Blessed are You, *Adonai*
Eloheinu Melech haolam...	...אֱלֹהֵינוּ מֶלֶךְ הָעוֹלָם	our God, Ruler of the universe...

Or, when the *b'rachah* applies to the performance of a mitzvah:

Baruch atah Adonai	בָּרוּךְ אַתָּה יי	Blessed are You, *Adonai*
Eloheinu Melech haolam	אֱלֹהֵינוּ מֶלֶךְ הָעוֹלָם	our God, Ruler of the universe,
asher kid'shanu b'mitzvotav	אֲשֶׁר קִדְּשָׁנוּ בְּמִצְוֹתָיו	who makes us holy with mitzvot
v'tzivanu...	...וְצִוָּנוּ	and commands us...

The Hebrew liturgy contains hundreds of different *b'rachot*. Not all, of course, are used in any given service. Some are said while performing specific mitzvot. Others are restricted to certain holidays. Many apply to special situations such as performing a circumcision, seeing a rainbow, hearing good news, or smelling the bark of a fragrant tree. Among the more familiar of these are *HaMotzi* (blessing over bread) and the Shabbat candlelighting:

For Bread

Baruch atah Adonai	בָּרוּךְ אַתָּה יי	Blessed are You, *Adonai*
Eloheinu Melech haolam	אֱלֹהֵינוּ מֶלֶךְ הָעוֹלָם	our God, Ruler of the universe,
hamotzi lechem min	הַמּוֹצִיא לֶחֶם מִן	who brings forth bread from
haaretz.	הָאָרֶץ.	the earth.

For Candlelighting

Baruch atah Adonai	בָּרוּךְ אַתָּה יי	Blessed are You, *Adonai*
Eloheinu Melech haolam	אֱלֹהֵינוּ מֶלֶךְ הָעוֹלָם	our God, Ruler of the universe,
asher kid'shanu b'mitzvotav	אֲשֶׁר קִדְּשָׁנוּ בְּמִצְוֹתָיו	who makes us holy with mitzvot
v'tzivanu l'hadlik ner	וְצִוָּנוּ לְהַדְלִיק נֵר	and commands us to kindle the
shel Shabbat.	שֶׁל שַׁבָּת.	lights of Shabbat.

In addition to the above forms, Jewish liturgy is filled with longer *b'rachot*—prayers that begin and end with the *b'rachah* formula, framing additional material. The blessing for reading the Torah is an example of a long *b'rachah:*

Baruch Atah Adonai	בָּרוּךְ אַתָּה יי	**Blessed are You,** *Adonai*
Eloheinu Melech haolam	אֱלֹהֵינוּ מֶלֶךְ הָעוֹלָם	**our God, Ruler of the universe,**
asher bachar banu	אֲשֶׁר בָּחַר־בָּנוּ	who chose us
mikol haamim	מִכָּל־הָעַמִּים	from among all other people
v'natan lanu et Torato.	וְנָתַן־לָנוּ אֶת־תּוֹרָתוֹ.	and gave us His Torah.
Baruch atah Adonai	בָּרוּךְ אַתָּה יי	**Blessed are You,** *Adonai,*
notein haTorah.	נוֹתֵן הַתּוֹרָה.	**Giver of Torah.**

Note how the Torah blessing begins and ends with the *b'rachah* formula. Another example of a long *b'rachah* (one that begins and ends with the *b'rachah* formula) is the *Yotzer,* which is said during the daily morning service:

Baruch atah Adonai	בָּרוּךְ אַתָּה יי	**Blessed are You,** *Adonai*
Eloheinu Melech haolam	אֱלֹהֵינוּ מֶלֶךְ הָעוֹלָם	**our God, Ruler of the universe,**
yotzer or	יוֹצֵר אוֹר	who forms light
u'vorei choshech	וּבוֹרֵא חֹשֶׁךְ	and creates darkness,
oseh shalom	עֹשֶׂה שָׁלוֹם	who makes peace
u'vorei et hakol.	וּבוֹרֵא אֶת־הַכֹּל.	and creates all things.
Hamei-ir laaretz	הַמֵּאִיר לָאָרֶץ	Who illuminates the earth
v'ladarim aleha	וְלַדָּרִים עָלֶיהָ	and all who dwell on it,
b'rachamim, uv'tuvo	בְּרַחֲמִים, וּבְטוּבוֹ	compassionately, and in His
m'chadeish b'chol yom	מְחַדֵּשׁ בְּכָל־יוֹם	goodness, each day
tamid maaseih V'reishit.	תָּמִיד מַעֲשֵׂה בְרֵאשִׁית.	renews the works of Creation.
Mah rabu maasecha Adonai!	מָה רַבּוּ מַעֲשֶׂיךָ יי!	How great are Your works, *Adonai!*
Kulam b'chochmah asita,	כֻּלָּם בְּחָכְמָה עָשִׂיתָ,	You do them all with wisdom,
malah haaretz kinyanecha.	מָלְאָה הָאָרֶץ קִנְיָנֶךָ.	the earth is filled with Your things.
Titbarach	תִּתְבָּרַךְ	May You be blessed,
Adonai Eloheinu	יי אֱלֹהֵינוּ	*Adonai* our God,
al shevach maaseih yadecha,	עַל־שֶׁבַח מַעֲשֵׂה יָדֶיךָ,	praising Your handiwork,
v'al m'orei or she-asita	וְעַל־מְאוֹרֵי־אוֹר שֶׁעָשִׂיתָ	and for the light of lights that You
y'faarucha selah.	יְפָאֲרוּךָ סֶלָה.	have made.
Baruch atah Adonai,	בָּרוּךְ אַתָּה יי,	**Blessed are You,** *Adonai,*
yotzer ham'orot.	יוֹצֵר הַמְּאוֹרוֹת.	**who forms the lights.**

In addition to *b'rachot*, there are many other types of prayers and readings. The full *Sh'ma,* for instance, is not a *b'rachah*. Rather, it's a doxology, or statement of belief, composed of three paragraphs from the Torah (Deuteronomy 6:4–9; Deuteronomy 11:13–21; and Numbers 15:37–41).

Another type of reading is taken from scriptural texts. An example of this can be found in Orthodox and Conservative prayer books, which include, as part of the introductory prayers of the weekday *Shacharit* (morning) service, a large section devoted to remembering the *korbanot* (Temple sacrifices). Passages from Exodus, Leviticus, and Numbers, as well as the Talmud and midrash, describing the various offerings and their preparations, comprise this section of the service.

The *Shacharit* (morning) service also includes a large set of hymns of praise, the *P'sukei D'zimrah,* poetic works from Chronicles, from Exodus (the Song of the Sea), and largely from the Book of Psalms, used to set a musical and reverent tone to the service. Among the songs in *P'sukei D'zimrah* is the *Ashrei* (Psalm 145), a beautiful and upbeat poem composed as an alphabetic acrostic (the opening letters of each line form the Hebrew alphabet). *Ashrei* is also the opening prayer of the *Minchah* (afternoon) service.

א *Ashrei yosh'vei veitecha,*	Happy are those who dwell in Your house,
od y'hal'lucha, selah.	they are ever praising You. Selah.
א *Ashrei haam shekachah lo,*	Happy are the people of whom this is true;
א *Ashrei haam she-Adonai Elohav.*	Happy are the people whose God is *Adonai.*
T'hilah l'David:	A psalm of praise of David:
א *Aromimcha Elohai HaMelech,*	I will exalt You, my God the King,
vaavarchah shimcha l'olam va-ed.	and I will praise Your name for ever and ever.
ב *B'chol yom avarcheka,*	Every day I will praise You,
vaahal'lah shimcha l'olam va-ed.	and extol Your name for ever and ever.
ג *Gadol Adonai um'hulal m'od,*	Great is *Adonai* and most worthy of praise,
v'ligdulato ein cheiker.	and His greatness no one can fathom.
ד *Dor l'dor y'shabach maasecha,*	Every generation will praise Your works,
ug'vurotecha yagidu.	and they will tell of Your mighty acts.
ה *Hadar k'vod hodecha,*	On the glorious splendor of Your majesty,
v'divrei niflotecha asichah.	and on Your wonderful works, I will meditate.
ו *Ve-ezuz norotecha yomeiru,*	They will tell of the power of Your awesome works,
ug'dulat'cha asaprenah.	and I will proclaim Your great deeds.
ז *Zeicher rav tuv'cha yabi-u,*	Remembering Your great goodness they will utter,
v'tzidkat'cha y'raneinu.	and of Your righteousness they will sing.
(etc.)	(etc.)

Another well-known prayer is the *Kaddish,* a version of which is recited by mourners. However, contrary to popular belief, the *Kaddish* is not a prayer about death. It isn't even written in Hebrew. The *Kaddish* is a doxology—a statement of belief—written perhaps in the first century B.C.E. in Aramaic, a language that is related to Hebrew. Aramaic is written in Hebrew characters, and most of its words contain roots familiar to Hebrew readers, but the spelling and grammar are altogether different. The *Kaddish* was originally used, in early talmudic times, as a sort of communal pledge said at the end of speeches and lessons. It entered the daily liturgy as a kind of bookmark separating each section of the service. It has been used as a mourners' prayer for most of its history, although its words say nothing about death. Rather, the *Kaddish* is a testament to God's holiness and the hope that God's reign on earth will come speedily.

Yitgadal v'yitkadash	יִתְגַּדַּל וְיִתְקַדַּשׁ	May His great name be
sh'meih raba	שְׁמֵהּ רַבָּא	magnified and sanctified,
B'alma di v'ra chiruteih	בְּעָלְמָא דִּי־בְרָא כִרְעוּתֵהּ	In the world that He created by His will;
V'yamlich malchuteih	וְיַמְלִיךְ מַלְכוּתֵהּ	And may His reign rule
b'chayeichon uv'yomeichon	בְּחַיֵּיכוֹן וּבְיוֹמֵיכוֹן	in your life and in your days
uv'chayei d'chol Beit Yisrael	וּבְחַיֵּי דְכָל־בֵּית יִשְׂרָאֵל	and in the lives of all the House of Israel
Baagala uvizman kariv	בַּעֲגָלָא וּבִזְמַן קָרִיב	Speedily and soon,
V'imru amen.	וְאִמְרוּ אָמֵן.	And we say, "Amen."

The *Siddur:* Structure of Hebrew Prayer

There are three worship services held daily: morning *(Shacharit),* afternoon *(Minchah),* and evening *(Maariv).* According to one midrash, these three services correspond to the three Patriarchs:

Shacharit (Abraham)   "Early the next morning Abraham got up and returned to the place where he had stood before *Adonai.*" (Genesis 19:27)

Minchah (Isaac)   "He went out to the field one evening to meditate, and as he looked up, he saw camels approaching." (Genesis 24:63)

Maariv (Jacob)   "When he reached a certain place, he stopped for the night because the sun had set. Taking one of the stones there, he put it under his head and lay down to sleep." (Genesis 28:11)

Shacharit (morning) is the longest of the three services, running approximately forty-five minutes to an hour, depending on the synagogue and any special sections that may need to be added. On Shabbat, Rosh Chodesh (New Moon), and various holidays, an additional service, *Musaf,* is added to *Shacharit,* in remembrance of the *musaf* sacrifice that was offered on special days during the time of the Temple. *Minchah* (afternoon) and *Maariv* (evening) are relatively short services, running approximately ten minutes apiece. Most synagogues combine *Minchah* and *Maariv* into a single twenty- to thirty-minute gathering.

An additional section is the reading from the Torah, added to the *Shacharit* service on Shabbat, Monday, and Thursday mornings. The *Hallel,* a section of six psalms (Psalms 113–118), is added to the *Shacharit* service on holidays and Rosh Chodesh.

We have seen that there are several sections added to the beginning *(Korbanot* and *P'sukei D'zimrah)* or end *(Musaf, Hallel,* and Torah reading) of a service. What then is the bare bones structure of a service? There are two groups of prayers that are essential to every service: the *Sh'ma Uvirchoteha* (*Sh'ma* and Its Blessings) and the *Amidah.*

Sh'ma Uvirchoteha (Sh'ma and Its Blessings).   This set of prayers has at its heart the *Sh'ma,* the two-line declaration of monotheism: "Listen Israel, *Adonai* is our God, *Adonai* is One!" Surrounding the *Sh'ma* are several prayers that form a unified message—a pattern of words—containing the core messages of Judaism.

Several of the prayers in the *Sh'ma Uvirchoteha* differ, depending on whether they are said in the morning or evening, but the structure remains the same. The basic pattern is as follows:

- *Bar'chu*—Call to Prayer
- *Yotzer Or/Maariv Aravim*—Creation: God in cosmology
  - *Ahavat Olam/Ahavah Rabbah*—God loves by teaching us Torah
    - *Sh'ma*—God is One
  - *V'ahavta*—We love God by learning Torah
- *Emet V'yatziv*—Redemption: God acts in history

Following is a graphic representation of the prayers of the *Sh'ma Uvirchoteha* and their meanings:

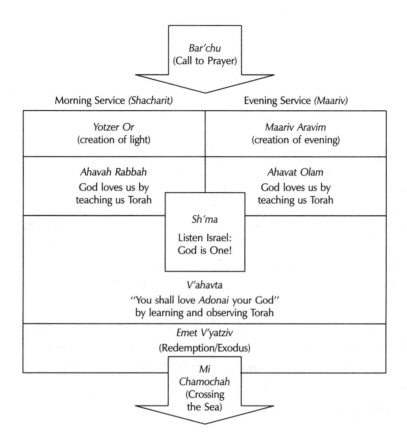

Amidah. The *Sh'ma Uvirchoteha* leads right into the next section of prayers, the *Amidah* (Standing) is also known as *T'filah* (Prayer) and *Sh'moneh Esreih* (Eighteen). These prayers are said silently to oneself while standing, and when a minyan (a quorum of ten) is present, they are repeated out loud by a reader. The daily *Amidah* contains nineteen *b'rachot*. There were originally eighteen (hence the name *Sh'moneh Esreih*), but in the first centuries of the Common Era, a nineteenth blessing was added. The Shabbat version of the *Amidah* contains, conveniently, seven blessings, with the thirteen intermediate petitionary prayers replaced by a single prayer sanctifying the Sabbath.

Types of Blessings	Daily T'filah Sh'moneh Esreih	Shabbat T'filah
Praises	1. *Avot (v'Imahot)* (Ancestors) 2. *G'vurot* (Strength) 3. *K'dushah* (Holiness)	1. *Avot (v'Imahot)* 2. *G'vurot* (Strength) 3. *K'dushah* (Holiness)
Requests	4. *Binah* (Wisdom) 5. *T'shuvah* (Repentance) 6. *S'lichah* (Forgiveness) 7. *G'ulah* (Redemtion) 8. *R'fuah* (Healing) 9. *Birkat HaShanim* (Prosperity) 10. *Kibbutz Galuyot* (Gathering of the Exiles) 11. *Din* (Justice) 12. *HaMinim* (Against Heretics)* 13. *Tzaddikim* (the Righteous) 14. *Binyan Y'rushalayim* (Building Jerusalem) 15. *Birkat David* (David's Reign) 16. *Kabbalat T'filah* (Acceptance of Prayer)	4. *K'dushat HaYom* (Sanctification of the Day)
Thanksgiving	17. *Avodah* (Service/Worship) 18. *Modim* (Thanksgiving) 19. *Shalom* (Peace)	5. *Avodah* (Service/Worship) 6. *Modim* (Thanksgiving) 7. *Shalom* (Peace)

*HaMinim is the nineteenth blessing added to the *T'filah* and is not generally included in Reform liturgy.

There is a logical sequence to the order of blessings in the *Amidah*. It opens with three benedictions of praise to God, starting with *Avot*, linking the person praying with Abraham. The requests follow, building up from individual petitions to two prayers of messianic hope. The final request is for the acceptance of prayer, which leads to the thanksgiving benedictions.

How Jews Pray

Rabban Gamliel says: A man should pray the Eighteen every day. Rabbi Y'hoshua says: The substance [abstracted short form] of the Eighteen. Rabbi Akiva says: If his prayer is fluent in his mouth, he should pray the Eighteen, but if not, the substance of the Eighteen. Rabbi Eliezer says: He that makes his prayer a fixed task, his prayer is no supplication. Rabbi Y'hoshua says: He that journeys in a place of danger should pray a short prayer, saying, "Save, *Adonai*, the remnant of Israel; at their every crossroad let their needs come before Thee. Blessed art Thou, *Adonai* who hearest prayer!"

Mishnah B'rachot 4:3–4

These passages from the Mishnah underscore an important tension in Jewish prayer: that of prayer on a set schedule versus praying when inspired. This tension is described by the two Hebrew terms *keva* (set, scheduled) and *kavanah* (intention). While prayer offered with proper intention is certainly preferable to prayers said begrudgingly, Jewish tradition (as we saw in chapter 10) stresses that action often leads to intention, that performance of a mitzvah—in this case prayer—can guide a person to inspiration.

When someone unfamiliar with traditional prayer observes a minyan in action, the body movements of the worshipers are likely to be perplexing to the onlooker. There are prayers during which they bend their knees and bow, prayers in which they take little steps, prayers in which they close their eyes, and even prayers in which they beat their chest. The most common gesticulation that one is likely to observe is the waving of the entire body from side to side or forward and back. The movement is called by the Yiddish word *shuckling,* an action that sometimes produces an almost trancelike state for the worshiper. These movements have a cultural basis, in that Jews are likely to follow the style of movement that they saw in their community of origin. *Shuckling* is generally more dramatic in an Orthodox minyan, but one can find similar movements among some congregations of Reform and Conservative Jews.

The Babylonian Talmud (*B'rachot* 28b) tells us that when one prays, one should bow until all the segments of his spine are separated. An explanation for this is found in a midrash on the following Proverbs passage:

> The spirit of man is the lamp of *Adonai,* searching all his innermost parts.
>
> Proverbs 20:27

When we pray, searching for our innermost parts, one body flickers like the flame of God's light, and each segment of spine separates and "flickers" in worship. Prayer is performed in many ways: in public and in private, beseechingly and adoringly, with music, song, dance, or in silence, on a set schedule and according to individual spirit. Regardless of how a Jew prays, prayer is a core form of religious expression and a central value in Judaism.

Prayer in World Religions

Hinduism and Buddhism

In the Eastern traditions, prayer is tightly bound with ritual, offerings, and meditation. Hindus and Buddhists typically pray before elaborately decorated altars, whether in their homes or in public temples. Statues or pictures of gods are often used as objects of focus for worship.

Below is a series of Morning Invocations said by a Hindu, calling on various gods and goddesses to guide and assist the individual through the day:

May there be peace on mortal, immortal, and divine planes. I meditate upon the most brilliant splendor of the Sun God. May he stimulate our intellect so that we are inspired to take the right action at the right time.

You are my mother and father. You are my relative and friend. You are my learning and wealth and you are my all—My Lord of Lords.

May good befall all, may there be peace for all, may all be fit for perfection, and may all experience that which is auspicious.

May all be happy. May all be healthy. May all experience what is good and let no one suffer.

May the lord protect us together. May he nourish us together. May our learning be luminous and purposeful. May we never hate one another. May there be peace, peace, and perfect peace.

O Lord, please lead me from the unreal to the real. Lead me from darkness to light, ignorance to knowledge. Lead me from death to immortality. May there be peace, peace, and perfect peace.

The following prayer calls on Ganesha, the elephant-headed son of Shiva, to clear away obstacles:

O, Lord Ganesha of the curved trunk and massive body, the one whose splendor is equal to millions of suns, please bless me so that I do not face any obstacles in my endeavors.

The word "prayer" doesn't always describe what Hindus and Buddhists do when performing religious rituals. A mantra is a word, a phrase, or hymn that is chanted or muttered for the purpose of focusing attention and producing some mystical effect. Mantras do not necessarily have verbal meanings and are usually untranslatable. Their meaning and effect are thought to work on a deeper, nonrational, nonliteral level.

The Sanskrit word *mantra* appears to be rooted in the same Indo-European root as "mind," "mental," and "memory." The Hindu mantra "AUM" (often spelled "om") is believed to encompass all sound, and slow, mindful chanting of it is believed to bridge waking consciousness with spiritual consciousness.

The Buddhist mantra *Om Mani Padme Hum* can be roughly translated to "*Om* the jewel in the lotus *hum.*" However, such an attempt at translation misses the deeper meaning of the mantra. According to the Dalai Lama (leader of Tibetan Buddhism),

226

chanting *Om Mani Padme Hum* is a means of transforming the impurity of human body, speech, and mind into the pure body, speech, and mind of a Buddha.

Tools are often used, both in Hinduism and Buddhism, to help the worshiper focus during prayer or meditation. These may include bells, chimes, incense, and paintings called yantras or mandalas. A yantra (which means "loom") or mandala ("circle") is a design using either geometric shapes or illustrations to depict abstract ideas.

Mandala, Tibet.

Tibetan Buddhists employ a tool called a prayer wheel in their worship. The prayer wheel, or *mani* wheel as Tibetans call it, is generally an object made of wood and metal, a cylinder attached to a handle with the words *Om Mani Padme Hum* (see above). The cylinder itself contains scriptures or

Prayer scroll, Tibet, 18th century.

mantras written on thin strips of paper. As the worshiper holds the prayer wheel by the handle and spins the cylinder, it is believed that the mantra releases compassion.

Christianity

During his Sermon on the Mount, Jesus instructed his followers on a variety of ethical and spiritual issues, including how to pray:

> And when you pray, do not be like the hypocrites, for they love to pray standing in the synagogues and on the street corners to be seen by men. I tell you the truth, they have received their reward in full.
>
> But when you pray, go into your room, close the door, and pray to your Father, who is unseen. Then your Father, who sees what is done in secret, will reward you.
>
> And when you pray, do not keep on babbling like pagans, for they think they will be heard because of their many words. Do not be like them, for your Father knows what you need before you ask Him.

This, then, is how you should pray:
> Our Father in heaven, hallowed be Your name,
> Your kingdom come, Your will be done, on earth as it is in heaven.
> Give us this day our daily bread.
> Forgive us our debts, as we also have forgiven our debtors.
> And lead us not into temptation, but deliver us from evil.
>
> Matthew 6:5–13

Out of that short teaching came the best known and possibly most important prayer of Christianity, the *Oratio Dominica*, better known as the Lord's Prayer. The formula of the Lord's Prayer is a simple one, based on Jewish prayer style. It consists of an opening address, followed by seven petitions, and closing praise (doxology) that was added later:

Address:	Our Father in heaven,
Praises:	Hallowed be Your name,
	Your kingdom come,
	Your will be done, on earth as it is in heaven.
	Give us today our daily bread.
	Forgive us our debts [or trespasses], as we also have forgiven our debtors.
	And lead us not into temptation,
	But deliver us from evil.
Doxology:	For Yours is the kingdom and the power and the glory, forever.

The saying of the Lord's Prayer was an essential element in Christian life from early times. Saint Augustine (354–430 C.E.) taught that the Lord's Prayer was *the* Christian prayer, to be said three times daily, as is the *Sh'ma* in Jewish worship. Various traditions arose for Christians to repeat the Lord's Prayer any number of times.

The rosary is a process of prayer repetition performed using a string of 150 beads (arranged in fifteen sets of ten). The name "rosary" is intended to conjure images of a well-tended rose garden. The number 150 corresponds to the number of hymns in the Book of Psalms.

In Roman Catholic tradition, one holds the string of rosary beads, using the beads as counters. With each bead, the Catholic says the Hail Mary (Ave Maria) prayer:

> Hail Mary, full of grace; the Lord is with thee.
> Blessed art thou among women and blessed is the fruit of thy womb, Jesus.
> Holy Mary, Mother of God, pray for us sinners, now and at the hour of our death.
> Amen.

Upon completion of each Hail Mary, the worshiper takes hold of the next bead, repeating the prayer. At the completion of each set of ten beads (and ten Hail Marys), the worshiper adds an "Our Father" (i.e., the Lord's Prayer).

If the Lord's Prayer is the most important prayer to Christians, the single most important prayer ritual is the Eucharist—Communion. Discussed in detail in the previous chapter, Communion is the consecration of bread and wine, representing the body and blood of Jesus, and the feeding of them to worshipers. While there may be some anthropological basis for this custom in Egyptian and Roman religion, the clearest source of Communion comes from the words of Jesus himself, as recorded in the Gospels. The Gospels of Matthew, Mark, and Luke—referred to as the synoptic Gospels because they provide parallel accounts of the life of Jesus—contain very similar accounts of the Last Supper. Here is the account from Matthew:

> On the first day of the Feast of Unleavened Bread, the disciples came to Jesus and asked, "Where do you want us to make preparations for you to eat the Passover?"
>
> He replied, "Go into the city to a certain man and tell him, 'The Teacher says: My appointed time is near. I am going to celebrate the Passover with my disciples at your house.'"
>
> So the disciples did as Jesus had directed them and prepared the Passover.
>
> When evening came, Jesus was reclining at the table with the Twelve. . . .
>
> While they were eating, Jesus took bread, gave thanks and broke it, and gave it to his disciples, saying, "Take and eat; this is my body." Then he took the cup, gave thanks, and offered it to them, saying, "Drink from it, all of you. This is my blood of the covenant, which is poured out for many for the forgiveness of sins. I tell you, I will not drink of this fruit of the vine from now on until that day when I drink it anew with you in my Father's kingdom."
>
> Matthew 26:17–20, 26–29

The Gospel of John—which does not follow the same structure as the synoptic Gospels, and thus probably derives from a different source—relates Jesus' teaching of the Eucharist differently. Jesus tells a crowd at a synagogue in Capernaum:

> "I am the living bread that came down from heaven. If anyone eats of this bread, he will live forever. This bread is my flesh, which I will give for the life of the world."
>
> Then the Jews began to argue sharply among themselves, "How can this man give us his flesh to eat?"
>
> Jesus said to them, "I tell you the truth, unless you eat the flesh of the Son of Man and drink his blood, you have no life in you. Whoever eats my flesh and drinks my

blood has eternal life, and I will raise him up at the last day. For my flesh is real food and my blood is real drink. Whoever eats my flesh and drinks my blood remains in me, and I in him. Just as the living Father sent me and I live because of the Father, so the one who feeds on me will live because of me. This is the bread that came down from heaven. Your forefathers ate manna and died, but he who feeds on this bread will live forever."

John 6:51–58

Communion is several things to the Christian: it is a reenactment of the sacrifice of Christ, it is a receiving of Christ's grace into one's own body, and like the sacrifices of ancient times, it is a sharing—a communion among people of a religious community and with God. In Roman Catholic and Eastern Orthodox Christianity, the priest has the power to consecrate the wine and bread, while in Protestant denominations, the entire Christian community, considered lay-priests, have the authority to perform the consecration.

Islam

Salat—prayer—is one of the Five Pillars of Islam. The Quran proclaims, "They have been commanded no more than this: To worship Allah offering Him sincere devotion" (Quran 98:5). The Quran does not provide the specifics of what prayers to say and how often they should be said. Muhammad prayed twice daily, at sunrise and sunset. Perhaps in imitation of Judaism, a third prayer service was added at midday, and it was customary to face toward Jerusalem when praying. Then, in 624 C.E., Muhammad declared a "break with Jews," asserting Islam's independence from Jewish ideas. Friday was declared to be the Sabbath instead of Saturday. Prayer was said five times daily (rather than the Jewish three) and always facing Mecca (instead of Jerusalem).

There are four steps of preparation for prayer:

1. Time: One must pay close attention to the schedule for prayer. There are five prayers daily: sunrise, midday, afternoon, sunset, and evening. In Muslim cities, a muezzin announces the Call to Prayers over loudspeakers.
2. Cleanliness: The Quran instructs: "When you rise up to prayer, wash your face and your hands as far as your elbows, and wipe your head and your feet to the ankles" (Quran 5:6). Even when water is not available, one should wash using sand as a symbolic cleansing. Clothing and prayer carpets should be checked for cleanliness before prayer.

3. Modesty: While it is customary to remove one's shoes, special care should be taken that one's sexual organs are not exposed.

4. *Al Qibla:* One must face toward Mecca when praying.

The prayer service involves a series of declarations of faith accompanied by physical movements: *al qayam* (rising), *ar rukuu* (bowing and touching knees), and *as sujuud* (kneeling to the ground so that one's forehead, palms of both hands, both knees, and toes of both feet are touching the ground).

For Muslims, the five-times daily service is not the burden it may seem to outsiders. *Salat* is a welcome break in the day, allowing the Muslim to pause, meditate, and refocus on God, all the while giving structure to the day. The entire ceremony is short, with regular services lasting under fifteen minutes. *Salat* for the Muslim is like a spiritual coffee break, five times a day.

Prayer serves many purposes, both inward and outward. It has the capacity to improve a person's health and well-being, to relieve, relax, and inspire. It serves to bring communities together, fostering friendship and fellowship. Like sacrifices, prayers are a bridge between humans and the Divine.

Chapter Thirteen

עַם יִשְׂרָאֵל

Am Yisrael

Nations and Peoplehood

> Out of all nations you will be My treasured possession.
> Although the whole earth is Mine, you will be for Me
> a kingdom of priests and a holy nation.
>
> Exodus 19:5–6

Jewish people sometimes refer to one another as "Members of the Tribe." The expression—while generally used jokingly—is telling. Why do Jews label themselves using a word normally reserved for American Indians? What is a tribe? Why do Jews differentiate themselves from non-Jews? Do other religious or ethnic groups do this? Is there a religious component to peoplehood?

This chapter will look at the role of community in Buddhism, Christianity, Islam, and two Native American tribes. It will then explore the meaning and value of *Am Yisrael*—the People of Israel—in Jewish tradition.

Word Histories

יִשְׂרָאֵל (*Yisrael,* **Israel**).   People typically associate the name "Israel" with the modern Middle Eastern state. Yet the word "Israel" has been in use for at least three thousand years, while the state only came into existence in 1948.

What did "Israel" mean during those three thousand years? Primarily it was a synonym for "Jew" or the Jewish community. The word first appears in the Bible when Jacob, after an encounter with an angel, is given the new name "Israel," from the root שׂ-ר-ה, *s-r-h* (to persist, exert oneself, struggle, or contend), "for you have striven with

God and with men, and have prevailed" (Genesis 32:29). From that event onward, Jacob was known by both Jacob and Israel. His children were referred to as the "Children of Israel," and by extension, all of Jacob's descendants are Israel's children, or Israelites.

When King Solomon died and his son Rehoboam was anointed king of Judah, a political leader named Jeroboam, together with a prophet named Ahijah, rebelled against the new king. A number of the Israelite tribes allied with Jeroboam and established a new kingdom called Israel, located to the north of Judah. The kingdom of Israel lasted about two hundred years, from 933 to 722 B.C.E., until it was conquered by Assyria.

עַם *(am)*. The Hebrew word עַם, *am* (people, nation) derives from the root ע-מ-ם, "to include," "to be comprehen-

> **Key Terms**
>
> **Community**. A group of people sharing a common background, interests, locality, and/or government.
>
> **Church**. The body of Christian believers. Also may refer to a particular denomination (e.g., Episcopal, Lutheran, Catholic) or to a specific building used as a Christian sanctuary.
>
> *Sangha*. Buddhist community. Strictly speaking, it refers to groups of Buddhist monks, but can also apply to the quality of community and cooperation.
>
> **Tribe**. A social division of people; a group consisting of a number of families or clans that share a common history, language, and/or ancestry.
>
> עַם *(am,* rhymes with "Tom"). People, nation, community.
>
> יִשְׂרָאֵל *(Yisrael)*. The Jewish people; all descendants of the patriarch Jacob.
>
> קְהִלָּה *(k'hilah)*. Assembly, congregation. From root, ק-ה-ל, "to come together or assemble." Also used in the form *(kahal)* קָהָל.

sive." It is related to the Hebrew preposition עַם, *im* (with) as well as the Arabic word *umma* (people, religious community). It must be made clear that עַם means "nation" in the sense of a group of people with common background, culture, and/or language, and *not* "nation" in the modern sense of a sovereign country.

Nation. The meaning of the English word "nation" has changed significantly. It has an odd relationship with the words "country" and "state." "Nation" shares the same root as "nature," "native," "natal," and "nativity." All these words have to do with birth or with qualities we are born with. "Nation" originally meant the large group of people into which you are born. "Country," by contrast, referred to land, and "state,"—related to "status," "stand," and "stature,"—has to do with condition or possession. Of the three words—country, nation, and state—only "state" implicitly involves a government.

Church. The word "church" never actually appeared in the Christian Bible in its original Greek. Ironically, "church" comes from the Greek *kuriakon*, meaning "[house] of the lord." The Greek Christian Bible frequently used the word εκκλησια *(ekklesia)*, which meant "gathering," and applied both words to any public gathering of people and to the community of Christian believers. In English translations of the Christian Bible, the word *ekklesia* is replaced with "church." It is not certain precisely when and how "church" came to be used in the dual sense of "community of believers" and "building for worship," but today it is used in both senses.

Synagogue. "Synagogue" also has Greek origins and appears about sixty times in the Christian Bible (as συναγωγη, pronounced "su-na-go-gey"), applied to Jewish houses of worship. "Synagogue" is a fairly precise translation of the Hebrew *kahal* or *k'hilah,* being a gathering or coming together of people. Modern synonyms for "synagogue" include the Hebrew terms *beit k'nesset* (house of gathering), *beit midrash* (house of study), *beit t'filah* (house of prayer), and in Sephardic communities, *kahl* (from *kahal*), as well as the Yiddish term *shul* (from the German for "school") and, in American Reform (and sometimes Conservative synagogues), "temple."

Gentile. "Gentile" comes from the Latin *gentilis* (belonging to the same clan, race, people, nation) and is related to "gentle" and "genteel" in the medieval sense of being well-born, or a "gentleman." These words, in turn, share ancestry with words such as "gene," "genetic," "pregnant," "genus," and "kin."

Pagan. "Pagan" comes from the Latin *pagus,* a rural district, out in the country. Hence, "pagan" referred to people who come from "out there." The word "heathen" has a similar origin, being Old English for "coming from the heath," or from the woods or uncultivated fields. Both "pagan" and "heathen" are now derogatory terms for barbaric people who do not acknowledge the God of Judaism, Christianity, or Islam.

גוי *(goy)*. *Goy* is a Hebrew word meaning "nation" and in the Bible is applied to both Israelite and non-Israelite populations. In Genesis 12:2, God promises to make Abraham a *goy gadol,* "a great nation," and in Exodus 19:6, God says that Israel is a *goy kadosh,* "a holy nation." Elsewhere in the Bible, *goy* is frequently used in the sense of comparing the people of Israel to all other nations. In later biblical writings, *goy* came to mean "non-Jewish nations," and in postbiblical times, it came to mean "non-Jew." While the word itself does not confer positive or negative value, in modern usage it is generally considered a derogatory term.

Us and Them: Issues of Ethnicity and Tribalism

Somewhere in the genetic code of all mammals—possibly all life—is the gene for the capacity to discriminate. This is a good thing. Without discrimination, we would be unable to recognize edible plants from poisonous ones, safe routes from perilous ones, our own species from any other.

Early in human development, after we have imprinted the images of our parents and have learned to identify members of our family from strangers, we begin to develop the sense of "us" and "them." This is a crucial step in forming our own identities, worldviews, culture, and sense of belonging to a community.

When discrimination goes out of control, we find ourselves enmeshed in irrational hatreds, feuds, wars, racism, sexism, and other xenophobic (fear or hatred of the stranger or foreigner) behaviors. It is natural and appropriate for individuals to have affinity toward people who share the same language, culture, and physical characteristics, but there is a narrow border between ethnic pride and ethnocentric bigotry.

Religions wrestle with this dichotomy of particular versus universal, clannish insularism versus global ecumenism. While religions often teach messages of harmony and unity of all people, religion has also been accused of building walls that separate people.

Community and Culture as Religious Concepts

Just as the *Sh'ma* is central to Jewish belief, and the *Shahada* is central to Islam, the *Tisarana* (Threefold Refuge) is the core prayer of Buddhism:

> I take refuge in the Buddha,
> I take refuge in the dharma,
> I take refuge in the *sangha*.

Buddha, dharma, and *sangha* are also referred to as the *tiratana* (three gems) of Buddhism. *Buddha* refers to the Enlightened One, the Teacher; *dharma* means "teaching," and it is the collection of wisdom and lessons attributed to or based on the Buddha; *sangha* is "community."

Judaism has something similar to the *tiratana*: the concept of God, Torah, and Israel, considered the three foundations of Judaism. One could easily make the case that the Christian Trinity—Father, Son, and Holy Spirit—demonstrates the same paradigm.

Judaism	Buddhism	Christianity
God	Buddha—Enlightened Teacher	Father—God
Torah	Dharma—teaching	Son—Jesus Christ
Israel	*Sangha*—community	Holy Spirit—pervading the community of believers

Islam is unique in being able to spread its message to so wide an audience with cultures as diverse as those of Southeast Asia, Africa, Persia, Pakistan, and the United States, not to mention Arabia. Yet despite the cultural variance within the Islamic community, there is a strong value of peoplehood—called *umma*—that one finds, for example, in the multitudes who make pilgrimage to Mecca each year.

Lastly, it is nearly impossible to think about the American Indians without calling to mind the rich culture and close-knit communities that are their heritage. An individual Indian and his or her tribe are an interconnected unit.

Native American Culture: The Tribe

"Indian" is a misnomer when used to describe pre-European indigenous people of the Americas. Christopher Columbus and his crew, thinking they'd discovered a western route to India when they landed on Cuba, coined the term. Cuba turned out not to be the eastern edge of Asia, but the name "Indian" stuck. The people called "Indians" call themselves by a variety of names—often by the name of their clan, tribe, or nation. However, generally, when describing themselves as an entire group, they prefer the term "American Indian"—or simply "Indian"—over the popular political term "Native American."

Archeological evidence suggests that Indians gradually migrated across the Bering Strait twenty to thirty-five thousand years ago. They appear to be ethnically related to the people of Central Asia. Linguistically, they are not a unified group, but seem to come from several unrelated language groups.

The Indians are not a single people, but are a diverse, interwoven tapestry of ancient and modern cultures. Thus, it's difficult to generalize any tribe's characteristics. The central unit of most Indian communities is the clan, an extended family comprised of several households related by blood.

A tribe is a group of clans that are ethnically, linguistically, and religiously similar. Often a tribe is defined by a specific territory in which they live. The U.S. government recognizes 560 tribes (within the forty-eight contiguous states and Alaska). Each has its own unique culture, history, and political structures.

It is difficult to separate innate aspects of Indian culture from those that were imposed on them by "white" culture. Tribal membership was once much more fluid than it is today, and much more a product of cultural identity than of economic benefit. Today, to apply for membership to a particular tribe or reservation, one must provide a Certificate of Degree of Indian Blood (CDIB), indicating a hereditary link to the tribe. Typically tribes require that applicants have at least one-quarter tribal blood—in other words, at least one grandparent who was a full-blooded member. Unfortunately, this notion of blood percentage is a Western invention, imposed by U.S. government agencies for determining who is entitled to Indian land rights and other benefits. Attachment to the tribe is integral to Indian identity, but these blood-quantum distinctions are usually more a matter of finance and politics than of spiritual identity.

Sioux

The Sioux are one of the largest and most well known Indian nations. With heroes like Sitting Bull and Crazy Horse, their military victory at Little Big Horn and their bloody defeat at Wounded Knee, and famous rituals like the Sun Dance and the Ghost Dance, the Sioux have done much to deserve their fame. Even the word "tepee" comes from the Sioux language.

The Sioux are not so much a tribe as they are a confederacy of three nations, each composed of several tribes grouped together because of linguistic similarities. The Sioux have had many cultural elements, including their name, imposed on them from the outside. "Sioux" is the shortened form of "Nadowesioux," the Ojibway term for "enemy." The Sioux prefer the names of their individual tribes or linguistic divisions, names like Dakota, Lakota, and Nakota, Mandan, Crow, Osage, and Wahpeton.

The Oglala tribe is part of the Lakota, or Western Sioux Nation, which migrated from Minnesota to the Great Plains region. The Oglala live primarily on the Pine Ridge Reservation in South Dakota. Pine Ridge, established in 1889, is the second largest reservation in the United States, with approximately 38,000 residents, of which 17,800 are enrolled members of the Oglala tribe.

Beadwork on a Sioux jacket, North America.

The following chart shows the various Sioux tribes, as well as the bands of the Oglala:

Nations	Tribes	Bands
Lakota (Teton, "Prairie Dwellers," or Western Sioux)	Oglala	Payabya Tapisleca Kiyuksa Wajaja Itesica Oyahpe Wagluhe
	Sicangu	
	Hunkpapa	
	Miniconjous	
	Sihasapa	
	Itazipacola	
	Oohenupa	
Dakota (Santee—Eastern Sioux)	Mdewakantonwon Wahpeton Wahpekute Sisseton	
Nakota ("Yankton")	Yankton Upper Yanktonai Lower Yanktonai	

(Nation: Sioux)

During the eighteenth and nineteenth and well into the twentieth centuries, White American culture was fairly effective at eliminating the Sioux cultural identity. The "Americanizing" efforts took three forms: (1) converting the Lakota from hunter-gatherers to farmers, (2) Christianizing the Lakota, and (3) education, requiring Indian children to attend boarding schools that taught Western culture.

The Indian Reorganization Act of 1934 brought a Western-style tribal government to the Pine Ridge Reservation, consisting of a five-member Executive Committee and sixteen-member Tribal Council. Social activities on the reservation include powwows, rodeos, races, and public feasts. Stories are still passed on, and the Lakota language is experiencing a renaissance.

Navajo

The Navajos, with 270,000 members, is the largest Indian nation in the United States. About 60 percent of the Navajo people live within Navajo territory, 26,110 square miles (slightly larger than the state of West Virginia), spanning parts of Arizona, New Mexico, and Utah. The Navajo are classified with the Athabascan linguistic family, which primarily includes nations that settled in Alaska and northwest Canada (Tlingit, Eyak, and Haida), as well as the Apache in the

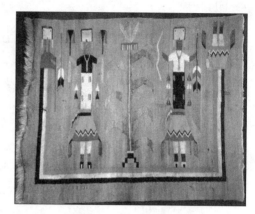

Navajo blanket, 19th century.

Southwest. Sometime between 900 and 1350 C.E., Navajo ancestors and their Apache cousins migrated to the Southwest.

While the Apache remained hunter-gatherers, by the early 1600s the Navajo had settled into an agrarian lifestyle, modeled in part on the Pueblo Indians, from whom they learned the arts of weaving, cultivating corn, and raising livestock. Yet they retained much of the individualistic flair of their Apache cousins, as opposed to the sense of communal unity found in Pueblo communities. It is also worth noting that both Apache and Navajo acquired their names from outside their own nation. Spanish settlers named both nations: the Apache using the Zuni word for "enemy," and the Navajo using the Tewa word for "cultivated arroyo." The Navajo's own name for themselves is Diné, meaning "people."

Clans are the core unit in the Diné culture. A Navajo is considered part of his or her mother's clan. When introducing themselves, Navajo people give their name, where they are from, and the name of their mother's clan and their father's clan. Members of the same clan are considered brothers and sisters even if there is no blood relation. Thus, it's considered incestuous and strictly forbidden to marry within one's clan.

Because of the personal connections established between a Navajo and his mother's clan, his father's clan, his grandparent's clan, and his spouse's clan, there is a tight sense of networking among Navajos. Just as two Jews who meet might play "Jewish geography," identifying common friends or relatives, two Navajos who meet for the first time will play a similar game of contacts.

A clan is comprised of many individual families. A traditional nuclear family (wife, husband, daughters, sons-in-law, unmarried sons, and grandchildren) might live in a hogan, an earth-covered, dome-shaped lodge. The hogan is more than a house—it is a home in the most religious sense. Special rules determine its construction: the door must always face east, it has six or eight walls, and so on. The hogan is sacred and should never be abandoned. Yet, if a person dies in his or her hogan, it becomes a house of the dead and must never be lived in again.

There are over 130 Navajo clans, with some of the major clans being the Towering House People, the One-Walk-Around Clan, the Bitter Water Clan, the Mud Clan, the Red-Running-Into-the-Water Clan, the Water's Edge Clan, the Cliff-Dwelling Clan, the Water-Flows-Together Clan, and the Black-Streaked-Wood People. To be considered a member of the Navajo nation, a person must be at least one-quarter Navajo, and at least one parent must be one-half Navajo, demonstrated by a CDIB (Certificate of Degree of Indian Blood) card.

Buddhism: The Sangha

The Buddhist community is embodied in the *sangha,* counted as the third of the three gems. Buddhism would never have become a global religion, but would have remained an obscure story of one man's enlightenment, had the Buddha (Siddhartha Gautama) not taught his message (dharma) and created the Buddhist community *(sangha).* According to the Pali texts, several weeks after his enlightenment, he was contemplating the difficulty of enlightenment when the Hindu god Sahampati visited him. Initially inclined to retire from human interaction with his newfound awareness, the Buddha was convinced by Sahampati to teach his wisdom to others:

> The Blessed One [Buddha], having understood Brahma [Sahampati]'s invitation, out of compassion for beings, surveyed the world with the eye of an Awakened One.... The Blessed One saw beings with little dust in their eyes and those with much, those with keen faculties and those with dull, those with good attributes and those with bad, those easy to teach and those hard, some of them seeing disgrace and danger in the other world....
>
> Then Brahma Sahampati, thinking, "The Blessed One has given his consent to teach of Dharma," bowed down to the Blessed One and, circling him on the right, disappeared right there.
>
> Samyutta Nikaya 6:1—The Ayacana Sutta

The Buddha's first sermon was delivered to a group of five monks, explaining the "middle path" to enlightenment and the Noble Eightfold Path. With the teaching of these five monks, the first *sangha* was formed:

On one occasion the Blessed One was staying at Varanasi in the Game Refuge at Isipatana. There he addressed the group of five monks:

"There are these two extremes that are not to be indulged in by one who has gone forth. Which two? That which is devoted to sensual pleasure with reference to sensual objects: base, vulgar, common, ignoble, unprofitable; and that which is devoted to self-affliction: painful, ignoble, unprofitable. Avoiding both of these extremes, the middle way realized by the Tathagata [the Buddha, describing himself in third person]—producing vision, producing knowledge—leads to calm, to direct knowledge, to self-awakening, to Unbinding. And what is this middle way...? It is this Noble Eightfold Path: Right View, Right Resolve, Right Speech, Right Action, Right Livelihood, Right Effort, Right Mindfulness, Right Concentration. This is the middle way realized by the Tathagata that—producing vision, producing knowledge—leads to calm, to direct knowledge, to self-awakening, to Unbinding.

Samyutta Nikaya 56:11—Dhammacakkapavattana Sutta

A *sangha*, properly speaking, is a group of Buddhist monks, or *bhikkus*. The *bhikkuni-sangha*, a group of female monks, or nuns, was instituted owing to the intervention of the Buddha's cousin and friend, Ananda.

On the one hand, the Buddhist notion of community is somewhat exclusive. One is not part of the proper community without taking the *bhikkus'* vows, shaving one's head, wearing plain robes, and eating only what passersby place in your rice bowl.

Yet, in a broad, abstract sense, *sangha* means living a life guided by the values of collaboration, friendship, friendliness, courtesy, and generosity. This applies to the monastic *sangha* as well as what Buddhists refer to as the "Noble *Sangha*" (*Ariya-Sangha*), those who have fully realized the Four Noble Truths and the Eightfold Path, which may include laypeople as well as monks and nuns.

When asked if laypeople could be part of the Noble *Sangha*, the Buddha answered that there were, in fact, more noble lay disciples than noble monks. The following story demonstrates the importance of the lay community. When a young homeowner named Sigala asked the Buddha how a layman can live a good life, the Buddha responded:

"Generosity, sweet speech,
Helpfulness to others,
Impartiality to all,
As the case demands.
These four winning ways make the world go round...."

When the Exalted One had spoken thus, Sigala, the young householder, said as follows:

"Excellent, Lord, excellent! It is as if, Lord, a man were to set upright that which was overturned, or were to reveal that which was hidden, or were to point out the way to one who had gone astray, or were to hold a lamp amidst the darkness, so that those who have eyes may see. Even so, has the doctrine been explained in various ways by the Exalted One.

"I take refuge, Lord, in the Buddha, the dharma, and the *sangha*. May the Exalted One receive me as a lay follower; as one who has taken refuge from this very day to life's end."

Digha Nikaya 31—Sigalovada Sutta

Another story has Ananda asking the Buddha, "Lord, is it true that good spiritual friends are fully half of the holy life?" The Master replied, "No, Ananda, good spiritual friends are the whole of the holy life. Find refuge in the *sangha* community."

Christianity: The Church

When most people hear the word "church," their first image is of a building—a place where people go to pray. Church is this and much more. Within Christianity, it is impossible to separate the ideas of God's spirit and God's grace from the community of human beings that comprise the Church.

In Christian biblical theology, "Church" has three broad meanings: (1) all people who, from the beginning of the world, have believed in the One True God (a group that includes Noah, Abraham, Moses, and in theory, all Jews and Muslims); (2) the earthly community of believing Christians; and (3) the future kingdom of God, comprised of all believers, living and dead, who will be part of God's eternal kingdom.

Early Christians—and to a large extent, Christians up to the present—view the Church as a continuation, fulfillment, and improvement on the relationship between God and Israel. While the "Old Covenant" was with the people of Israel, the "New Covenant" is with all nations. "Church" goes beyond the walls of any building and the borders and bloodlines of any nation. The Church is universal.

For Christians, the covenant between God and Israel is the foundation for the New Covenant of Jesus. Church fathers saw authentic human relationships with God in the stories of Abraham, Moses, and the prophets of Israel, and they wanted to maintain this link between old and new. However, the Israelite covenant—the Torah—was unfulfilling for early Christian thinkers. For the early Christian thinkers, Torah was unable to remove sin from the human soul. In his Letter to Hebrews, Paul writes:

> Christ has obtained a ministry which is as much more excellent than the old as the covenant he mediates is better, since it is enacted on better promises.
>
> For if that first covenant had been faultless, there would have been no occasion for a second.
>
> Hebrews 8:6–7

Paul continues:

> The days will come, says the Lord, when I will establish a new covenant with the House of Israel and with the House of Judah; not like the covenant that I made with their fathers on the day when I took them by the hand to lead them out of the land of Egypt; for they did not continue in my covenant, and so I paid no heed to them, says the Lord. This is the covenant that I will make with the House of Israel after those days, says the Lord: I will put My laws into their minds, and write them on their hearts, and I will be their God, and they shall be My people.
>
> Hebrews 8:8–10

Peter supports the idea of the Church being a continuation of Israel by using a midrashic style of proof texts:

> For in Scripture it says: "See, I lay a stone in Zion, a chosen and precious cornerstone, and the one who trusts in him will never be put to shame" [Isaiah 28:16]. Now to you who believe, this stone is precious. But to those who do not believe, "the stone the builders rejected has become the cornerstone" [Psalm 118:22], and "a stone that causes men to stumble and a rock that makes them fall" [Isaiah 8:14]. They stumble because they disobey the message—which is also what they were destined for.
>
> But you are a chosen people, a royal priesthood, a holy nation, a people belonging to God, that you may declare the praises of Him who called you out of darkness into His wonderful light [Psalm 118:23].
>
> I Peter 2:6–9

For Peter, the New Covenant is the very thing that unites diverse nations as one people:

> Once you were not a people, but now you are the people of God; once you had not received mercy, but now you have received mercy.
>
> I Peter 2:10

Saint Peter by Masaccio, 15th century.

The Christian idea of Church is that of a body of people imbued with God's spirit and given God's grace. The notion that God's spirit pervades the Church must be stressed. According to Christian belief, it is the single element that distinguishes the Church from any other grouping of people.

The Christian Bible uses an array of metaphors to describe the Church:

- God's flock (Luke 12:32; Acts 20:28; I Peter 5:2–3)
- God's chosen remnant (Acts 15:17; Romans 11:5)
- People of God (II Corinthians 6:16)
- Kingdom of God (Colossians 4:11; Revelation 1:6; 5:10)
- Temple of God (I Corinthians 3:16–17; Ephesians 2:21)
- Bride of Christ (Ephesians 5:23; Revelation 19:7; 21:9)
- Body of Christ (Ephesians 5:23; Colossians 1:18, 24)

These various metaphors serve not only as links to imagery in the Hebrew Bible, but also as illustrations of how God's spirit is present in the Christian community.

> Do you not know that you are God's temple and that God's spirit dwells in you?...
> For God's temple is holy, and that temple you are.
>
> I Corinthians 3:16–17

Paul's message in the above passage almost resembles the idea in the Hindu Upanishads emphasizing that the individual's atman (soul) is really the Brahman (universal soul). Paul brings together past and future in the following passage, which also describes the Church as the abode of God's spirit:

> You are fellow citizens with the saints and members of the household of God, built upon the foundation of the apostles and prophets, Christ Jesus himself being the cornerstone...in whom you also are built into it for a dwelling place of God in the spirit.
>
> Ephesians 2:19–22

In the following passage, Paul describes the Church as both the Bride of Christ and as the Body of Christ:

> The husband is the head of the wife as Christ is the head of the church, his body, of which he is the Savior....No one ever hated his own body, but he feeds and cares for it, just as Christ does the church—for we are members of his body.
>
> Ephesians 5:23, 30

One becomes a member of this community by accepting Jesus—an act of asserting and internalizing faith. Simply by announcing with sincerity before Christian witnesses that one believes in Christ, a person becomes Christian and part of the Church.

Rituals of baptism and Communion serve as vehicles for accepting the grace and spirit. As discussed in chapters 11 and 12, Communion—or Eucharist—is an act of literally ingesting God's spirit in the form of the Host wafer and wine. Few modern rituals are as potentially powerful and as genuine as the act of Communion in bringing together God and believers.

There is one aspect of Christian community building that is a problem area for Jews. Christianity, especially in its evangelical and "born-again" movements, is very active in its mission to convert non-Christians to Christianity. Often these proselytizing efforts present Judaism in ways that Jews find very demeaning and that imply that the Jewish religion is inferior and incomplete. Despite the ignorance and misconceptions missionaries have of Jewish beliefs, they are seeking to bring Jews into the Christian fold out of what they see as love and to perform an act in keeping with their religious belief. However, for Jews these efforts are offensive and insensitive.

Islam: al-Umma

In the Muslim world, clan, tribe, sect, and race all play important roles but are subservient under *Dar al-Islam,* "the abode of Islam," the universal religious community of Muslims. Islam grew out of Arabic culture and continues to bear a distinct stamp of Arabism. Still, the majority of Muslims are not Arab. They are a world community that includes North Africans, Persians, Indonesians, Pakistanis, and Americans, to name a few. The identification of a Muslim with his or her clan or country does not preclude identification with the Muslim world at large.

One becomes a part of *al-Umma*, the nation of Islam, simply by performing the first of the Five Pillars—namely, by declaring with sincerity of heart that "there is no God but Allah and Muhammad is His prophet."

Of the Five Pillars of Islam, four are clearly communal activities. *Salat, zakat, siyam* (fast on Ramadan), and hajj are all behaviors done in groups. Prayer *(salat)*, while it may be performed alone, is generally performed in large groups, the preferred model. *Zakat* (alms) and *sadaqa* (charity) are practices intended to benefit the many. *Siyam* (fasting), far from being a solemnly solitary observance, is one that brings the Muslim community together, particularly when the sun goes down and families gather together for the nightly *iftar* (break-fast). And finally, hajj is the most profoundly communal event in Islamic life, when a person converges with hundreds of thousands of co-religionists at the central and holiest spot in the Muslim world, the Kaaba in Mecca.

The Arabic *al-Umma* is precisely translated as "the people." The concept of *al-Umma* is something of a cross between the Christian idea of a body of believers and the Jewish idea of a nation. It is a people made up of many nations, with Allah and the words of the Prophet Muhammad at its core. *Umma* is sometimes used as a synonym for religion. The Quran says:

> All people are a single nation.
> Quran 2:213

Islamic scholars understand this passage as referring to the generations of men who lived between Adam and Noah. They were a single people, united by their close relationship with God. But after the time of Noah, the people began to disperse, becoming many nations, no longer united with one theology.

> So Allah raised prophets as bearers of good news and as warners, and He revealed with them the Book with truth, that it might judge between people in that in which they differed; and none but the very people who were given it differed about it after clear arguments had come to them, revolting among themselves; so Allah has guided by His will those who believe in the truth about which they differed and Allah guides whom He pleases to the right path.
> Quran 2:213

This passage, as interpreted by Islamic scholars, teaches that at some primordial period, all people shared a single creed *(milla)* and religion *(din),* but after the time of Noah, they came to disagree, and ceased to be a single *umma.* The basis of *umma* is one of belief and religion.

The official doctrine of Islam reveals it as a highly democratic and egalitarian religion. There are no priests in Islam. Despite the monarchies and oligarchies that rule many Arab nations today, the Quran is explicit in pointing out that such types of rule are a mistake and an affront to Allah:

> Have you not considered the chiefs of the children of Israel after Musa [Moses], when they said to a prophet of theirs: Raise up for us a king, [that] we may fight in the way of Allah. He said: May it not be that you would not fight if fighting is ordained for you? . . .
>
> Surely the sign of His kingdom is, that there shall come to you the chest in which there is tranquility from your Lord and residue of the relics of what the children of Musa [Moses] and the children of Haroun [Aaron] have left, the angels bearing it; most surely there is a sign in this for those who believe.
>
> Quran 2:246, 248

In practice, caliphs, sultans, kings, and ayatollahs rule Islamic communities. But in theory, it is the *umma* that rules itself. Thus, the Muslim people are, like the Christian Church, a people that go beyond national or racial boundaries and are united in faith. Being subservient to Allah and the teachings of His prophet, the *umma* becomes an ideal community:

> You are the best of the nations raised up for [the benefit of] men; you enjoin what is right and forbid the wrong and believe in Allah; and if the followers of the Book had believed it would have been better for them; of them [some] are believers and most of them are transgressors. . . .
>
> They are not all alike; of the followers of the Book there is an upright party; they recite Allah's communications in the nighttime and they adore [Him]. They believe in Allah and the last day, and they enjoin what is right and forbid the wrong and they strive with one another in hastening to good deeds, and those are among the good.
>
> Quran 3:110, 113–114

Both Islam and Christianity use Judaism as the measuring stick for human relationships with God. While both see their own religions as improvements on Judaism, it is instructive that it is the Jewish people they are comparing themselves to. It is also important to note that historically, when Christian and Muslim attempts to absorb the Jewish people failed, Christians and Muslims responded with violence toward Jews. This was true even in the case of the Protestant Reformation in the sixteenth century.

The Jewish People: Am Yisrael

When Jewish people come together to celebrate, the air is often filled with the smell of food, the chatter of laughter, and the sound of Old World melodies, in spirit if not in fact. But what precisely are Jews as a group? They have been variously labeled as a religion, a nationality, an ethnicity, and a race. None of these classifications is fully adequate.

If "Jewishness" were determined by religion alone, then—as with any other religion—a Jew who stops believing in God or ceases participating in Jewish religious life would no longer be a Jew. It is impossible to be a Christian without belief in Christ. One cannot be a Buddhist without rudimentary acceptance of the Four Noble Truths and the Eightfold Path. A Muslim who denies the oneness of God and the truth of Muhammad's prophecy would cease to be Muslim. Yet, there are many people who identify strongly as Jews despite their lack of affiliation or participation in religious life—sometimes for generations. The Jewish people is filled with avowed atheists who still consider themselves Jewish.

"Nationality" generally refers either to the country of a person's citizenship or the country of origin of one's family. Jews living in Montreal may consider their nationality as Canadian, or—if their ancestors came from Russia, France, or Scotland—as Russian, French, or Scottish. They may also identify their nationality as Jewish despite the fact that there was no Jewish country a person could come from until the mid-twentieth century. Ironically, in the former Soviet Union—a nation established ostensibly as a social equalizer—the passports and identification cards of Jews marked their nationality as Jewish regardless of whether they were living in Russia, Ukraine, or Belarus.

Ethnicity usually implies external cultural commonalities like language, food, and music. Yet there are Jews whose families have never spoken Yiddish—or Hebrew. One community of Jews may never have tasted a bagel, a matzah ball, or gefilte fish, while another may never have tried kubbeh, malawah, or falafel. "Jewish music" can refer to klezmer, Ladino ballads, or Middle Eastern melodies. Furthermore, Jews are a people of many cultures: Sephardic, Ashkenazic, Israeli, Yemenite, even North American.

Throughout the ages, Jews have often been classified as a race. Sometimes this classification was benign, and at other times used with malicious intent. If "race" implies a group of people united by a common history, then Jews are a race. But "race" generally implies a group of people with common genealogical lineage and common genetically transferred physical traits. Human beings display genetic variations of skin tones, hair types, facial characteristics, and body stature. Anthropologists in the seventeenth and eighteenth centuries categorized people into a handful of "races" like Negroid, Caucasoid, Mongoloid, and Australoid. These categories are now widely disputed by scientists as having little basis in genetic science. Many Jews "look Jewish," in that they display clusters of common physical characteristics associated with Jews: hair, skin tone, facial shape. But many non-Jews display the same characteristics, just as many Jews display characteristics that counter the stereotypes. Much of what we consider today as Jewish physical traits are really Eastern European characteristics. More often than not, categorizing Jews—or any other group—as a race is merely an excuse to isolate, persecute, or in the worst case, commit genocide.

Religion, nation, ethnic group, and race—none of these is completely adequate to describe the Jewish people. Perhaps the best label is one that we borrow from the Reconstructionist Jewish Movement: Judaism is a religious civilization. Jews are the people within that civilization who share a common history and a common destiny.

The Israelite Nation

Jews get their name from the tribe of Judah, a name attributed to Jacob's fourth son, and in turn the name for the Jewish kingdom, which reigned roughly from 1028 to 586 B.C.E. Another name for Jews is the people of Israel. In the Bible, the name Israel is a synonym for Jacob, a second name given to him by an angelic being in Genesis 32:

> Jacob was left alone, and a man wrestled with him till daybreak.
>
> When the man saw that he could not overpower him, he touched the socket of Jacob's hip so that his hip was wrenched as he wrestled with the man. Then the man said, "Let me go, for it is daybreak." But Jacob replied, "I will not let you go unless you bless me."
>
> The man asked him, "What is your name?"
>
> "Jacob," he answered.
>
> Then the man said, "Your name will no longer be Jacob, but Israel, because you have struggled [sarita] with God [Elohim] and with men and have overcome."
>
> Genesis 32:25–29

250

"Israel," then, is "one who struggles with God." In the Bible, the twelve sons of Jacob (and by extension, all his descendants) are thus the "Children of Israel," or Israelites. The Bible tells us that eleven of Jacob's sons and his two grandsons from Joseph were the progenitors of the tribes of Israel. By this definition, all Jews, whether descended from Judah, Levi, or any other tribe, are Israelites.

An Israelite tribe is a group of families who believe they are descended from common ancestors—the sons or grandsons of Jacob who provide the names of the tribes: Reuben, Simeon, Levi, Judah, Issachar, Zebulun, Benjamin, Dan, Naphtali, Gad, Asher, and the two half-tribes of Manasseh and Ephraim. When Assyria conquered the Kingdom of Israel (the Northern Kingdom) in 722 B.C.E., most of the tribes were scattered and lost. Those who remained were the people of Judah (the Southern Kingdom) together with portions of the tribes of Levi, Benjamin, and scattered others. It is impossible to say with certainty whether the members of any given tribe are actually descended from any one of Jacob's sons.

During the Exodus from Egypt, Jacob's descendants were not the only people to escape to the Sinai:

> And the people of Israel journeyed from Raamses to Succoth, about six hundred thousand men on foot, besides women and children. A mixed multitude also went up with them, and very many cattle, both flocks and herds.
>
> Exodus 12:37–38

The Hebrew term עֵרֶב רַב *(eirev rav)*, translated here, as "a mixed multitude" is an interesting one. It suggests that along with the descendants of Jacob and his sons, a number of other unrelated tribes accompanied Israel during their return from Egypt. Among the important non-Israelites who became integral to the Israelite community was Caleb, a Kenezite whose people were apparently absorbed into the tribe of Judah, who accompanied Joshua on a reconnaissance mission into Canaan (Numbers 13–14). The Gibeonites were a Semitic nation that joined the Israelites during the time of Joshua. Resident aliens who lived among the Israelites were accepted with varying degrees, though the Torah itself gives a mixed message about this. On the one hand, it warns that associating with foreigners will contaminate Israelite culture and religion:

> When *Adonai* your God brings you into the land you are entering to possess and drives out before you many nations—the Hittites, Girgashites, Amorites, Canaanites, Perizzites, Hivites, and Jebusites, seven nations larger and stronger than you—and when *Adonai* your God has delivered them over to you and you have defeated

251

them, then you must destroy them totally. Make no treaty with them, and show them no mercy. Do not intermarry with them. Do not give your daughters to their sons or take their daughters for your sons, for they will turn your sons away from following Me to serve other gods, and *Adonai*'s anger will burn against you and will quickly destroy you.

Deuteronomy 7:1–4

On the other hand, we are told:

The stranger who sojourns with you shall be to you as the native among you, and you shall love him as yourself; for you were strangers in the land of Egypt.

Leviticus 19:34

Am Yisrael Chai

The tension illustrated by the two biblical passages in the preceding section remains as common today as it was in the time of Moses. Jews are called on to treat non-Jews with beneficence, at the same time protecting their own culture and identity from being watered down by the influences of outside cultures.

Many Jewish observances implicitly (and some explicitly) serve to set Jews apart from their neighbors in order to preserve their uniqueness. This is certainly the case with the kosher dietary laws, as well as the biblical prohibitions against idolatry and marrying foreigners. Among Shabbat observances is the עֵרוּב *(eiruv)*, a boundary, typically the borders of a town or city, beyond which a Jew cannot travel during Shabbat. While the primary purpose of an *eiruv* is the avoidance of activities prohibited on Shabbat, one of the obvious side effects is that it keeps Jewish communities geographically together.

Jewish literature is filled with mitzvot and proverbs that emphasize the Jewish value of community. Among the classic passages that tell of the Jewish value of community are the following:

Dedication of a synagogue in Alsace by George Emanuel Opitz, ca. 1820.

וְאָהַבְתָּ לְרֵעֲךָ כָּמוֹךָ.

V'ahavta l'rei-acha kamocha.
Love your neighbor as yourself.
Leviticus 19:18

The Golden Rule is often attributed to Jesus, but it is easy to forget the original source. "Love your neighbor" made its first appearance in Leviticus. While the original implication was that "neighbor" meant fellow Israelites, the rule was never limited to that. In Deuteronomy 10:19 we are specifically instructed to "love the foreigner" (וַאֲהַבְתֶּם אֶת־הַגֵּר, *v'ahavtem et-hager*). The word *ger*, incidentally, evolved in meaning from being a foreigner or stranger to being a proselyte, that is, one not born of the Jewish people but who has joined them.

הִנֵּה מַה־טּוֹב וּמַה־נָּעִים שֶׁבֶת אַחִים גַּם־יָחַד.

Hineih mah tov umah na-im, shevet achim gam yachad.
Behold how good and nice, brothers sitting together in unity.
Psalm 133:1

This verse from Psalms, in its simplicity and upbeat innocence, has become intertwined in Jewish folk culture through countless musical adaptations. Any child attending religious school or Jewish summer camp will come away familiar with one or more songs based on this verse, often sung around campfire friendship circles.

כָּל יִשְׂרָאֵל עֲרֵבִים זֶה בַּזֶה.

Kol Yisrael areivim zeh bazeh.
All Israel is interdependent.
Babylonian Talmud, *Sanhedrin* 27b

This passage is especially rich in meaning, precisely because it is difficult to translate. The difficulty lies in the word *areivim*, which here probably means "mingling." Thus a literal, word-for-word translation would read, "All Israel is mingling, this [one] with that [one]." Yet *areivim* has many alternative meanings, two of which we have already encountered in this chapter.

עֵרֶב רַב *(eirev rav)*.   A mixed multitude. As we read a couple pages back, the mass of people who accompanied Moses out of Egypt were called an *eirev rav*, "a mixed multitude." In this instance, the term *eirev* suggests something like the American "melting pot" idea, in which many cultures mingle to form one nation. An example of this is the Latin statement *e pluribus unum*—"out of many, one"—found on U.S. currency and national seals.

עֵרוּב *(eiruv)*.   A boundary or encirclement used to maintain and define a community during Shabbat.

עֶרֶב *(erev)*.   Evening. According to the Jewish method of measuring and reckoning days, sunset is the point at which one day mingles with the next.

עֲרָבָה *(aravah)*.   Willow. The willow branch used with *hadas* (myrtle), *lulav* (palm), and *etrog* (citron) in the celebration of Sukkot is called *aravah*, a word that applies to all willow trees. (Aravah is also the name of the rift valley that includes the Dead Sea and regions to the east and south. This usage seems to be related to *arav*, the Arabic people.)

עֵרַב *(eirav)*.   To mix, combine, weave. This verb is used in the Bible and in rabbinic writings to describe mixing or blending of wines, flours, parts of fish, and letters of different sizes, and the weaving together of different types of fabric. The form *arov* is used to describe swarming insects during the Egyptian plagues (Exodus 8:17).

עָרַב *(arav)*.   To vouch for, guarantee, make surety for someone. It is this verb that supplies the meaning for the talmudic passage *Kol Yisrael areivim zeh bazeh*. Throughout Bible and rabbinic writings, this verbal root applies to all sorts of exchanges that today would include bail bonds, pawns, and loans.

עָרֵב *(arav)*.   To sweeten, gladden, humor. In the Bible this passive verb applies to the pleasing qualities of offerings and meditation and to the sweetness of food and sleep. The Talmud exhorts that "at all times, a person should have a sweet *[m'urevet]* disposition toward others" (Babylonian Talmud, *K'tubot* 17a).

A People Chosen

The belief in Israel's chosenness is an essential tenet of Judaism. Modern Jews sometimes find this notion embarrassingly ethnocentric. This response is understandable, but it overlooks the deeper meaning of chosenness. The Jewish people were not *chosen* to be superior to other people. They were *chosen* for a task: to make the world a better place by realizing the values of ethical monotheism. In response to the rhetorical anti-Semitic rhyme "How odd of God to choose the Jews," Maurice Samuels wrote, "It was not at all odd, the Jews chose God."

Despite certain setbacks, the Jewish mission has been very effective. From a tiny fraction of the world's population, more than half the people in the world now espouse monotheism. Both Christianity and Islam are, in a very real sense, the children of Judaism.

The mission of Israel is like a shofar. Its blast can travel far and wide, carrying a deep and resonant message. But in order to make any sound come out of it, we have to blow into the small end. The mission is universal, but it begins at home, in the particular.

And so we come full circle. To be an effective Jew, one has to be a part of the Jewish community. Being a Jew means having a home to come home to. In order to know our home—the culture or "tribe" from which we came—it is important to know the words and ideas that we hold as a group, and how those words and ideas differ from those of our neighbors. Jewish knowledge involves understanding the *Jewish* meanings of belief, spirit, God, angels, messiah, life, holiness, stories, observances, sacrifice, prayer, and peoplehood. These are the words that define us. These are the words upon our heart.

Am Yisrael chai.

Photo Credits

The UAHC Press is grateful to Art Resource, NY for granting permission to use the following images:

Art Resource, NY: p. 7 King David Playing the harp, in an initial. Padua, Italy, ca. 1500. Inv.: Divers V, 349 (402 VI). Photo: R.G. Ojeda. Musée Condé, Chantilly, France. © Réunion des Musées Nationaux/Art Resource, NY; p. 20 13th century C.E. Indra. Bronze figure. From Ladakh (?), India. 12th-13th c. Private Collection. © Art Resource, NY; p. 22 Prince Siddhartha. Tacoste schist. Pakistan, Swat valley, North-West frontier. Ghandara period, Kushan dynasty, 4th c. (CT30962). Victoria and Albert Museum, London, Great Britain. © Victoria and Albert Museum, London/Art Resource, NY; p. 23 Confucius (c.551-479 B.C.E.). 17th C.E. Chinese scroll painting. Bibliotheque Nationale, Paris, France. © Snark/Art Resource, NY; p. 32 Prayer book. Written by Aryeh Judah Loeb ben Elhanan Katz for Michael ben Meir ha Levi of Innsbruck in honor of his wife and their children. Vienna, 1716-17. Ink, gouache on vellum. 209 folios. Gift of Evelyn and Bob Roberts, JM79-85. The Jewish Museum, New York, NY, U.S.A. © The Jewish Museum of New York/Art Resource, NY; p. 36 Pisano, Giovanni (1248-c. 1314). Statue of Plato. Museo dell'Opera Metropolitana, Siena, Italy. © Alinari/Art Resource, NY; p. 37 Catlin, George (1796-1872). Tobacco, an Oglala Chief. Oil on canvas, 73.7 x 60.9 cm. Teton Dakota. Smithsonian American Art Museum, Washington, DC, U.S.A. © Smithsonian American Art Museum, Washington, DC/Art Resource, NY; p. 44 The god Horus, wearing the red crown of Lower Egypt. Shown as a falcon, Horus is the sky-god, image of the living pharaoh. The Pharaoh is represented as Osiris after his death. Relief from one of the chapels off the Hypostyle Hall, Great Temple of Seti (13th B.C.E.), Abydos. Temple of Seti I, Abydos, Egypt. © Erich Lessing/Art Resource, NY; p. 48 Athena, copy after Phidias. Greek sculpture. Museo Archeologico Nazionale, Naples, Italy. © Alinari/Art Resource, NY; p. 50 Ganesha. Stone figure. National Museum, New Delhi, Delhi, India. © Nimatallah/Art Resource, NY; p. 51 13th century C.E. Surya. Temple erected by Narasingh Deva I (1238-65), Ganga dynasty. Temple of the Sun, Konarak, Orissa, India. © SEF/Art Resource, NY; p. 53 18th century C.E. Krishna child with his mother Yashoda. School of Tanjore, 18th c. Museum of the Hanging Gardens, Bombay, Maharashtra, India. © SEF/Art Resources, NY; p. 57 Koran revealed to Mohammed during a battle. © Art Resource, NY; p. 63 Blake, William (1757-1827). Moses & the Burning Bush. Victoria and Albert Museum, London, Great Britain. © Victoria and Albert Museum, London/Art Resource, NY; p. 72 Chagall, Marc (1887-1985) © ARS, NY. Jacob Wrestling the Angel. Oil on canvas, 1960-66. Photo: Gerard Blot. Musee National message biblique Marc Chagall, Nice, France. © Réunion des Musée Nationaux/Art Resource, NY; p. 80 Raphael (1483-1520). Vision of Ezekiel. Galleria Palatina, Palazzo Pitti, Florence, Italy. © Nimatallah/Art Resource, NY; p. 81 Cavallini, Pietro (c. 1250-1330). Seraphim. Detail from the Last Judgment. Fresco. S. Cecilia in Trastevere, Rome, Italy. © Scala/Art Resource, NY; p. 85 English. Archangel Gabriel holding palm and book, flanked by two donors. Book of Hours. England (East Anglia), c. 1325-c. 1330 C.E. M. 700, f. lv. The Pierpont Morgan Library, New York, NY, U.S.A. © The Pierpont Morgan Library/Art Resource, NY; p. 93 Gilgamesh. Assyrian relief from Palace of Sargon II, Khorsabad. 8th B.C.E. Louvre, Paris, France. © Giraudon/Art Resource, NY; p. 104 Great Buddha, Todai-ji Temple. Japan. 745-752 AD. Todaiji Temple, Nara, Japan. © Werner Forman/Art Resource, NY; p. 106 Johnson, William H. (1901-1970). Haile Selassie, 1945. Smithsonian American Art Museum, Washington, DC, U.S.A. © Smithsonian American Art Museum, Washington, DC/Art Resource, NY; p. 113 Ishtar. Alabaster. From Babylon. Seleucid period, 4th B.C.E. Louvre, Paris, France. © Scala/Art Resource, NY; p. 114 Osiris, god of death and resurrection. Wallpainting in the vaulted tomb of Sennutem in the cemetery of Deir el-Medina. 18th dynasty. Tomb of Sennutem, Deir el-Medina, Tombs of the Nobles, Thebes, Egypt. © Erich Lessing/Art Resource, NY; p. 119 Vasilievic, Jovan (18th c.). Christ Enthroned. 1745. Icon. Monastery, Krusedol, Serbia and Montenegro. © Erich Lessing/Art Resource, NY; p. 130 Lao Tse, 2nd of the "Three Pure Ones." Chinese Taoistic scroll painting. Watercolor on paper (102 x 262 cm). Religions Collection, Castle, Marburg, Germany. © Foto Marburg/Art Resource, NY; p. 132 "Fuji from the Mountains of Izu." 12 1/4" x 8 3/4". Collection of The Newark Museum, John Cotton Dana Collection. Inv.: 00.121. The Newark Museum, Newark, New Jersey, U.S.A. © The Newark Museum/Art Resource, NY; p. 136 The ritual robes and equipment of a shaman displayed on a model. The shaman's equipment consists of a carved staff, a rattle, a necklace, and a bear claw crown. Tsimshian, Northwest Coast of America. Canadian Museum of Civilization, Ottawa, Ontario, Canada. © Werner Forman/Art Resource, NY; p. 141 Scale model of Jerusalem and the Second Temple at the time of King Herod the Great (ca. 20 B.C.E.). The picture shows the Temple compound. Holy Land Hotel, Jerusalem, Israel. © Erich Lessing/Art Resource, NY; p. 153 The scribe Ezra rewriting the sacred records. Codex Amiatinus, fol. 5 r. Jarrow, early 8th C.E. Biblioteca Laurenziana, Florence, Italy. © Scala/Art Resource, NY; p. 157 Open shrine with dressed Torah scrolls. Spanish Synagogue, Prague, Czech Republic. © Scala/Art Resources, NY; p. 175 Two young ascetics or brahmans with their hands raised in a gesture of reassurance. Relief. Grey schist. From Butkara, Pakistan. Gandhara style. Inv. 1184. Museo Nazionale d'Arte Orientale, Rome, Italy. © Scala/Art Resource, NY; p. 182 Bosch, Hieronymus (c. 1450-1516). Last Judgment. Detail from the table of the Seven Deadly Sins. Museo del Prado, Madrid, Spain. © Erich Lessing/Art Resource, NY; p. 184 Page from the Koran. Islamic art, Turkey. Musée Condé, Chantilly, France. © Giraudon/Art Resource, NY; p. 195 Human sacrifice. From "Codex Magliabechiano." B.R. 232 c. 70 r. Aztec manuscript. Biblioteca Nazionale, Florence, Italy. © Scala/Art Resource, NY; p. 197 Franchi, Alessandro (1838-1914). Jewish sacrifice. Duomo, Prato, Italy. © Scala/Art Resource, NY; p. 207 Rosary. Enamelled gold. English, 1500. (CT619B). Victoria and Albert Museum, London, Great Britain. © Victoria and Albert Museum, London/Art Resource, NY; p. 215 Prayer book. Badge with initials C.M. on binding and two clasps. Silver repousse, from Venice, 1772. 5.4 x 17.4 x 11.7 cm. Photo: J.G. Berizzi. Musée du Judaisme, Paris, France. © Réunion des Musées Nationaux/Art Resource, NY; p. 227 top Mandala Vajravarahi. Tibetan Tangka, 54 x 35 cm. Inv.: MA 1633. Musée des Arts Asiatiques-Guimet, Paris, France. © Réunion des Musées Nationaux/Art Resource, NY; p. 227 bottom 18th century C.E. Praying mill (Mari' Khor lo) with inscription in ranja characters "Om Mani Padme Hum" and containing a long prayer scroll. 18th C.E. Oriental Tibet. Gilded bronze, h.: 26.5 cm; diam. 8.5 cm. Inv.: MG 21698. Photo: Arnaudet. Musée des Arts Asiatiques-Guimet, Paris, France. © Réunion des Musées Nationaux/Art Resource, NY; p. 238 Beadwork decoration on a sleeveless jacket showing fighting between an Indian and a white man. Plains Indians, Sioux. British Museum, London, Great Britain. © Werner Forman/Art Resource, NY; p. 240 Blanket based on sand painting design. Two supernatural "holy people" flank the sacred maize plant, gift to mortals. They are enclosed by a rainbow arc. Navajo, 19th century. © Werner Forman/Art Resource, NY; p. 245 Masaccio (1401-1428). Saint Peter baptizes a neophyte. Brancacci Chapel, S. Maria del Carmine, Florence, Italy. © Erich Lessing/Art Resource, NY; p. 252 Opitz, George Emanuel (1775-1841). Dedication of a Synagogue in Alsace, c. 1820. The Jewish Museum, New York, NY, U.S.A. © The Jewish Museum of New York/Art Resource, NY.

The UAHC Press is also grateful to Artists Rights Society for granting permission to use the following image:

Artists Rights Society: p. 72 Mark Chagall, "Jacob Wrestling with the Angel" © 2003 Artists Rights Society (ARS), New York/ADAGP, Paris.